Democratic Politics in Latin America and the Caribbean

Jorge I. Domínguez

Democratic Politics in Latin America and the Caribbean

The Johns Hopkins University Press / Baltimore and London

BLH 6425- 8/2

To Leslie, Lara, and Edward

© 1998 The Johns Hopkins University Press
All rights reserved. Published 1998
Printed in the United States of America on acid-free paper
07 06 05 04 03 02 01 00 99 98   5 4 3 2 1

The Johns Hopkins University Press
2715 North Charles Street
Baltimore, Maryland 21218-4319
The Johns Hopkins Press Ltd., London

Library of Congress Cataloging-in-Publication Data will be found
at the end of this book.
A catalog record for this book is available from the British Library.

ISBN 0-8018-5752-x
ISBN 0-8018-5753-8 (pbk.)

Contents

Preface

This book includes chapters that I have written for other books; only this preface, the introduction, and the conclusion have not been published before. The idea of a book on democratic politics came to me rather late; I had thought of myself as a scholar of authoritarian regimes and discovered the coming of democratic politics in Latin America and its endurance in the Anglophone Caribbean edited book by edited book.

Dozens of colleagues have made this book a reality. I am, of course, solely responsible for mistakes in fact and analysis, but the book's debt to other scholars is much greater than usual. Chapters 3 and 5 were co-authored with Jeanne Kinney Giraldo and James A. McCann, respectively; their intelligence, ideas, and hard work gave meaning and substance to these texts. These were fruitful and enjoyable intellectual partnerships, from which I learned immensely.

Chapters 1, 2, 3, 4, and 6 synthesize the work of other scholars; these chapters were originally introductions or conclusions to edited books, my task being not unlike that of a rapporteur, seeking to call attention to and, to some degree, summarizing themes that emerge in the other chapters (and often in other papers prepared as part of the project of which the edited book was one product). For that reason, my co-authors in those books may with justice claim that all the errors are mine and all the insights theirs. To these various co-authors I owe a debt of both scholarship and friendship.

Special thanks go to my co-authors of the edited book on Central America, where the original version of chapter 2 appears. These writers have been practitioners of government and politics and have contributed to helping their countries make the transition to democracy. Special thanks go as well to my co-authors of the edited book on technopols, where the original version of chapter 4 appears. At the time, all were graduate students, thus demonstrating that one reason for teaching is to learn from one's students.

These reprinted chapters appear basically in their original form. I have, however, corrected errors of fact and done some updating. The original chapters included many references to the chapters of other authors, acknowledging their specific contributions. I have dropped these references and recommend that readers consult the original edited books.

All my scholarly work has been supported by Harvard University's Center for International Affairs, under whose auspices this book is published. More recently, my work has also been supported by Harvard's David Rockefeller Center for Latin American Studies, directed by John Coatsworth.

My work for chapters 1 and 2 was supported by the World Peace Foundation and its executive director, Richard Bloomfield. The World Peace Foundation published the books in which these chapters first appeared. My work for chapters 3 and 4 was supported by the Inter-American Dialogue, of which I am a founding member and associated fellow. Chapter 3 evolved as part of a project co-directed with Abraham F. Lowenthal under the oversight of the Dialogue's president, Peter Hakim. The project was funded by the National Endowment for Democracy and the Mellon Foundation. Chapter 4 began with a suggestion from the president of the Dialogue, Richard Feinberg. Both books in which the chapters first appeared were published under the auspices of the Inter-American Dialogue; the one in which chapter 4 first appeared was also published under the auspices of Harvard's Center for International Affairs.

The work for chapter 5 depended on the professionalism and generosity of Richard W. Burkholder, vice president of the Gallup Organization, and Ian M. Reider, president of IMOP/Gallup Mexico, for allowing us to use three of their polls. My field research in Mexico was supported by two Fulbright Distinguished Lecturer grants, in 1983 and 1988, and by the hospitality of the Centro de Estudios Internacionales, El Colegio de México, directed respectively by Blanca Torres and Soledad Loaeza. The writing of the text was supported in part by the Inter-American Dialogue; the book in which the chapter first appeared was published under the auspices of Harvard's Center for International Affairs.

My work for chapter 6 was done under contract with the Cuban Research Institute of the Center for Latin American and Caribbean Affairs of Florida International University. The project director was Lisandro Pérez. The overall project, in turn, was funded by the U.S. Department of State and the U.S. Agency for International Development. These papers have not been published, though they are publicly available from the Cuban Research Institute.

I am very grateful to all of these persons and institutions for facilitating my research.

Democratic Politics in Latin America and the Caribbean

Introduction

The Argentine epic poem, *Martín Fierro*, first published in 1872, gives a good account of a common view of Latin American politics and government. Early on in Martín Fierro's life, he was gang-pressed into military service. He was physically beaten and exploited. He was forced to work for the private gain of the commanding officer, not for public purposes. He was not paid. Though he was promised a release in six months, he was not released for more than a year. The quality of the training was poor; the instructors were ignorant. Soldiers were not issued weapons; ammunition was sold off illegally. No wonder Martín Fierro concluded: "If that is government service, I don't like its ways."[1]

Ineptitude, abuse, deceit, corruption—these are traits of the high and mighty who have lorded over the peoples of these countries. Banal, routine authoritarian rule has long been the quotidian experience of Latin Americans, punctuated by moments of ever-greater brutality. In the early 1980s, U.S. policy toward Latin America was also premised on the worldview that dictatorship was to be expected in Latin American cultures and that U.S. policies should, therefore, accommodate authoritarian rulers.[2]

Contrary to that legacy, democracy and democratization have blossomed in Latin America and have endured in the Anglophone Caribbean in the 1980s and 1990s. Thus, the possibility of studying democratic politics in Latin America and the Caribbean is a dream come true. When I began my academic career in the early 1970s, most Latin American countries were under authoritarian rule; though authoritarian structures had become more bureaucratic than in Martín Fierro's time, Fierro would have recognized familiar pathologies. The trend toward authoritarianism spread and deepened in the years immediately following. A torture pandemic gripped much of Latin America in the mid-1970s.[3] During those same years, doubts were commonly expressed in the Anglophone Caribbean about the prospects for democratic politics. This book could not have been imagined.

Much is still wrong in Latin American and Caribbean countries, and the conditions of life of a great many citizens remain deplorable. The quality of democratic governance is highly uneven; some political systems barely pass minimal tests to warrant being labeled democratic. But major liberalizing and democratizing changes in public life have already had important positive consequences; these civilian governments have also pursued more effective economic policies than the authoritarian regimes they replaced.

In Latin America and the Caribbean in the 1960s and early 1970s, much of the political left—to its subsequent regret—undervalued what it called formal or bourgeois democracy. Many paid with their lives for that error in judgment. Today, with few and isolated exceptions, the hemisphere's political left values democratic politics as the first defense of the weak and the best chance to advance its social, economic, and political objectives. The political right in the same era—in a blunder of epochal proportions—believed that only reliance on brute force could protect the values it held dear. Their countries suffered heavily for that error in judgment. Today, with few and isolated exceptions, the hemisphere's political right has discovered that democratic politics is the most efficient instrument to win power and advance its own objectives.

Scholars of the Soviet Union and European communism have been chided for their failure to anticipate the breakdown of communist regimes in the late 1980s and early 1990s; the norms and structures of ruling communist regimes seemed likely to endure. Scholars of Latin America could be chided for expecting authoritarianism to endure and democracy to break down; the culture and structures of authoritarianism seemed just as likely to linger in this region.

A collection of distinguished essays by leading scholars, *The New Authoritarianism in Latin America*, focused on a new and harsher form of authoritarianism.[4] Its analysis concentrated on Argentina, Brazil, Chile, and Uruguay, though its title hinted at continental coverage. This book was published, however, a year after the Dominican Republic effected its first-ever government transition to rule by the opposition party and in the year that Ecuador effected its transition from a military to a civilian government; a similar process was under way in Peru, culminating in another transition in 1980.[5] Indeed, a better judgment would have been that Latin America would continue to experience contradictory trends—and that authoritarianism might or might not appear or persist.[6]

In the 1980s scholars of Latin America expected the new democratic regimes to break down and fail, though no regime had—and none has. "As in the past," wrote Karen Remmer in 1985, "the significance of recent regime shifts has been exaggerated at the expense of contrapuntal developments. . . . A far more likely outcome is a period of political volatility characterized by the breakdown of a significant number of established regimes, both democratic and authoritarian."[7] Two years later, Mitchell Seligson accurately noted that "the prevailing view among scholars is that democracy and authoritarian rule have oscillated throughout an extended series of cycles . . . and that this pattern of oscillation . . . is likely to continue."[8] In a similar vein, Adam Przeworski, writing in 1991 about Latin America and Eastern Europe, argued that "democracy in the political realm works against economic reforms." Economic reforms "can advance quite far under democratic conditions," he wrote, "but they are politically destabilizing."[9]

The transformation of politics in Latin America, the consolidation of a democratic consensus in the Anglophone Caribbean, and the able performance of many democratic governments in fashioning economic policies made this book intellectually possible. Most of Latin America's democratic governments have carried out economic reforms more effectively than their authoritarian predecessors and have remained stunningly resilient despite many problems.[10] The naysayers have not been proven right. Indeed, even if democratic governments were to be overthrown tomorrow, the history of democratic politics in the 1980s and 1990s is already noteworthy.

I have been no more prescient than my scholarly colleagues, however; I, too, did not expect the political pattern of the recent past.[11] Only the title of chapter 1 formally records my surprise at the turn of events during the past quarter-century, but in fact I undertook the work that follows in order to better comprehend why the unexpected became so commonplace. In the next section, I explore some reasons for this surprise.

The Surprises

The social and economic conditions of the Anglophone Caribbean would seem to have doomed the countries of this region to a breakdown of democratic governance. Vulnerable to international economic fluctuations and plagued by myriad social and economic problems, these small island countries seemed ripe for violence, instability, and military coups. In fact, such breakdowns have occurred only rarely. The Anglophone Caribbean is the only part of the so-called Third World to have, with few exceptions, sustained democratic political systems since decolonization and independence, beginning in the 1950s. As a democratic group, these Caribbean countries clearly outperformed former European colonies in Africa and Asia as well as Latin American countries. It is the purpose of chapter 1 to explain why.

In various Central American countries in the late 1980s and early 1990s, those in power agreed to give up their power to their adversaries. In the 1970s, no one would have forecast this outcome. In preceding decades, El

Salvador, Guatemala, and Honduras suffered nearly uninterrupted military rule, directly or through civilians dependent on military power; Nicaragua had been governed by three members of the Somoza family since the early 1930s. In the 1970s and 1980s, internal and international wars ravaged Nicaragua, El Salvador, and Guatemala. That peace and democratic politics came to these countries in the 1990s seems a miracle. Chapter 2 seeks to explain this result.

The democratic experiences of Latin America and the Caribbean present four political surprises: the vitality of political party life, the institution of effective market-oriented economic policies, the construction of barriers against military coups, and the failure to institute constitutional reform. These are the subjects of chapter 3, but the reason for surprise is worth sketching here.

The early 1990s witnessed the collapse of Italy's Christian Democratic Party, the split and sharp decline of Japan's mighty Liberal Democratic Party, and the dramatic rout of Canada's Progressive Conservative Party. At the moment of their crushing defeat, all three parties were in power; in Italy and Japan, the Christian Democrats and the Liberal Democrats, respectively, had been governing uninterruptedly since shortly after World War II. For at least two decades, scholars had been tracking such partisan realignment and dealignment, many arguing that political parties were growing weaker, even irrelevant, in the advanced industrial democracies.[12]

Democratic politics is more fragile in Latin America and the Caribbean than in the industrial democracies, and so the demise of parties and party systems in these regions might have been even more marked than in the industrial democracies. And yet only in Peru has such a demise occurred, when the APRA Party (American Popular Revolutionary Alliance) went from victory in the 1985 presidential election to virtual insignificance in the 1990s. Latin America and the Caribbean suffer from severe crises of representation and other ills, but politicians and parties are more successful than their counterparts in advanced industrial democracies at eliciting the consent of the governed.

In the 1970s there was a pervasive, and seemingly well-grounded, pessimism about the capacity of democracies to implement economic policies that were sound and that would foster economic growth. Indeed, that was a key message of the brilliant book that set the scholarly agenda for research on South American countries during that decade: Guillermo O'Donnell's *Modernization and Bureaucratic-Authoritarianism: Studies in South American Politics.*[13] Democratic pessimism was directed not only at Latin America, however; a justly famous report to the Trilateral Commission, reflecting upon the ineffectiveness of democratic governance in the United States,

Western Europe, and Japan, was suffused with the same sentiment.[14] Some of the pessimism regarding the contradictions between the market and democracy lingers.[15] And yet the surprise of the 1990s is the capacity of democratic political systems in Latin America and the Caribbean—from Bolivia to El Salvador, from Argentina to Costa Rica, from Guyana to Jamaica—to adopt sound economic policies, most of them superior to those of the authoritarian regimes of the region's recent past. Chapters 3 and 4 present an argument for the compatibility, in contemporary Latin America, of democracy and market economies.

Latin America, in particular, could have been called the land of the unfree and the home of the coup, so common were military dictatorships and coups in the middle decades of the twentieth century. And yet, not since 1976 (in Argentina) has a civilian president elected through constitutional means in a free and fair national election been overthrown by the armed forces in any Ibero-American country—a stunning advancement toward the establishment and consolidation of democratic politics. Moreover, though early evidence (reported in chapter 3) shows that the military retained excessive independence from the civilian executive and congress and that it had impressive prerogatives for decision making even in nonmilitary areas, more recent evidence suggests that the autonomy and the prerogatives have eroded. Civilian control over the military is gradually becoming more widespread and effective.

Flush from these successes in providing channels of partisan representation, fashioning market-oriented economic policies, and preventing military coups, such competent democratic leaders might have been expected to refashion the state to better serve the needs of these countries. Thus another surprise is the failure, for the most part, of attempts at constitutional reform that would make a real difference in the quality of governance. The fundamental institutions of government in Latin America and the Caribbean are not yet up to the tasks of effective democratic governance.

Democracy is both a collective process and a personal experience. It is a personal process for politicians and government officials who must make it work and for the citizens who casts ballots on election day. The long-term experience of democratic politics in Latin America and the Caribbean gave little reason to hope that politicians and mass publics would act to advance the cause of effective democratic governance and sound economic policy. Populist leaders who succeed in fooling the mass public time and again are well documented in the scholarly and popular literature on Latin America and the Caribbean.

Thus yet another democratic surprise of the 1980s and 1990s is that many politicians, and the mass public in several countries, learned from past mistakes in economic policy and sought to fashion a course relying on market-oriented economic policies. In country after country, classic "populist" politicians and parties, who could be held responsible for many of the economic ills in their respective countries, changed course decisively and, for the most part, effectively. This was true of President Víctor Paz Estenssoro and the National Revolutionary Movement (MNR) in Bolivia in the mid-1980s; of Prime Minister Michael Manley and the People's National Party in Jamaica in the late 1980s; of President Carlos Menem and the Peronista Party in Argentina in the early 1990s; of the parties of the left in Chile in the 1990s; and of President Cheddi Jagan and the People's Progressive Party in Guyana in the 1990s. Another important and effective policy change occurred in Costa Rica's largest party, Liberación Nacional, in the 1980s. And in Brazil, to the shock of his critics, Fernando Henrique Cardoso embraced market-oriented economic policies to a greater extent than his previous scholarly record might have suggested.[16] In Venezuela and in Mexico, the turnaround was less complete and less successful, but both President Carlos Andrés Pérez in Venezuela and the majority factions in Mexico's Institutional Revolutionary Party (PRI) took important steps to correct past mistaken economic policies. And, as chapter 6 notes, even Cuba's Fidel Castro has made important changes in economic policies. The capacity of political leaders to learn from the past and to act creatively and decisively is the focus for the analysis in chapter 4.

Politicians have learned more than economics, however. Some who were once high officials in military governments, such as Argentina's Domingo Cavallo, in later years came to make major contributions both to sound economic policy and to the consolidation of democratic politics. A political party founded in close association with right-wing violent gangs, El Salvador's Nationalist Republican Alliance (ARENA), became an agent of the country's democratization in the 1990s. These themes are discussed in chapters 2 and 4.

The mass public, despite the derision of antidemocrats, has also learned. In the late 1980s and early 1990s, electorates in nearly all Latin American and Caribbean countries turned relentlessly against ruling political parties that had performed badly. But by the mid-1990s, the same electorates learned to reward with reelection parties that had performed well—Chile's Concertación Democrática, Argentina's Menem and the refurbished Peronistas, Jamaica's People's National Party, and El Salvador's ARENA, among others. These themes are explored in chapters 1, 2, and especially 3.

There is evidence of yet another surprise with regard to the democratic behavior of the mass public in Mexico: Mexicans are much less authoritarian than their reputation has it. That reputation was well deserved: there were strong authoritarian traits in Mexico's political culture decades ago. But Mexican public opinion has been changing steadily, and Mexicans were ready for democracy sooner than their country's leaders. The evidence for authoritarian values in Mexico's past and for the trend toward democratic values by the 1990s is presented in chapter 5.

Mexico remains one of only two (along with Cuba) nondemocratic Ibero-American countries. Given Mexico's soft authoritarianism of the 1950s, with its subsequent political openings, Mexico seemed a candidate for early democratization (note the repeated use of the phrase "in transition" in the titles of scholarly books about Mexico published during the past several decades).[17] In the 1970s, many scholars and ordinary citizens celebrated Mexico's willingness to give asylum to political and intellectual exiles from the tougher dictatorships to its south, though Mexico was much less generous to the mass of refugees from Central America's wars.[18] Mexico's democratization, alas, has been long delayed. The argument of chapter 5 is that Mexico's transition to democracy may, at last, be at hand, and that ordinary Mexicans are important actors in bringing about this outcome.

Finally, there is the beginning of political change in Cuba, which is edging away from a very tough authoritarian regime toward a more porous authoritarianism and, perhaps, toward democratic politics. For someone whose first book documented the apparent consolidation of a seemingly stable authoritarian regime in Cuba, this is a welcome shock.[19] Cuba's "transition to somewhere" is still in its early stages. Consequently, chapter 6 combines an analysis of aspects of Cuba's transition already under way with comparatively informed speculation about Cuba's possible alternative futures.

The Themes

The chapters that follow explore several enduring themes that help to explain the likelihood of democratic practices in Latin America. In this section, I call attention to the more general themes.

Two International Explanations

International explanations help to account for the pattern of domestic politics in Central America and the Caribbean. International structural explanations for domestic outcomes focus on the impact of the international system within the boundaries of states.[20] Central America and the Caribbean comprise small countries bordering the United States. Their size makes them vulnerable to international political, economic, societal, and military forces. The proximity to the United States has given the U.S. government a disproportionate impact in shaping the internal affairs of its neighbors.

Major power competition throughout the twentieth century and, in particular, the Cold War international system shaped the choices of the U.S. government and of elites in the small countries. The characteristic effect was to facilitate the rise and continuance of authoritarian regimes of diverse stripes, unless U.S. power was deflected by a major power that the United States did not consider its main adversary. (In the Caribbean, this was the United Kingdom.) These authoritarian regimes, of varying degrees of harshness, sometimes attempted to justify and legitimate themselves as the small nation's best defense against attacks on its sovereignty by the United States. Only such tough regimes, its advocates argued, could guarantee the unity of purpose and the concentration of resources necessary to resist U.S. power. The experiences of Cuba, Nicaragua, and Grenada fit this pattern (as did Mexico's, to a more limited extent).

In principle, the U.S. government preferred democratic outcomes in the domestic politics of its small neighbors, but it was unwilling to risk supporting them if democracy would open the country to influence by a major U.S. rival—Germany in the first half of the twentieth century and the Soviet Union during the Cold War years. If the choice was between a loyal and stable authoritarian regime and an adversarial or unstable democratic regime, the United States typically chose the first, even if at various times it also sought more open, hopefully democratic, political systems.[21] Thus, the U.S. armed forces at one point or another during the twentieth century (and occasionally repeatedly) occupied the Dominican Republic, Haiti, Cuba, Nicaragua, and Panama to fill alleged power vacuums that might have made these countries easy prey for European powers. When in the 1930s the United States lowered its military profile and withdrew its troops, strongmen seized and held dictatorial power in the Dominican Republic, Cuba, and Nicaragua; some of these men had been trained in the United States, and many of them were at some moment endorsed by the U.S. government. The United States also had, at various times, an important military presence in Guatemala, Honduras, and El Salvador. From the end of World War II until the mid-1970s, and again in the early 1980s, in different instances the U.S. government supported dictatorships throughout most of Central America and in Cuba, Haiti, and the Dominican Republic, in the belief that local anticommunist despots would prevent domestic turmoil and Soviet penetration. During these years, in practice, the United States was only rarely on the side of democratization.[22]

The fate of the even smaller and more vulnerable countries of the Anglophone Caribbean was different because they belonged to the British empire until the late 1950s and, in the case of the smaller islands, later. The United Kingdom shielded these countries from the syndrome just described. Except for Guyana and Grenada, in which the United States intervened to undo Marxist regimes (indirectly in Guyana in 1964 and directly in Grenada in 1983), these countries escaped the brunt of the Cold War's effects on domestic politics. Their long-term ties to the United Kingdom (as explained in chapter 1) shaped their domestic democratic politics, which featured strong labor unions and strong labor parties. Further, by the late 1970s and throughout much of the 1980s—a later phase of the Cold War—the United States came to see the Anglophone Caribbean democracies as barriers to worse political outcomes and, therefore, supplied significant economic assistance to their governments. This pattern marked the Carter and Reagan presidencies.

In the late 1980s and early 1990s, the international system changed, but an international structural explanation still applies to trends in the domestic politics of these countries. With the collapse of the Soviet Union and Cuba's consequent debility, the international system was transformed. Bereft of credible enemies, the U.S. government had no reason to spend money to ward off extracontinental powers from its southern neighbors and no motivation to support tyrants in their domestic politics. In the Anglophone Caribbean, therefore, the United States cut its foreign aid budget. In Central America, it came to prefer negotiated peace, democratic regimes (even with the participation of the political left), and a reduction in the size of the military. An international structural explanation thus distinguishes between the Anglophone Caribbean and Central America by historical moment and helps to account for the changes in the late 1980s and early 1990s in the Caribbean and Central America (see chapters 1 and 2)—democratization in Central America and more troubled times in the Caribbean.

South American countries were never as closely involved with the United States as were Central America and the Anglophone Caribbean, and their governments came to regard the Soviet Union not as a threat but as a balancer of U.S. power.[23] Nonetheless, some of the same international system effects are evident in the evolution, between the 1940s and the 1980s, of dictatorship and democracy in Venezuela, Colombia, Ecuador, Peru, Chile, Uruguay, and Brazil. The United States did not oppose, and at times supported, the establishment and maintenance of dictatorships until near the end of the Cold War, at which time the United States became a force for the establishment and consolidation of democracy (see chapter 3).

A quite different international explanation (which I term ideational and discuss especially in chapter 4) refers to the impact of international pools of ideas as they help legitimate, change, and mold domestic political, economic, and military practices. At any given moment, certain international ideas predominate; at some critical juncture, new leaders ("idea carriers") come forward with new ideas. For example, in the 1940s democratic politics and import-substitution industrialization were the predominant international pools of ideas available to Latin American and Caribbean countries; these were borrowed from Europe and North America and were communicated through the United Nations Economic Commission for Latin America.[24] These ideas became attractive, intellectually and practically, in response to a first critical juncture: the shared experience of the Second World War; the war was portrayed as an alliance of democracies and as an experience that valued economic self-sufficiency.

In the 1960s and early 1970s, national security doctrines and export-promotion policies became the dominant international pools of ideas. The Cuban revolution was the second critical juncture. The impact of the Cold War was at last fully felt in the Americas: governments believed they had to respond by combating communism and accelerating economic growth. U.S. concern with counterinsurgency nurtured the spread of national security ideas in Latin America, while the World Bank and the Inter-American Development Bank pushed export promotion in the region.

The third critical juncture was the so-called international debt crisis of the 1980s, when Latin American governments were mainly authoritarian. The crisis made politicians and publics receptive to new ideas and to replacing dictatorships that were failures in economic policy and brutal in their politics. The dominant international pools of ideas by then were democracy and markets, which were powerfully ensconced in North America and Western Europe. As chapter 4 explains, these ideas spread throughout Latin America and the Caribbean—slowly at first and then, as the debt crisis deepened, rapidly and comprehensively. The major U.S. contribution to the cause of democracy in these countries would prove to be the training obtained at U.S. universities by students from Latin America and the Caribbean, who then became secular missionaries on behalf of the ideas they had learned.

International structural explanations identify the boundaries of possibilities and constraints shaping each political regime. International ideational explanations give specific policy content in politics and economics.

Political Craftsmanship

In the making of democratic politics, "the high degree of indeterminacy embedded in situations where unexpected events (*fortuna*), insufficient information, hurried and audacious choices, confusion about motives and interests, plasticity, and even indefinition of political identities, as well as the talents of specific individuals (*virtù*), are frequently decisive in determining the outcomes."[25] Political craftsmanship is a central feature not only of the making of democracies but also of the practice of democratic politics. Such craftsmanship is important to the transition toward democratic politics; the discussion about Central America in chapter 2 makes this point. But the continuing importance of political craftsmanship for sound democratic politics is key to the story of Latin American and Caribbean democratic politics and goes well beyond the mode of the transition to democracy or the particular deals that might have been struck to make it happen.

In the Anglophone Caribbean, the construction and reconstruction of bargains to undergird political and economic practices is a thread running through the history of these countries since independence and largely accounts for the civil quality of this region's politics (see chapter 1). In South America, the practice of democratic politics—since the return of such regimes, beginning in the late 1970s—has rested on considerable political creativity. In particular, as analyzed in chapter 3, the transformation of party systems in nearly all South American countries has sought to provide new channels for representation without undermining the constitutional foundations of democratic regimes. This is an unparalleled accomplishment in the South American experience, for previous similar transformations of party systems and forms of representation characteristically followed military coups or were the deliberate outcomes of authoritarian rulers. This was the case, for example, in Chile in the early 1930s, in Argentina and Brazil in the mid-1940s, and in Peru and Venezuela in the 1950s. In the 1980s and 1990s, in contrast, new political parties emerged independent of their prior experience of military rule, and the weights of parties were reshuffled without political violence. This happened in Argentina, Uruguay, Brazil, and Venezuela, and a similar experience was evident in Mexico.

Political craftsmanship is also an important explanation for the lack of success, in recent years, of military coups against constitutional civilian presidents in Ibero-American countries. Presidents as different as Carlos Menem and Raúl Alfonsín in Argentina, Carlos Andrés Pérez in Venezuela, and León Febres Cordero in Ecuador successfully resisted coup attempts. Political parties and civic associations have mobilized to defend democratic politics time and again in recent years.

This book breaks with one persistent scholarly tradition, however. Much social science work on Latin America has long eschewed the mention of proper names. Structural analyses (Marxist and otherwise) mark much of the scholarship on these countries, and these analyses often contribute valuable insights. But they deemphasize the role of individuals. Even Guillermo O'Donnell and Philippe Schmitter, despite their celebration of the role of *virtù* in democratic transitions, speak of the making of democracies in abstractions. They use the proper names of other scholars far more often than they cite those of politicians.

In contrast, this volume seeks also to shed light on individuals who have reoriented the history of their countries and who are, therefore, master political craftsmen. I name names. In the maintenance of democratic politics in the Anglophone Caribbean and in the transition toward peace and greater political openings in Central America, real human beings have mattered. In making the creative connection between markets and democracy, specific individuals are key to understanding and explaining the outcome. The roles of specific statesmen are part of chapters 1 and 2, but they are particularly central to the analysis of the role of technopols, as defined and analyzed in chapter 4.

Democratic politics is, indeed, about people of flesh and blood, not just abstract social processes. And democracy is in a fundamental sense the government of the people. Consequently, in another break with the bulk of scholarly work on democratization in Latin America, this book ponders the extent of democratic beliefs in the mass public (chapter 5) and the trends over time.

Ultimately, the principal effect of political craftsmanship is to reduce the uncertainty of which O'Donnell and Schmitter have written and to make it possible for *virtù* to overcome *fortuna*.[26] The reduction of political uncertainty is at the heart of the political success of Anglophone Caribbean democracies—business and labor, government and opposition, Christians and Muslims knew the rules of the democratic game. Uncertainty reduction, understandably, became a focus of the effort of Central American political craftsmen to make the transition from authoritarian rule, for only in that way would the hitherto powerful yield their power. Long-term, stable, rational expectations are the main connection between markets and democracy that motivates the technopols. And the process of uncertainty reduction may open the door to democratization in Mexico and Cuba.

Democracy demands of all acceptance of some uncertainty. Citizens do not know in advance who will win the elections. But to tolerate that uncertainty, politicians craft substantive deals and procedural bargains and accord material and symbolic payoffs to assure most participants that their lives and other interests are not in grave danger in advance of celebrating the sacraments of democracy on election day.[27] That is the key test of *virtù* and a key contribution of politics to democracy.

I The Caribbean Question

Why Has Liberal Democracy (Surprisingly) Flourished?

In *Society and Democracy in Germany*, one of the more influential books published about Germany after the Second World War, Ralf Dahrendorf began by asking what the "German Question" was.[1] For Germans, Dahrendorf suggested, the German Question was one put to foreigners: Why was Germany divided and how could it be reunited? Many Germans thought that the German Question focused on the role of the German people in international affairs. For Dahrendorf and, he said, for many non-Germans, there was a different German Question: Why had liberal democracy (surprisingly) not flourished among Germans?

In the nineteenth century, Germany had seemed to be very much a part of the culture of the West, which had given birth to liberal democracy in Western Europe; Germany's economic resources were on the forefront of Europe. Germany's transition from the empire to the Weimar Republic seemed at the time no more traumatic than other European transitions to democracy: the Weimar Constitution seemed to enshrine many of the West's values of liberty and democracy. Dahrendorf's own German Question, therefore, sought to understand why liberal democracy had not taken root under the empire, why it failed so spectacularly in the 1930s, and why this happened among a people once seen as good candidates for liberal democratic politics?

There is, perhaps, a Caribbean Question, and to its exploration I turn. As for the Germans in their history, so too for many in the Caribbean (the islands, the Guianas, and Belize)[2] the Question has been and remains at the international level: Why is the Caribbean so divided and above all why has there not been a better integration? For example, analysts at times assess the role of the Eastern Caribbean states in their international environment, giving special attention to integrative efforts among the member countries of the Organization of Eastern Caribbean States (OECS).[3] There is understandable concern about regional security in the Caribbean and about the internationalization of corruption and violence, with special attention to the international dimensions of the drug traffic problem. There are many differences between the German and Caribbean cases, even beyond the fact that the OECS does not threaten to conquer the world; above all, Caribbean scholars and decision makers do not insist on political unification but focus, instead, on pragmatic questions for which regional policy options are reasonable and also appropriate.

Many outside the Caribbean also consider the Question from an international perspective. This is the way in which the major powers and, above all, the U.S. government have thought about this region; at times it has seemed as if the region's sea lanes mattered more than the region itself.[4] Across the centuries, for the major powers the Caribbean has been an arena for competition. Trends in the international economy and in international politics have always had a major impact on the Caribbean.

The Caribbean Surprise

From a comparative perspective, however, there is another Caribbean Question: no other region in what has been called the Third World has had, for so long, so many liberal democratic polities. Democracy is defined by its free and fair elections, held at regular intervals, in the context of guaranteed civil and political rights, responsible government (i.e., accountability of the executive, administrative, and coercive arms of the state to elected representatives), and political inclusion (i.e., universal suffrage and nonproscription of parties). Elections must be competitive, and guarantees of rights must be embodied in a convention of constitutionalism, that is, the presumption that political change should only occur in accordance with rules and precedents.

The Caribbean's capacity to sustain liberal democratic polities is impressive. Since independence (beginning with Jamaica and Trinidad and Tobago in 1962) ten of the twelve (Guyana and Grenada excepted) Anglophone Caribbean countries have consistently held fair elections and have been free of unconstitutional transfers of power. Also since independence nearly all of the ten consistently constitutionalist Anglophone Caribbean countries have witnessed at least one election as a result of which the governing party peacefully turned power over to the hitherto opposition party; in Barbados, Belize, Jamaica, and Trinidad and Tobago, this democratic achievement has occurred thrice.[5] Since 1978 the transfer from government to opposition has also occurred three times in the Dominican Republic, where there have been no unconstitutional transfers of power since the 1978 election.

This Caribbean achievement is far superior to that of Latin America and also to that of the countries of Africa and Asia that acquired their formal independence from European powers after the Second World War. Former

British colonies have had a better record than the former colonies of other major powers at sustaining liberal democracy.[6] It is noteworthy, however, that the former British colonies in the Caribbean have also had a far superior capacity to sustain liberal democratic polities than most former British colonies in Africa and Asia and have done so with much less violence. Nigeria and Uganda, plagued by military coups and civil war, became independent within the same time span as Jamaica and Barbados, which have suffered no coups and no civil wars. There is no Caribbean analog to Sri Lanka's sustained ethnocommunal violence. And in the Caribbean, too, the Dominican Republic's transition to democratic politics in the late 1970s preceded most of Latin America's democratic transitions of the decade that followed. Thus, even from a comparative perspective it is a surprise that the Caribbean has so many liberal democracies.

The surprise goes beyond such international comparisons. The Dominican Republic's transition to democracy occurred after the decades' long rule of Rafael Leónidas Trujillo, a type of despotic experience that has not elsewhere fostered liberal democracy. Puerto Rico's domestic democratic institutions have been vitalized by twenty-six uninterrupted elections in the twentieth century. Moreover, the level of electoral participation by Puerto Ricans in Puerto Rico puts to shame the level of electoral participation by U.S. citizens on the mainland. The engagement of Puerto Ricans in the politics of their island resembles electoral participation in Europe far more than it does that in mainland United States. The vigor of political competition among Puerto Rico's principal parties may be unsurpassed anywhere.

Thus, some favorite explanations for the flourishing of democracy in the Third World do not explain these cases. The Dominican Republic's liberal democracy is not the mature fruit of decades of cultural-historical nurturing. Nor is Puerto Rico's vigorous, electorally participative, liberal democracy to be explained as derivative of politics in the United States. Nor can one explain the practice of liberal democracy in the Anglophone Caribbean merely as what might be expected among former British colonies. Why, then, has liberal democracy (surprisingly) flourished in the Caribbean?

Economic Arguments

One long-standing explanation for the consolidation of liberal democracy has been level of economic development. For the world as a whole that argument has always been somewhat useful because highly economically developed countries are, indeed, much more likely than poor countries to have consolidated liberal democracy. But the argument has also been somewhat problematic; the Caribbean experience illustrates why. For the sake of standardization, let us rely mainly upon data for the World Bank's 1990 report.[7]

At first blush the Caribbean confirms the proposition that wealthier countries are more likely to have liberal democratic regimes. In 1988 U.S. dollars, the gross national product (GNP) per capita of every Anglophone Caribbean country but Guyana was above $1,000. Guyana was the only Anglophone Caribbean example of sustained authoritarianism since independence; authoritarian rule lasted roughly from the falsification of electoral lists prior to the 1968 election to the first-ever opposition party victory in 1992. Moreover, as compared with the Anglophone Caribbean, Nicaragua, El Salvador, Honduras, and Guatemala all had lower GNP per capita levels, again illustrating that the prospects for stable liberal democracy are poorer for poorer countries. Moreover, with one of the world's lowest GNP per capita levels, the poorest Caribbean country is Haiti, which has also been the one country in the region with the longest experience of authoritarian rule.

The relationship between levels of economic development and liberal democracy in the Caribbean is much weaker than the above facts suggest, however. The Dominican Republic's GNP per capita was about the same as that of Guatemala. Jamaica's GNP per capita was only slightly above that of Guatemala. Though in the late 1980s Guatemala took some important steps toward democratization, Jamaica has never experienced the grip of military power that Guatemala has, nor has the Dominican Republic since the late 1970s; nor has either experienced the thirty-five-year civil war that Guatemala suffered. In the same vein, St. Lucia, Dominica, and Grenada differ little in their GNP per capita, yet only Grenada has experienced such authoritarian episodes as Eric Gairy's latter years in power and the New Jewel Movement. Suriname is much more economically prosperous than St. Lucia, Dominica, or St. Vincent and the Grenadines, but only Suriname experienced nearly continuous military rule in the 1980s.

What, then, of the effect of economic growth rates on the endurance of liberal democracy? In the 1970s and 1980s the economic growth rates of the Caribbean were not good. Guyana, Haiti, the Dominican Republic, Suriname, and Trinidad and Tobago had a lower gross domestic product (GDP) per capita at the end of the 1980s than at the beginning; Jamaica's GDP per capita at the end of the 1980s was lower than it had been in 1970.[8] Thus it may be argued that faltering rates of economic growth could "cause" regime changes—or at least political violence. Jamaica's 1980 election, for example, was marked by high levels of political violence, in part in response to a deteriorating economy. Guyana's economic decline was associated with its trend toward further authoritarian rule. The fall of the Duvalier dynasty in Haiti could have been related to faltering economic performance. In the early 1980s, riots in the Dominican Republic were related to austerity measures adopted after negotiations between the International Monetary Fund and the Dominican government. Suriname was governed mainly by its military arm during its decade of economic decline. And the government of Trinidad and Tobago was nearly overthrown by a mutiny in 1990.

And yet the relationship between trends in economic growth as "cause" and democratic stability as "effect" is muddled at best. The governments of the Dominican Republic and of Trinidad and Tobago were not overthrown despite their economic troubles. If economic explanations for political stability were dominant, the Trinidadian government should have fallen in 1983 or 1984, when GDP per capita fell massively and abruptly. In 1980 the opposition's victory in the Jamaican elections was recognized, and despite continuing economic troubles in the 1980s, political violence in Jamaica declined over the decade. Military government began in 1980 in Suriname after a decade of economic growth.[9] Nor was the government of Barbados overthrown in 1974, when the inflation rate seemed to spiral out of control—an acceleration of the rate of inflation as statistically worrisome as that which preceded the 1964 military coup in Brazil. Nor were some of the better economic performers among the OECS countries free from political violence.

A final illustration of the insufficiency of economic arguments is to compare the political regimes of countries at comparable levels of GNP per capita: the Dominican Republic and Egypt, Jamaica and Cameroon, Trinidad and Tobago and Gabon. Though Egypt, Cameroon, and Gabon have been among the more open political systems in their regions, for the same level of economic development and even in some ways comparable kinds of economic activity, the countries of the Caribbean are much more liberal democratic. Thus we should remain surprised that, given the Caribbean's levels of economic development, liberal democracies have flourished as much as they have.

Though he made only passing references to the Caribbean, perhaps Samuel Huntington has characterized best the relationship between economic performance and political regime as it bears on the Caribbean: it is indeterminate. Most Caribbean countries have a level of economic development in or near what Huntington calls the "transition zone," in which high enough "economic development compels the modification or abandonment of traditional political institutions; it does not determine what political system will replace them."[10] By Huntington's assessment of the economic argument, among the Caribbean's independent states only Barbados and the Bahamas appear wealthy enough to be considered safe as liberal democracies. More generally, the Caribbean's comparatively high level of economic development by Third World standards seems to make liberal democratic politics more likely than, say, in Africa and even in much of Latin America (although the GNP per capita level of several OECS countries, Belize, and Jamaica is below that of South American countries), but one cannot explain the marked success of liberal democracy in the Caribbean just in such economic terms.

The Armed Forces

In order to ponder why liberal democracy, surprisingly, has flourished in the Caribbean, let us consider the role of the armed forces. The military has played a major role in preventing the installation and consolidation of democracy in the Third World; in the Caribbean, military apparatuses were small upon independence and, typically, remained so. One feature of the Westminster model (that is, the legacy of British constitutional practices in some of its former colonies), which has played such a key role in the Anglophone Caribbean, is civilian supremacy. This is an important institutionalist point (to which I return in a later section).

A related but different argument—that big armies undermine democracies—does not find support, however. Consider the evidence from the U.S. Arms Control and Disarmament Agency about "militarization," measured as armed forces personnel per one thousand people.[11] At first blush there appears to be a clear relationship between high rates of militarization and the probability of dictatorship. In the mid-1980s only the three Caribbean countries under sustained authoritarian rule—Cuba, Guyana, and Suriname—had more than five soldiers per one thousand people. All the liberal democracies had lower levels of militarization.

And yet the relationship between militarization measured in this way and the nature of the political regime is muddled as well. One of the Caribbean's most stable liberal democracies has been Barbados, which did not have armed forces (only police forces) upon independence. In 1979 the Barbados Defense Force was founded.[12] In the first half of the 1980s the Barbadian rate of militarization rose to between three and four soldiers per one thousand people, a rate about the same as that of Chad and higher than that of Haiti or Ghana, none of which is an example of democracy or stability. The Barbadian rate was also twice as high as those of Jamaica and of Trinidad and Tobago, both of which experienced higher levels of domestic political violence. Jamaica and Trinidad and Tobago increased slightly their rate of militarization from the 1970s to the 1980s, reaching levels comparable to those of other former British colonies such as Ghana and Uganda, neither of which exemplified democratic order. Militarization so measured does not distinguish countries in terms of the likelihood of democracy or stability.

Consider other examples. From the mid-1970s to the mid-1980s the Dominican Republic and Haiti had stable rates of militarization, but the Dominican rate was three times that of Haiti's. And yet it was the Dominican Republic that made the earlier and smoother transition to democratic politics. The cases of Guyana and Suriname are interesting. Suriname's rate of militarization was stable (about 2.8 per 1,000 people) for the years prior to Desi Bouterse's coup in 1980. The rate of militarization doubled only after the coup; thus the increase in the rate does not "explain" the prior coup. Guyana's level of militarization jumped from below 3 in 1975 to above 9 since 1977, but that was in response to Forbes Burnham's choices, not the result of a coup. The militarization of the Guyanese system of government under Burnham ultimately reflected the corruption of a civilian system rather than its displacement by military rule.

In brief, higher rates of militarization accompany the consolidation of dictatorships in the Caribbean (except in Haiti), but the origins of Caribbean dictatorships must be found in factors other than the relative size of the armed forces or the change in their size.

Overthrowing the Government: Unconstitutional Attempts

Liberal democracy might have endured in the Caribbean because no one had bothered to try to seize power. And yet Caribbean constitutionalism has been tested all too frequently. In 1969 there was a black power uprising in Curaçao that led to the dispatch of Dutch marines. In 1970 there was a black power uprising in Trinidad in which parts of the army were included.[13] In 1976, Sidney Burnett-Alleyne attempted to invade Barbados with forces organized in Martinique (where French authorities arrested and convicted him); in 1979, Burnett-Alleyne made a second attempt to overthrow the Barbadian government.

Also in 1979 the New Jewel Movement seized power in Grenada, combining aspects of a putsch with those of a popular uprising. In that same year St. Vincent's prime minister, Milton Cato, requested and received Barbadian military support to repel an invasion of Union Island by a group called the Movement for National Liberation. There was also a coup attempt in Dominica in 1979. In 1980 sixteen noncommissioned officers, led by Desi Bouterse, seized power in Suriname. The political violence that accompanied Jamaica's elections in 1980 (and some of the political rhetoric during that contest) raised doubts regarding Jamaica's democratic regime.

In 1981 two coup attempts were made against the government of Prime Minister Eugenia Charles in Dominica; these were defeated, thanks in part to the dispatch of Barbadian military forces. (As a result of these coup attempts, Charles's government abolished the standing army.) In 1983 a military coup overthrew Prime Minister Maurice Bishop's government in Grenada, technically the only successful military coup ever in the Anglophone Caribbean; this was followed by the invasion of Grenada by U.S. and some Anglophone Caribbean forces.

In July 1990 an uprising by the Jamaat-Al-Muslimeen resulted in the kidnaping of Trinidad's prime minister, A. N. R. Robinson, and many of his ministers and nearly toppled the government; Trinidad's army overcame the uprising and defended the constitutional government.[14] In December 1990 a military coup overthrew Suriname's weak civilian government. From 1986 to 1994 considerable political instability, punctuated by military coups and other violent uprisings and capped by a U.S. military occupation in 1994, marked Haitian politics.

Moreover, since the Second World War the Caribbean has been the area in the Americas most marked by international, conventional, military confrontations. Leaving aside events pertaining mainly to U.S.-Cuban relations, the United States invaded (a) the Dominican Republic in 1965, (b) together with several Anglophone governments, Grenada in 1983, and (c) under United Nations auspices, Haiti in 1994. Guyana and Belize have faced serious attempts by Venezuela and Guatemala, respectively, to lay claim to much or all of their national territories. In 1980 a Bahamian coast guard boat was attacked by a Cuban air force plane, which killed several crew members (the only conventional military attack ever made by Cuba on one of its neighbors).

The record is discouraging: Is the Caribbean, but for the grace of God, not unlike Latin America and the rest of the Third World? Why has liberal democracy (surprisingly) flourished in so many of these islands?

Toward an Answer

Habits of Societal Resistance to Centralized Power

The Caribbean is the only part of the world (with the partial and interrupted exception of Rwanda) where the descendants of slaves govern sovereign countries. For the Commonwealth Caribbean, this legacy may have placed a premium on freedom in the emergent political culture. For those who may have heard at home stories from their grandparents about the consequences of highly concentrated power, the arguments on behalf of freedom may not be abstract; the distrust of political claims that would install illiberal regimes is marked.

The abolition of chattel slavery elsewhere in the Americas did not, however, much alter the racial identity of rulers even a century after abolition. Even today Puerto Rican elites have difficulty coping with the country's Afro-Caribbean legacy. There is a lingering racism in the Dominican Republic's political life, often expressed as a distrust of "Haitians"; Dominican President Joaquín Balaguer (1966–78, 1986–96) asserted his country's Spanish heritage by making a major effort to celebrate the quincentenary of Columbus's voyage. Fewer changes occurred, therefore, in the social structure of the Hispanic than in that of the Anglophone Caribbean to foster the distrust of centralized power, and it is in Cuba and in the Dominican Republic where the harshest dictatorships have been founded.

Outside of Haiti and the Hispanic Caribbean, the pattern of resistance to slavery in Caribbean societies may also have contributed to a social structure more resistant to centralized rule. In the densely forested Guianas and in mountainous Jamaica, slaves escaped from their masters and formed communities that did not recognize central power. The trickster figure of Afro-Caribbean folklore and the extensive use of humor through musical and other forms of expression are living symbols of resistance to those who have too much power.

The slaves brought from Africa had no common language. They combined European and African languages to give birth to the French-based Creole languages of Haiti, Martinique, Guadeloupe, and Dominica; to the English-based Sranan (or Taki-Taki) and Djukatongo of Suriname; to the English Creole of Jamaica; and to the Portuguese-based Saramakatongo of Suriname and Papiamentu of the Netherlands Antilles. These languages did not belong to the elites, even if they learned them. In the Hispanic Caribbean the only analog is the endurance of Spanish as Puerto Rico's non-imperial language.

Africans and their descendants were equally creative in adapting European religions, and in this regard the Hispanic Caribbean was no exception. Afro-Caribbean religiosity today is strong and complex. In contemporary Cuba, Afro-Cuban religions probably command greater fidelity than any other system of belief. In the English and Dutch Caribbean a variety of Protestant denominations, indigenous religious communities, Roman Catholicism, Hinduism, and Islam have all taken root; probably no comparably small part of the world is so religiously pluralistic as well as so intensely religious. These are among the dimensions of what Anthony Maingot has called "conservative societies," which value the right to one's own beliefs and the ownership of private property—for a house lot or to raise food.[15] These habits of thought and behaviors with regard to religion and property are inhospitable to the ambitious plans of dictators. This Caribbean social structure is especially receptive to challenges from below (not necessarily in a revolutionary sense) to affirm the worth of religion, culture, and social mores in the face of state power.[16]

In contrast, ethnocommunal pluralism may be as adverse to liberal democracy in the Caribbean as it is worldwide. Studies from many countries indicate that the likelihood of consolidating liberal democracy is much greater in societies with a low degree of subcultural pluralism and much lower in societies with marked or extreme pluralism.[17] The latter have often been marked by civil discord (as in Lebanon and Cyprus) or by authoritarian rule to control such pluralism (as in the Soviet Union from the 1920s to the 1980s). Among the independent countries in the Caribbean, the societies with the most extreme ethnocommunal pluralism have been Guyana and Suriname, which were both under authoritarian rule for many years. Indeed, over the years race has explained a great deal about political behavior in Trinidad and Tobago; until the 1986 election very few blacks felt that it was legitimate for them not to vote for the Peoples National Movement, founded and led by Eric Williams until his death.[18] The ethnocommunal constraints on Trinidadian politics have made change and accommodation harder. On normative grounds, the case on behalf of liberal democracy as a preferable system for the management of such ethnocommunal cleavages is of course strong, but that is not to say that this is a frequent outcome.[19]

In sum, the Caribbean's habits of societal resistance were generally favorable for liberal democracy, but the experiences of the largest islands and of the Guianas indicate that such societal factors do not by themselves establish and consolidate liberal democracy.

The Statist Bargain

For Karl Marx, John Stuart Mill, and Alexis de Tocqueville, among others, capitalism and full democracy were at best an odd couple, if not strongly contradictory. But, in fact, the wedding between capitalism and universal and equal suffrage under representative government is at the heart of liberal democracy as it has come to exist. One explanation for this outcome has been the Keynesian welfare state.[20] Labor accepts the logic of profitability and markets as means to allocate resources in exchange for a sustained rise in living standards, along with the exercise of political rights. Business supports the welfare state to buy peace. Keynesianism becomes a positive-sum game of economic growth with economic security in which capitalists and workers acknowledge that they need each other. Profits are needed for investment, which is the guarantee of future jobs and future income, which will enrich makers of goods and increase demand, which will yield greater profits.

This welfare state was an aspect of the Caribbean's economic success during the 1960s. Thanks mainly to factors external to the Caribbean, the region's economies grew and were able to benefit the elites and the masses.[21] (In this way, this particular economic argument helps to explain the timing of Caribbean's democratic consolidation.) Building on trends begun during the Second World War, primary and secondary education expanded in the Anglophone, Francophone, and Dutch Caribbean, in Cuba, in Puerto Rico, and somewhat later in the Dominican Republic. The levels of literacy, and of schooling beyond literacy, achieved in many of these countries are impressive.

One way to assess the Caribbean's record is to compare some of the welfare achievements of Caribbean liberal democracies with those of nondemocratic regimes at comparable levels of economic development. For example, the Côte d'Ivoire is somewhat wealthier, more populous, and larger than the Dominican Republic, but both are small, primary, goods-producing countries, with about the same GNP per capita and vulnerable to international price fluctuations in very few products. In the mid-1980s the rate of illiteracy in the Dominican Republic was less than half that in the Côte d'Ivoire, and the life expectancy of Dominicans was thirteen years more than that of Ivoiriens. Trinidad and Tobago and Gabon have comparable populations and about the same GNP per capita; both are oil producers, and neither had a good economic growth record from the mid-1960s to the mid-1980s. And yet in the mid-1980s the rate of illiteracy in Trinidad and Tobago was one-tenth that of Gabon, while the life expectancy in Trinidad was fourteen years more than in Gabon. Jamaica's GNP per capita is comparable to Botswana's, another former British colony and one of Africa's few democratic regimes. At the end of the 1980s, Jamaica's infant mortality rate was one-quarter that of Botswana. Though Colombia is a bit wealthier than Jamaica and has had a much higher economic growth rate, in the late 1980s, Jamaica's infant mortality rate was also one-quarter that of Colombia's.[22]

Caribbean states invested the income derived from favorable international circumstances (high prices for commodities, new investments in tourism and other sectors, and foreign aid) to improve the standard of living for many Caribbean citizens. The Caribbean state was the midwife: economic growth gave birth to social welfare. Because this practice continued in the 1960s even after independence in the larger countries of the Anglophone Caribbean and in the 1970s in the Dominican Republic as it gradually democratized (through high sugar prices, high foreign aid, and high remittances from foreign emigrants), the allegiance of citizens to democratic states was enhanced: democracies delivered material gain.

In this way, the political economy of Caribbean states differed from that of the small states in Western Europe.[23] Small European states fashioned domestic political and economic arrangements, including creation of a welfare state, to maintain social peace but also to ensure their ability to survive on their own in the international system (from which they could not expect financial donations and which could even engulf them in war) by means of the cohesion of their polities and the competitiveness of their economies. Small Caribbean states began with the premise that their economies were uncompetitive (except for primary products) but that their strategic location would generate protection from friendly major powers (sparing them the costs of defense) and the funds to pay for their welfare states.

There was, however, a less happy but equally important face to the welfare state in the Caribbean. With their externally originated resources, Caribbean governments also built an apparatus that protected their economies from international competition while using both subsidies and government jobs to distribute income and employment. In some cases, as in the Dominican Republic, the result was a massive, but irrationally constituted, state apparatus. In other cases, especially Puerto Rico in the 1940s, a strategic design for the state's role was in greater evidence. The consequences for economic policy and performance are enormous.

The corruption of the welfare state was necessary for the kind of democratic politics built in the region. Joaquín Balaguer's presidencies were the hallmark of machine politics. Machine politics can function in democratic or authoritarian settings, but the latter are typically neither totalitarian nor among the harshest bureaucratic authoritarian regimes. Machine politics is inherently distributive, seeking to include, albeit with unequal gains, the many people needed to build political support. Machine politics was a key factor in the Dominican transition from Trujillo's monopoly of resources to liberal democratic politics. So too in the Anglophone Caribbean: political parties have traditionally maintained the loyalty of their supporters in large part through patronage. That patronage has often benefited poor people. And in racially divided societies such as Trinidad and Guyana, parties were avenues for jobs and contracts for those associated with victorious parties.

Patronage did not benefit only the poor. It often benefited the business community, which was the direct beneficiary of the structures of protection against imports and of direct subsidies to their operations. In the agricultural and livestock sector, the state created the conditions for legal, successful business cartels.[24] Moreover, by relying on relatively high commodity prices in the 1960s and early 1970s and on foreign aid in the late 1970s and early 1980s (net external transfers to Caribbean countries rose from U.S. $542 million in 1978 to $1,142 million in 1982),[25] the liberal democratic states were able to tax business less than would otherwise have been necessary to pay for education and health services, for the costs of import substitution and cartel-fostering protection, and for patronage of various kinds and for various beneficiaries.

Another feature of the statist bargain that obtained the allegiance of Caribbean business elites to the newly independent liberal democratic regimes was that many firms did not have to work so hard to be profitable.[26] The Caribbean states built walls around their economies to guarantee profits higher than justified by competitive efficiency. For somewhat more venturesome firms, CARICOM (the Caribbean Common Market) provided a slightly wider market that was still highly protected. Liberal democracy was good for business: politicians sought to include everyone.

Even in Puerto Rico the state government is big. Puerto Rico's government was designed in the early 1940s by U.S. and Puerto Rican social democrats; it is the only place under the U.S. flag where the state has had such a large role in the economy. In recent years, new ways have been designed to use state power to foster the allegiance of Puerto Ricans. Many of those who have supported statehood hope that the U.S. federal government will bankroll Puerto Rican welfare rolls (especially through food stamps) indefinitely. To those who support commonwealth status, the complex financial provisions and tax exemptions of the U.S. Internal Revenue Code have long represented key attempts to harness the state's power for the sake of Puerto Rico's economic growth.

From the 1960s to the mid-1980s the statist bargain on behalf of democracy sought to provide gains for the many—the worker and the business owner—while exporting the costs of running such states to the international economy via commodity prices or foreign aid. Parties were the institutional brokers for such distributive politics; allegiances to them depended to a large degree on the expectation of particularistic benefits. These states by and large did not threaten the society's habits of resistance in religion, language, or property ownership. They could be big because they were not lordly. They had to be capacious to construct democratic politics. By the late 1980s commodity prices were down; net external transfers to the Caribbean had turned negative. Caribbean liberal democracy had flourished, not surprisingly, thanks to what economists call inefficiencies. It had depended to a large degree on the kind of state that these countries can no longer afford.

The Institutionalist and Leadership Arguments

Perhaps most important of all to the establishment and consolidation of liberal democracy has been the intersection between political institutions and political leaders. As noted above, the statist bargain could also buttress certain kinds of authoritarian rule, and the habits of resistance in the society could be overcome under certain conditions, as they were in Haiti, Suriname, and Guyana. The simple form of the international argument—British legacies—was insufficient to explain why liberal democracy was more enduring in the Anglophone Caribbean than in Anglophone Africa or Asia.

The argument still begins, however, at the international level, but with a special focus on the impact of the international system on institutional development in the Caribbean. In the 1930s there were mass uprisings in Central American and Caribbean countries. In Central America (except in Costa Rica), in Cuba, and in the Dominican Republic, dictatorships emerged (at times with U.S. acquiescence or even explicit support) as a response to the crisis. In the Anglophone Caribbean, British colonialism opened up the political system instead; the process of decolonization was long and deliberate but also democratic in its direction. Thanks to the British Empire, the Anglophone Caribbean handled in much less repressive ways problems that some Central American countries have yet to settle.

Another dimension of the connection between the international system and local institutional development has been highlighted by Maingot: the role of political leaders and of available international ideologies to fashion the new institutions in the context of imperial decolonization.[27] For the French, decolonization meant even fuller Antillean assimilation into France; in 1946 the French Antilles became French departments. Political leaders in the French Antilles thus reconstructed the political parties of metropolitan France, responding in part to the ideologies prevalent on the French mainland, including those of the Communist Party.

For the Dutch, the important thing was to allow for various forms of voluntary choice, which nonetheless retained the tie to the Netherlands. Dutch elites and the elites in the Netherlands Antilles and Suriname worked hard to forge consociational agreements, that is, agreements among elites of the various ethnic and religious communities that sought to establish democracy and to guarantee certain rights and privileges to all, while constraining some features of mass democracy.[28]

For the British, decolonization was motivated in part by the desire to reduce the costs of empire. Institutionally, the Westminster model was already in place and working toward a political opening. Certainly attractive were its constitutional guarantees of government by rule and precedent, its civilian supremacy (given that local politicians had no military experience), and its bureaucratic neutrality (at least until politicians could get a better grip on administration). The analysis of the Westminster model suggests that what matters for stable democracy is less the size of the armed forces and more the institutionalized pattern of civilian elite supremacy over military elites. And the political ideology that West Indian politicians most readily picked up in Britain was Fabian: to promote social welfare and redistribution through a state built on a democratic process via competitive elections.

Anglophone Caribbean politicians learned as well that defeat in elections, and the turnover between government and opposition, while never pleasant (no politician likes to lose an election) were not necessarily life threatening. The concept of an official, loyal Opposition (with a capital O) may have been among the United Kingdom's most valuable institutional legacies to these colonies. The Opposition was honored for its necessary and constructive role; its leaders were not killed—they were paid to do their job. And programs that politicians implemented while in government often survived their election defeat. The norms of democratic competition were learned.

These institutions and procedures could take root in part because of the very long tradition of British rule. Unlike in Africa and in Asia, British rule in the Caribbean had been uninterrupted for centuries. The colonies of exploitation founded by the British Empire in the Caribbean had deracinated the African population and created new peoples, who were themselves products of empire. There was no preimperial society to overcome; that had been done centuries before by means of the slave trade and the cruelty of slavery, the past's bloody legacy to the constitution of liberty today.

For the United States, the shift toward a commonwealth in Puerto Rico was bolstered by the belief that Puerto Ricans wanted it. Puerto Rico's new institutions were not just a replica of those of states in the United States; they were also a policy legacy from the New Deal's ideology. Luis Muñoz Marín's Popular Democratic Party shared many of the political attitudes then prevalent in the British West Indies. The developmentalist state flourished more in Puerto Rico in the 1940s than in the U.S. mainland under Roosevelt in the 1930s because Rexford Tugwell and Muñoz Marín, colonizer and colonized, agreed on it more than the U.S. Supreme Court agreed with Franklin Roosevelt.

A further feature of institutional development has been the democratic role of labor unions especially in the Anglophone Caribbean. Labor expressed mass rage in the 1930s, but labor unions channeled protests through more peaceful channels in later years. The connection between the labor unions and many political parties on various islands provided the foundation for both democratic transition and consolidation. To some extent, the development of trade unionism and its connection to a political party was the particular contribution of the British Labour Party's active engagement in support of Caribbean democracy. At independence the Anglophone Caribbean's party-union complex was firmly established in terms of electoral effectiveness and as one pillar of the democratic order.

More generally, in some countries social class cleavages played a constructive role in the establishment and consolidation of Caribbean liberal democracy. The existence of such cleavages facilitated the creation of competing political parties, while the ideological convictions and leadership skill of key politicians contained the potentially divisive effects of such cleavages. In ethnocommunally divided societies, of course, many parties were founded, and they operated on such societal segmentation. In other countries, political leaders built multiclass coalitions, often around patronage, that set the foundations for political competition. In any case, moderate but effective party competition became the norm (except in Guyana).

In short, the disposition of the United States and, especially, the United Kingdom to grant substantial autonomy and, eventually, independence to many countries was manifest in an institutional, ideological, and leadership context, from elite to mass, that strengthened the foundations of liberal democracy. Leaders discovered that they could accomplish their welfare goals by democratic means through institutions that had proven democratically resilient in other international settings. These leaders acted through political institutions that did not threaten the society's religious and cultural institutions, which were themselves vigorously pluralistic. Unions and parties tied citizen allegiances to the newly independent democratic states at moments of world economic expansion. For various reasons, including but not limited to the articulation of social cleavage differences, leaders founded and led competitive parties that for the most part were politically moderate. The statist bargain brought business, initially distrustful of the experiment, into the democratic coalition.

The point is not that the Caribbean's political leaders were born democrats (though many have indeed been convinced democrats). It is that the international and institutional factors—even in an authoritarian international setting such as that of colonial empires—set constraints that made domestic authoritarian outcomes less likely while inducing political leaders to learn about democratic politics.

Consolidating Democratic Politics

The consolidation of democratic rule followed mainly from the combination of these institutional and leadership factors, but other factors became important as well. For one thing, the international system came to play a new, different, and ultimately constructive role. One reason that the many violent and unconstitutional attempts to overthrow governments failed is that international actors intervened in time on democracy's side. This has happened so often that it can no longer be described as simply good luck; it is the pattern of international behavior in this subsystem.

Prime Minister Charles's government in Dominica owed its survival more than once to timely arrests or weapons seizures by the U.S. Federal Bureau of Investigation. The Barbadian government was assisted at one moment by similar timely action by French security forces in Martinique.

Barbados has given military help to Dominica and St. Vincent and the Grenadines. And although the government of Trinidad did not request foreign military intervention in 1970 or 1990, it received ample and public political backing from its neighbors. In this context, the most controversial international intervention—the 1983 invasion of Grenada—is consistent with the norms that have evolved in the Caribbean international subsystem to privilege democracy over nonintervention (the opposite of the norm that had been common in Latin America).

This democratizing role for the Caribbean's international subsystem is also an explanation for the Dominican Republic's democratic transition in 1978. As the counting of the ballots stopped, the U.S. government made it clear that it expected the results of the election—the opposition victory—to be honored. The participative effects of machine politics, under U.S. pressure, completed the transition toward a fuller democratic opening.

A less dramatic and less discernible probable international effect has been emigration. The Caribbean has a long history of migration: among the islands, to the European metropolis, and to the United States. Emigration might also have been a way for these countries to export without coercion some of the social basis for an opposition that might have placed even greater strains on the system. Emigration in fact has made democratic politics more difficult to mount in Cuba; in general, emigration helps to explain order more than it does competition. But the maintenance of political order in a region where liberal democracy is the norm has as an indirect effect the fostering of a democratic order.

Apart from such international factors, the Caribbean has been blessed with remarkable political leaders.[29] It must have been difficult for Michael Manley in 1980 and Edward Seaga in 1989 to acknowledge defeat, but they did. In Barbados, too, leaders of both major political parties have had to accept electoral defeat at various times. It must have been difficult for Trinidad's People's National Movement (PNM) in 1986 to acknowledge defeat for the first time since independence, but it did. So too have political leaders in the Eastern Caribbean time and again. Most impressive of all was Puerto Rico's Luis Muñoz Marín, who in the mid-1960s, in order to bring about a leadership transition beyond the party's founder, had to impose his will on the Popular Democratic Party so that it would not nominate him again.[30] Moreover, political parties in the larger countries—Trinidad and Tobago, Jamaica, Barbados, the Dominican Republic, and Puerto Rico— have all witnessed a transition of power within the party at least once since independence (in Puerto Rico's case, since commonwealth; in the Dominican Republic's case, since the key 1978 election).

Parliamentary institutions have also served the Anglophone Caribbean well. A relatively smooth political transition has occurred upon the prime minister's death twice in Barbados and once in Trinidad. The new prime minister in each case was, in turn, politically strengthened by having to form his own government, not just inheriting the mantle of the deceased predecessor. Perhaps an even better test of the utility of parliamentary institutions occurred in 1982 in St. Lucia. In January the prime minister resigned under pressure from a heterogeneous coalition (which even included the chamber of commerce and middle-class groups) that accused the government of corruption and abuse of power; parliament was dissolved. The caretaker government was led by a member of the smallest of St. Lucia's three parties, a politically radical party, in part because this party had not been the source of the government crisis. In the end, the moderate parties won the election.[31] In Latin America this scenario might have led to a coup. Or an embattled president might have stayed in office, presiding over policy drift. Few would have trusted the most radical party to play the caretaker role and then to turn power over peacefully to its ideological opponents.

On the other hand, some Caribbean countries might have been less well served by the first-past-the-post (or single-member-plurality) system of electoral representation typical of Anglo-American electoral law. Parties at times win too many or too few seats relative to their share of the electorate. In countries that are ethnically deeply segmented, this can present serious problems of citizen allegiance. In 1986 in Trinidad, for example, the PNM won nearly one-third of the votes but not quite one-tenth of the seats, which means that other parties were overrepresented. In other elections, of course, the PNM had been overrepresented. For different reasons, the Jamaican Labour Party swept the 1984 parliamentary elections; had the electoral rules been closer to proportional representation—something like the German two-vote system—the willingness of Jamaica's opposition (which had boycotted the elections) to participate in the elections might have been greater.

Finally, mass-media institutions and key intellectuals have played important roles in defending freedom of expression. Though the personal and institutional behavior of some intellectuals and of some mass-media institutions may be subject to criticism, and though some of that behavior may at times have been self-serving and even abusive, and though the printed press in much of the Caribbean has had a marked probusiness predilection, freedom of expression, including freedom of the press, is essential to liberal democracy. Important examples, therefore, of the decline of democratic liberty are the murders of Rupert Bishop in 1974 in Grenada and of Walter Rodney in 1980 in Guyana. And an equally important example of the preservation of democratic liberty is the decision of Michael Manley's government, in the late 1970s, not to shut down the *Daily Gleaner* when the *Gleaner* stood up for its own pluralistic vision of Jamaica's polity.

Austerity, Insecurity, Democracy, and Markets: New Questions

As the 1990s began, the international economic situation was adverse for most of the Caribbean. In 1990 recessions began in the United States and the United Kingdom. They were triggered in part by the sudden rise in the price of petroleum, which benefited Trinidad and Tobago at a critical moment after the July 1990 attempt to overthrow its government but which hurt most of the region. Recessions typically lead to reduced spending on Caribbean tourism, as U.S. consumers cut back on nonessentials, and to decreased international demand for products exported by Caribbean countries (including lower industrial demand for bauxite and alumina), hence depressing prices.

Even before those recessions, the economic outlook was problematic. Net external transfers to the Caribbean had fallen steadily from a high of U.S. $1,142 million in 1982 to $15 million in 1988. Net transfers from the United States alone fell from a high of $353.5 million in 1984 (the aftermath of the intervention in Grenada) to a low of –$44.5 million in 1988.[32] Given the constraints of the U.S. budget deficit and the demands for economic aid to democratize Eastern Europe and the former Soviet Union, consolidate peace in the Middle East, and fight Andean drug trafficking, the United States is not likely to make large, new commitments of economic assistance to the Caribbean. In 1992, moreover, Caribbean banana producers lost their preferred access to the U.K. market when the single European market was completed. In short, the economic constraints on the Caribbean have tightened.

Insecurity, Democracy, and Drug Traffic

With declining domestic and international economic resources, Caribbean states could become more vulnerable to drug trafficking opeerations and their politicians and government officials more vulnerable to the lure of drug money. Can liberal democracy survive these threats?

Drug traffic operations already threaten the Caribbean's security, society, and political order.[33] In 1984, a commission of inquiry in the Bahamas concluded that at least one minister had corruptly accepted funds from known drug smugglers. In March 1985 the head of government of the Turks and Caicos Islands and two of his ministers were arrested in Miami for facilitating the transshipment of drugs to the United States. In 1990 a commission of inquiry in Antigua-Barbuda heard evidence alleging that Prime Minister Vere Bird's son, Vere Bird Jr., himself a government minister, had facilitated the transfer of weapons to a Colombian drug traffic organization.

Among the threats earlier in the 1980s against Dominica's stability was the possibility that the island might be seized to serve as a drug haven. Thus, the problems range from the possibility that a country might be seized by force to facilitate future drug traffic, to normal corruption, to the purchasing of a government, such as in the Turks and Caicos.

One Caribbean response to the drug traffic threat has been the development of a regional security system. Scholars and citizens continue to debate the wisdom of this development. At issue is not the need for some means to enforce law and order but the configuration, size, command structure, and sovereign authority of the regional security system. Connections between this problem and the Caribbean's worsening economic difficulties raise two questions. Can the incomes of politicians and government officials rise to make them less subject to the temptations of drug corruption? Can these countries pay for a regional security force?

The Caribbean's New Question: The Effects of the New Economic Strategy on Democracy

In the Anglophone Caribbean, one general response to the grim economic agenda has been to attempt to shrink the size of the state and its role in the economy and to rely more on market forces and on the role of private business. Here, I focus on some consequences of this new strategy for the survival of democracy in the Caribbean.

The Caribbean's emerging strategy depends on the entrepreneurship of its business firms to generate growth in international markets and on the toughness and skill of its politicians and administrators to cut government expenditures and subsidies (so that each country can afford its state) and to create a regulatory environment conducive to market-led economic growth. To put it differently, the new strategy requires terminating the statist bargain, discussed earlier, because Caribbean countries can no longer export its costs to foreign consumers and to foreign governments. But can Caribbean societies and political institutions preserve liberal democracy while terminating the statist bargain? This could be the Caribbean Question for the new century.

The behavior of Caribbean business firms does not augur well for the prompt ending of the statist bargain. There is pessimism about the current capacity and skill of Caribbean business firms to compete in global markets.[34] Anglophone Caribbean business firms remain attached to protected markets; so too does Puerto Rican business. Are Caribbean capitalists afraid of capitalism? Will they continue seek the state's protection as they did under the statist bargain? But given budget cuts and patronage reduction, such protection would mean not just participation in distribution, consistent with aspects of the old system of patronage, but redistribution on behalf of business.

The behavior of some politicians in the Hispanic Caribbean seems no more hopeful. Joaquín Balaguer won reelection as Dominican president in 1990 and again in 1994 by running a government based on personalist, pork barrel politics. All major Puerto Rican formal status options seem also to be connected to policy hopes that seek to make even more use of the state for the sake of economic welfare.

In the Anglophone Caribbean, however, politicians and government officials have been taking more vigorous steps to terminate the statist bargain and to behave in ways consistent with the new economic strategy. If these politicians are to succeed in a liberal democratic setting, they need political support. Stable democracies everywhere require strong political parties. And yet many political parties in the Caribbean have relied on patronage in exchange for electoral support. As politicians cut back on patronage, as required by the new economic strategy, what will be the new bases for voter loyalty and party organization?[35] The proportion of loyal party voters in Jamaica was declining by the end of the 1980s: if there is less patronage to distribute, it is more difficult to retain voter allegiance.[36] Can democratic regimes survive if the partisan institutions that have been at the heart of politics no longer provide organized political support and opposition?

Moreover, many political parties in the Anglophone Caribbean historically relied upon labor union support to generate general political support. And yet labor union militancy and power have weakened, too; whatever their ills, labor unions have been one of the foundations of Caribbean democracy. With weakened labor unions, what will channel into peaceful avenues the discontent that is a normal part of politics and that could become abnormally severe if economic circumstances deteriorate?

The Caribbean's demography is still characterized by youthfulness: the average age of its citizens is still generally in the midteens. This exacerbates problems of high social expenditures, unemployment, underemployment, and political disenchantment, since young and underemployed people were involved in the 1969 and 1970 black power uprisings in Curaçao and Trinidad. Demography cannot be remade overnight. Will such people threaten the stability of Caribbean democracy again and even more because the parties and the unions can no longer channel protest as effectively as they did in the past?

In Trinidad and Tobago, in particular, the efforts to reduce government patronage have had adverse effects for the stability of racial politics in a society in which citizens have expected their parties to favor their ethnic community with government jobs and other forms of economic support. The government's economic austerity policies have already resulted in severe ethnic dislocations, including an attempt in July 1990 to overthrow the government. Similar violence, protesting economic austerity measures, occurred years earlier in the Dominican Republic. The government of Suriname actually fell in December 1990.

Even the possible valuable economic contributions of private direct foreign investment may present some problems for liberal democracies under economic stress. Such foreign firms may choose to invest in the Caribbean because they find labor markets attractive; if so, they may prefer even weaker labor unions with even fewer connections to political parties. Some Anglophone Caribbean business sectors may fear the coming of such foreign firms, either because they worry about the direct competition or because they fear that foreign firms will soak up all the investment incentives that Caribbean states can afford.[37]

Foreign firms tend to be large; Caribbean countries are small. Under these conditions, these countries could become vulnerable to the "Dutch disease," that is, the development of one sector so that island costs are pushed up to the point at which other sectors are rendered uncompetitive. The political analog of Dutch disease is the company town, the overwhelming political domination of a single firm of the affairs of the community and the combination and concentration of political and economic power to the detriment of democracy.

What, then, could be a new bargain between politics and markets? The Caribbean's new economic strategy rests on according a "privileged position" to business.[38] While such an outcome is at odds with the Fabian traditions common in the West Indies and with the New Deal statist tradition of Puerto Rico, business has already been greatly influential in all of these countries as well as in the Dominican Republic. The new strategy seeks, however, to tilt further toward business. The legitimization of business power will require, in due course, that local business elites prove they can generate economic growth. But the legitimization of business power cannot await some hypothetical economic boom of the twenty-first century. A new political bargain is required to enable liberal democracy to survive while the new economic strategy is at work. Such a bargain could rest on three foundations.

First, the shrinking of the state has occurred in a capricious and cavalier fashion, giving priority to current expenditures and cutting capital expenditures. Maintenance has been neglected; government services are insufficient, and thus the quality of services and of the infrastructure required to resume economic growth has eroded. There is a need to increase the government's capital expenditures to improve services and infrastructure that benefit economic reactivation as well as the population as a whole. Second, for the public at large, such improvements would represent an early benefit of the new strategy and thus would increase the likelihood of the public's support of the parties committed to it. But the new strategy must also focus on one of the Caribbean's premier assets, namely, its people. To be consistent with the new strategy, educational policy needs to focus on training in skills for which there are jobs, because there are business needs for those jobs. Educational policy also needs to focus on increased investment in university education, which not only would garner political support and be socially appropriate but also would contribute to the new economic strategy. Third, to finance these increased expenditures consistent with an export promotion strategy, governments need to reform their fiscal strategies to provide inducements for the growth of exports in goods and services, while raising revenue by penalizing the diversion of resources away from export-oriented investments toward nontraded activities such as real estate.

Politicians and government officials should reorder their priorities accordingly: national and international businesses, foreign governments, and international financial institutions should support increased government capital expenditures, a different as well as renewed commitment to education, and fiscal reform. Liberal democracy cannot survive if all the pillars on which it was built are destroyed, unless they are replaced with new foundations. Society's habit of resistance to dictatorship could be used against the liberal democratic order: in the Anglophone Caribbean, the public's impatience became evident in the second half of the 1980s and first half of the 1990s, as government after government on island after island were defeated in elections. The institutions and procedures on which Caribbean liberal democracies have been built would not withstand much greater levels of hostility in the postpatronage, poststatist circumstances unless gains become evident.

For business and political elites, the challenge is to legitimize an even more privileged position for business, as other democracies elsewhere have. That requires efficient economic growth and also establishing the foundations of an effective and capable state that delivers quality services and generates and maintains a necessary infrastructure to serve not only economic growth but also the public as a whole. For the production of these public goods, the democratic state receives and deserves the allegiance and support of its citizens.

2 Democratic Transitions in Central America and Panama

From the late 1970s to the early 1990s, revolutionary wars broke out in Nicaragua, El Salvador, and Guatemala, and a revolutionary movement reached power in Nicaragua. These countries also became the object of international competition, drawing the attention of the Soviet Union, many European countries, Canada, Japan, and many Latin American countries including Cuba. The United States deepened its involvement in the domestic politics of Central America and Panama, actively supporting military efforts to overthrow Nicaragua's Sandinista government and eventually invading Panama to overthrow its government. At the same time, Central America and Panama suffered an acute economic crisis, caused in part by these wars; the crisis worsened as a result of sharp drops in the international price of coffee in the late 1970s and the late 1980s. In the early 1980s, the U.S. economic recession had a severe negative impact on these countries, which depended greatly on the U.S. economy.[1]

Central America and Panama made serious strides to transform their politics and their economies. In the late 1970s, there were society-led transitions in Nicaragua and, at least at the outset, in El Salvador: Social forces—with guns—overpowered the government and other elite actors. In the next decade, Nicaragua and El Salvador engaged in another regime transition that involved intensive negotiations between government and opposition as well as violence and the broad mobilization of social forces. On the other hand, throughout the 1980s there was a slow-moving, regime-led political transition shaped by the elite in Guatemala (and, in different ways, in Honduras). Panama began with a similar kind of transition in the 1970s, but in the 1980s there was a turn to a society-led effort to overpower the military, culminating with a U.S. invasion in 1989. All these countries (including Honduras and Costa Rica) made moderate to major transitions in the organization of their respective economies.[2]

To shed light on the perhaps surprising but now clear trend toward freer politics and freer markets throughout these countries, I concentrate this analysis on the still imperfect but ongoing processes of democratization and political and economic liberalization in these countries. I focus on the four countries of the region in which the transition to democracy has been the most difficult and the most violent: El Salvador, Nicaragua, Guatemala, and Panama. (Unless otherwise specified, discussions of Central America includes only Guatemala, El Salvador, and Nicaragua.) Several questions guide this analysis. Why do the powerful yield their power? How do conscious actors construct political liberalization and democratization? What rules or arrangements do they design to bring these things about? What is the behavior of economic elites in political and economic liberalization?

Following Guillermo O'Donnell and Philippe Schmitter, by political liberalization I mean "the process of making effective certain rights that protect both individual and social groups from arbitrary or illegal acts committed by the state or third parties."[3] By economic liberalization, I mean a turn toward market-oriented economic policies. By democratization I mean the shift to toward democracy, as defined in the introduction.

Launching Democratization

Central America and Panama share important similarities in their recent political processes, despite structural differences that set their experiences apart from those of other countries. In exploring these similarities and differences, I find four common factors that help to explain the beginning of democratization: military force, rational choices in response to a state of war, international pressure, and severe economic crisis.

The Necessity of Military Force to Begin Democratization

At key junctures in the 1970s and 1980s in Guatemala, El Salvador, Nicaragua, and Panama, the powerful yielded power only because military force defeated them. The starting points of the processes of democratization that, with gains and setbacks, have been under way in these four countries since 1979 were the defeats at war of General Anastasio Somoza Debayle in Nicaragua in 1979 and of General Manuel Antonio Noriega in Panama in 1989, as well as the military coups that deposed General Carlos Humberto Romero in El Salvador in 1979 and General Fernando Romeo Lucas García in Guatemala in 1982. In each of these cases, military force did not merely depose a ruler; it also ended a regime. The personal dictatorships and tight oligarchies that had governed these countries would not be reconstituted; the rules of authoritarian imposition were replaced by a greater pluralism.

Despite their different histories, the use of force was necessary to begin democratization in all four countries because tenacious rulers clung to power. Prior to 1968, civilians had played an important and continuous role in Panama's government, whereas the Somoza dynasty and military offi-cers had played such roles in the other three countries. Somoza and Nor-iega, however, showed few signs of surrendering power unless forced to do so. In Guatemala, the fraudulent "election" of Defense Minister General Angel Aníbal Guevara in March 1982 signaled an intention to continue with an unchanged regime and triggered the coup that overthrew President Lucas. In El Salvador, President Romero's exacerbation of the use of force and his unresponsiveness to reform preceded the October 1979 coup.

At various moments in the late 1970s and in the 1980s, in Turkey, Nige-ria, Peru, and Ecuador, military officers willingly and peacefully turned power over to civilians. The same pattern of a military government negoti-ating its exit from power was evident in Honduras in 1980 and in Guate-mala in 1985; this might have occurred in Panama if General Omar Torrijos had lived. The critical point here, however, is that in Guatemala, El Salvador, Nicaragua, and Panama, democratization required the use of military force at a key juncture.

Military force has been used outside this region, of course, to initiate the processes of democratization. In the late 1950s in Colombia and Venezuela and in 1974 in Portugal, for example, military coups opened the way to eventual democratization. Defeat in war is also an important part of the explanation for the democratization of the Axis powers after World War II and, in more recent times, in Greece and Argentina. The reason to call atten-tion to the role of military force in opening the path toward democratiza-tion in the four countries studied in this chapter is to identify some shared characteristics of these four transitions that situate them at one extreme of the spectrum of paths toward democratization. The peaceful transitions toward democracy evident from the 1970s to the 1990s in India, Spain, Czechoslovakia, Hungary, Brazil, and Chile are quite different from those found in the four cases analyzed in this chapter, where politics has been played, comparatively, with unusual roughness.

From a State of War to a Democratic State

In Thomas Hobbes's *Leviathan*, political order is established as individuals recoil from a state of war that is "nasty" and "brutish." Though it is doubt-ful that Hobbes had Central America in mind, the decades-long civil wars in Nicaragua, El Salvador, and Guatemala surely meet his standards of wars that civilized people would wish to end.

Whereas in Hobbes's writing an authoritarian state is founded to end the state of war, in Central America the authoritarian state fueled the war. This outcome occurred even when those who made the decisions to limit dem-ocratic liberties might perhaps have preferred to do otherwise. For example, the Sandinista government responded to U.S. policy in the early to mid-1980s by limiting the opposition's liberties and political space and by subordinating all aspects of the Sandinista government project—including democratic changes—to the need to fight the war. In the long term, however, these antidemocratic policies strengthened the opposition and led more people to take up arms against the government.

Panama never faced such a civil war, mainly because the opposition chose a strategy of nonviolence.[4] Nonetheless, Panama's stark economic decline in the late 1980s as the United States imposed sanctions on the Noriega regime, and the increased repression of the opposition by the regime's forces, mark Panama also as a hardship case prior to regime change.

In all four cases, a key reason for democratization was the decision of significant elites that the state of war or the state of hardship had to end. The elites reached this decision for various reasons, to be sure, including their inability to repress the opposition and the international pressures and economic collapse to which the next two sections make reference. In the 1980s in Guatemala and Nicaragua, and in the early 1990s in El Salvador, those in government agreed with the axiom that Robert Dahl identified well in advance of their decisions: "The more the costs of suppression exceed the costs of toleration, the greater the chance for a competitive regime."[5] In Panama, the opposition to Noriega made the calculation that the state of hardship had to end; the opposition preferred U.S. intervention to Noriega's continued rule. (See related, more general discussion in chapter 3.)

In Guatemala, the decision of the army to move toward democratization featured an intermediate step: democratic politics was more likely to generate the political backing necessary to obtain resources from abroad and to defeat the insurgent left. Nonetheless, this very strategy required moving away from the pure reliance on Hobbesian force and the deliberate shift, albeit gradually and imperfectly, toward democracy.

Central Americans, therefore, sought to solve their Hobbes problem with a Dahl solution. For Hobbes, the solution to the state of war is to install an all-powerful Leviathan. Citizens of Guatemala, El Salvador, Nicaragua, and Panama had experienced such Leviathans and had found them wanting. For them, the solution was to democratize power as a means to end the violence and the hardship. Nevertheless, extensive political violence has been a part of the recent history of Guatemala, El Salvador, and Nicaragua; substantial violence was perpetrated in Panama by the Noriega forces and also during the U.S. intervention. Is such violence the midwife of democracy? To the contrary, Samuel Huntington reminds us; since the early 1970s successful democratization has been associated with low levels of violence. This has happened for a variety of reasons, but one is especially important: "The resort to violence increased the power of the specialists in violence in both government and the opposition."[6] Huntington's argument leads us to consider the possibilities for the future of these countries.

Democratization in these countries remains incomplete. Although in place since late 1989, Panama's government has yet to prove that it can govern effectively. In Nicaragua, the degree of contestation between government and opposition remains too acute, with recurring and severe incidents of political violence (though they are far short of civil war); the government is constrained in its capacity to implement its policies. In Guatemala, the civil war ended only in December 1996. The concentration of power in the military and the presidency remains far above what might be expected in a democracy. In May 1993, President Jorge Serrano Elías staged a coup against the Congress, the Supreme Court, and other independent civilian institutions. Although the attempt failed and constitutional government was preserved, the attempt and its aftermath underscore the fragility and limitations of Guatemala's democratization. In El Salvador, though, the January 1992 agreements that ended the war have been effective; only the future can tell whether it will consolidate its transition to democracy.

More pessimistically, these four countries may experience a reversal of democracy. Since the restoration of civilian rule, there have been several military coup attempts in Guatemala and Panama against civilian presidents, and in Guatemala civilian president Serrano even led one of them! Although these attempts failed, they indicate that much work needs to be done to secure civilian control over the military and even civilian allegiance to democratic practices. In all four countries, many people—former soldiers in all cases and former insurgents in three—have many weapons that can be, and to some degree are, used for private purposes but that could be used to destabilize the governments.

In any case, Guatemala, El Salvador, Nicaragua, and Panama stand at one end of the spectrum of countries that have made significant political openings. They have experienced war and hardship to a degree that is rare in recent times among countries that have democratized successfully. All four countries have witnessed elites seeking to make rational choices, however, with the hope that the experience of long and brutal wars and sustained hardship would indeed be the midwife for a democratic peace.

International Pressure: Induced to Be Free

In the recent past, international factors have had a persistent and pervasive role in regime transitions in these four countries.[7] Jimmy Carter's presidency (1977–81) and its policies in favor of human rights and democratization greatly weakened the support for established autocracies in the region.

Somoza, Romero, and Lucas were undermined in ways that led to their eventual forcible removal from power. In Panama an important political opening can be traced to General Torrijos's decision to create a domestic political environment that would facilitate U.S. Senate ratification of the Panama Canal treaties.

The Reagan administration's eventual support of human rights and democratization in this region derived in part from the need to build an ideological consensus to oppose Sandinista Nicaragua. By late 1983, the Reagan administration had dropped its opposition to, and instead embraced, many of Carter's policies on human rights and democratization. Curiously perhaps, its support for civilian rule in Central America may have been caused by the Sandinista revolution.

Historically, the United States has had an important presence in the domestic politics of these four countries. In Panama, the U.S. government ran the canal and occupied the large Canal Zone area in the heart of the country, necessarily becoming involved directly or indirectly in the country's politics in ways that were at times adverse to democracy. U.S. troops occupied Nicaragua earlier in the century and, upon their repatriation in the early 1930s, left dynasty founder Anastasio Somoza García in command of the U.S.-created National Guard. In 1954, the United States was a major factor in the overthrow of Guatemala's President Jacobo Arbenz. In El Salvador, the United States has also played an important role at key junctures in the twentieth century, though it did not assume as powerful a role as in the other three countries until the late 1970s.

Most recently, political openings evident in Nicaragua, Panama, and El Salvador are related to the end of the Cold War. By 1989 Nicaragua's governing party, the FSLN (Frente Sandinista de Liberación Nacional), decided to advance the date of the constitutionally scheduled national elections from November to February 1990 and to negotiate with the opposition an extensive set of mutually acceptable guarantees to ensure fairness and full participation. These Sandinista decisions aimed to change Nicaragua's domestic political environment in the hopes that the new Bush administration would not continue the U.S. policy of war on the Nicaraguan government. The Sandinistas lost these elections, however. An international argument is also essential to explain the change in Sandinista policies that led to these elections. Sandinista policies toward the opposition and toward the United States changed in part because the Sandinista leadership realized that it could not count indefinitely on Soviet economic assistance and that it could no longer count on further Soviet military aid.

By December 1989, the United States could invade Panama to remove Noriega without fear of Soviet retaliation. By late 1991, El Salvador's insurgent coalition, the Farabundo Martí National Liberation Front (FMLN), knew that it could no longer count on material assistance from the former communist countries of Europe or from the government of Nicaragua, thereby increasing the likelihood that it would agree to a settlement. Similarly, by late 1991, the U.S. government had made it clear to the armed forces of El Salvador that they would not get continued military aid to fight a war in which the United States was no longer interested.

"Historically," Laurence Whitehead has written thoughtfully, "Washington's most memorable experiences of promoting democracy overseas took place at the end of successful wars (1898, 1918, and 1945) when, of course, international forces were in a position to overwhelm domestic political tendencies."[8] The collapse of the Soviet Union is an international earthquake comparable to those victories—a point in common between the recent experiences in Central America and Panama and Whitehead's analysis. The main point of Whitehead's study, however, and of the series of which it is a part, is that international factors were rarely so important in promoting democratization.

The analytical issue might be put as follows: with regard to the explanatory pertinence of international factors, the transitions in Panama, Nicaragua, and El Salvador most resemble the transitions in Eastern Europe and differ from the transitions in South America and Southern Europe. The international shocks of the end of the Cold War had strong effects on the domestic politics of the countries in local international subsystems in which a superpower was especially prominent. Moreover, where countries are small and highly dependent not only on the international market but also overwhelmingly on the locally preeminent superpower, the leverage of outsiders to induce domestic change is strong. Even in the mid-1980s in Guatemala (the country most belatedly affected by the ending of the Cold War), the military government's decisions to move toward competitive elections and civilian rule were powerfully shaped by the effort to break out of the country's deep international isolation.

Thus, once again, the four countries examined in this chapter share certain common characteristics that situate them at one end of the spectrum of paths toward democratization: their regime changes cannot be explained without reference to international pressures to induce democratization and, in the case of Panama, to force it. The powerful were pressured to give up or to share their power and to do so by means of democratic elections and bargains.

Economic Crisis: The Blessings of Failure

The economies of Central America and Panama each collapsed at a moment that proved favorable for a democratizing political transition. The claims of authoritarian rulers that they deserved obedience because they had created the conditions for economic growth or for improved social welfare are familiar enough in the history of these countries. As living standards fell and the economy collapsed, authoritarian regimes weakened. For example, among other factors, the severe economic downturn in the late 1970s contributed to the demise of the Somoza dynasty in Nicaragua. El Salvador's economy, too, collapsed in the late 1970s and early 1980s. Economics was an important (though not the preeminent) factor motivating Guatemala's initial transition in the early 1980s. And a deep economic crisis accompanied Noriega's loss of support and preceded his overthrow. These countries were "blessed" with serious enough economic failures to discredit long-entrenched authoritarian regimes and, thus, to permit a transition to more open politics.

In addition, economic malperformance shaped the rhythm of politics in these countries even after the initial transitions. Nicaragua's severe economic difficulties weakened support for the Sandinistas and increased support for the opposition before the February 1990 national elections. One motivation of Guatemala's army in the mid-1980s to turn over power to civilians was the recognition of the country's economic troubles and the greater likelihood that civilians could gain international support to address them. El Salvador's deplorable economic circumstances contributed to the 1989 national election defeat of the governing Christian Democratic Party.

The uniformity of economic collapse as a factor favorable to political regime transition sets Central America and Panama apart from South America, where the relationship between economic crisis and political regime transition is far more variable: in the early 1980s Argentina's transition did occur in a context of severe economic crisis, but in the mid-1980s Brazil's political transition occurred during a business cycle upswing, while in the later 1980s Chile's political transition occurred during an economic boom.

Summary

These four factors—the necessity of military force to begin democratization, a severe state of war and hardship that eventually provokes rational choices toward change, international pressure to induce democratization, and a profound economic crisis—help to explain democratizing outcomes in Guatemala, El Salvador, Nicaragua, and Panama but also set them apart from the main examples of democratic transitions in South America, southern and Eastern Europe, and south and East Asia. Central America and Panama resemble only the disaster areas of the Cold War: Ethiopia, Angola, and Cambodia. And yet none of these countries is in those dire circumstances, because each chose Dahl to answer Hobbes. To understand their reasons for cautious hope, I turn to other factors.

The Construction of Certainties

"The process of establishing a democracy," Adam Przeworski has written, "is a process of institutionalizing uncertainty, of subjecting all interests to uncertainty." He argues that "democratic compromise cannot be a substantive compromise; it can be only a contingent institutional compromise. It is within the nature of democracy that no one's interests can be guaranteed."[9] He notes, for example, that in democratic politics voters can support the expropriation of private property and the dissolution of the armed forces. Indeed so, but as a practical matter no one loves uncertainty, and few are prepared to take steps toward the specific form of uncertainty that Przeworski (accurately) considers inherent to democracy. At issue, therefore, is the need to construct certainties, that is, to fashion formal and informal assurances for key actors that will lead them at a given point to risk democracy's uncertainties. The construction of certainties (featuring a mix of procedural and substantive dimensions) must precede the contingent institutional compromises that establish democracy, because without some certainties democratic uncertainty becomes unthinkable.

The Injection of Reformers

The opening and undermining of authoritarian regimes, many scholars believe, often starts with a split among the high officials of the regime between hard-liners and soft-liners or between standpatters and reformers.[10] In Central America and Panama, there has been a somewhat different pattern: at a key moment, regime outsiders were "injected" into the regime to become its leading soft-liners or reformers. The success of reform by regime injection has been variable.

The strategy of reformist injection was most long-lived in El Salvador. The October 1979 coup by young military officers featured not the displacement of the military in power but the introduction of civilians, formerly in the opposition, into the high echelons of government. Months later, the Christian Democratic Party, El Salvador's largest, divided over the strategy for democratizing the country. The party's foremost leader, José Napoleón Duarte, decided to work inside the regime; he became president of the militarily sustained junta and in 1984 was elected president of El Salvador.

A centerpiece of Duarte's strategy was to persuade the Salvadoran armed forces and the Reagan administration in its early years that civilians who had not been the historic allies of the military and who advocated important social and economic reforms could, nevertheless, be trusted to govern. In that way, Duarte sought to open political space in El Salvador and to enlist U.S. support for the task of democratizing the country. Duarte sought to establish civilian authority over the armed forces and to negotiate a settlement with the insurgents. He failed at the second and succeeded to some degree at the first only because of the strong support he received from successive U.S. ambassadors. Nonetheless, as the 1980s unfolded, the likelihood of a military coup declined in El Salvador, and important institutional changes were made gradually to further open up the nation's political space. The Salvadoran armed forces discovered that they did not need to depend exclusively on the most conservative civilian forces. The injection of Duarte (the man the armed forces had prevented in 1972 from assuming the presidency he probably won in those elections) into the regime made an important contribution to El Salvador's democratization.

Duarte and the Christian Democrats constructed certainty for El Salvador's armed forces. President Duarte demonstrated that he shared with military officers a commitment to the maintenance of public order and national sovereignty; Duarte worked hard, as well, to secure U.S. funding for the Salvadoran military. In this way the injection of Christian Democrat reformers into what in many ways remained a military regime reduced the uncertainties once felt by El Salvador's military about the prospects of civilian supremacy over the armed forces.

The strategy of soft-liner injection was more problematic in Guatemala. The March 1982 coup installed a military junta in power but placed at its head a retired officer, General Efraín Ríos Montt, who had been the Christian Democratic Party's presidential candidate in the 1974 elections; Ríos Montt had probably won those elections but had been prevented from assuming the presidency. The Guatemalan scenario thus had some similarities to the earlier Salvadoran case. Ríos Montt, no longer a Christian Democrat, introduced some important changes into the government's conduct and policies. And yet, the war was prosecuted more fiercely and with greater loss of civilian life than a parallel with Duarte might suggest. Ríos Montt also lasted in power for a much shorter time than Duarte; Ríos Montt was overthrown because he was unable to solve the economic problems and wanted to postpone elections to remain in power. Ríos Montt turned out not to be a reformer.

The strategy of soft-liner injection was perhaps most promising in Panama, though it eventually failed. Nicolás Ardito-Barletta had been out of

Panamanian politics for nearly six years, serving as World Bank vice president for Latin America, when he was invited to lead the official party in the 1984 presidential elections. He accepted the offer in order to open the way toward democratization and economic growth. During the election campaign, he secured support from parties that had previously opposed the government; he also secured pledges from the military commanders that, once he was elected, the military would return to the barracks, removed from routine public management.

Ardito-Barletta did not realize until much later, however, that the commanders had no intention of retreating to the barracks and that they were prepared both to commit electoral fraud to get him elected and to remove him from office should he displease them. Whereas Duarte in El Salvador had his own strong political party and clear U.S. backing in dealing with the military, Ardito-Barletta in Panama had no party of his own and weak U.S. backing. Consequently, Ardito-Barletta was less successful in reshaping his country's politics.

The effect of this failed injection of reformists into the Noriega regime was to accelerate the trend toward dictatorship and self-destruction, which would harden until the end of the decade. Ardito-Barletta's strategy was a calculated gamble, which could have worked—but did not. It was based on the intellectual premise, mentioned earlier, that Panama's military would understand that the costs of suppression were higher than the costs of toleration. They did not, and thus Ardito-Barletta was not able to construct the institutional certainties that might have made the Panama Defense Forces (PDF) responsive to democratization.

New Institutions and New Rules

In the three cases (Guatemala, El Salvador, and Nicaragua) in which significant steps were taken toward liberalization and democratization in the absence of a U.S. invasion, one factor in the political transition was the creation of new institutions and rules to provide assurances to all would-be voters.

The accomplishments of Guatemala's Supreme Electoral Tribunal have been impressive. Founded during the government of General Oscar Mejía Víctores, the tribunal prepared rules for the election of a constituent assembly in 1984 and then oversaw that election. Its credibility was enhanced by the fact that the Christian Democratic Party, long in opposition to the military governments and a victim of electoral fraud in the past, won the 1985 presidential elections. The tribunal's credibility was enhanced again in 1990 when it oversaw the rules and the election, which was won by the opposition—this time electing conservative Jorge Serrano to the presidency. In

May 1993, the tribunal firmly opposed President Serrano's failed coup attempt and, thus, protected the democratic regime. The establishment of this tribunal was an important innovation because its predecessor had been corrupt and had presided over repeated fraudulent elections. It may have become Guatemala's most respected institution.

Important changes in the rules of the game occurred in Nicaragua, as well. The opposition for the most part had boycotted the 1984 presidential elections. The Sandinista government knew that a repetition of that election would not serve political stability nor the legitimacy of a renewed Sandinista government (in the expectation, eventually proven mistaken, that the FSLN would win). One mistake made by the Sandinista government had been to neglect taking early and credible steps toward providing institutional guarantees. In late 1987, the Sandinista government began complex negotiations with opposition parties, economic and social groups, and the United States to create certainty about procedural fairness for the February 1990 elections. Nicaragua's sovereign government even accepted extensive formal international inspection of the election. These new rules made the election possible.

There were also several important institutional changes in El Salvador. As the 1980s progressed, the organs of the state—especially the Legislative Assembly and the Supreme Court—became willing to recognize existing social movement organizations. The mass media developed and became more professional and diverse. Political parties became permanent organizations, not merely vehicles convoked at election time, and thus became able to make agreements and to follow through on them. The procedures to administer elections were greatly improved; there was a new electoral registry, voting cards were given to citizens, and computers were introduced to make the count accurate and fast. In the late 1980s, the democratic left recognized the significance of these changes in institutions and rules and, thus, decided to reenter electoral contests.

In all three countries, the new institutions and rules created the necessary procedural certainties for participants to be willing to live with the uncertainties of electoral outcomes (about which Przeworski has written). All three countries had a long tradition of electoral fraud prior to 1979; indeed, rational people had to act on the expectation that elections would be fraudulent unless proof was given to the contrary. The new institutions and rules had to be transparent and to embody the means to settle normal electoral disputes. In that way, they could break the expectations about electoral fraud. Where there were no such institutional guarantees, as in Panama's 1989 national election, the electoral results were not credible.

Creating a Reliable Opposition

These changes in institutions and rules enabled a legal opposition to emerge. In all four countries, opposition leaders understood the utility of demonstrating to those in office that the opposition could be trusted to remain nonviolent and to abide by the laws, in that way seeking to create the certainty that an opposition campaign would not be disruptive nor would its victory lead to revenge against defeated incumbents. An important "certainty" was the assurance that, if those within the regime acted to bring about changes, they would not suffer.

The least successful but most far-reaching of these opposition campaigns occurred in Panama.[11] Panama's National Civic Crusade adopted a nonviolent strategy and remained apart from political parties. It concentrated its protest on Noriega. By its nonviolent commitment and its focus on Noriega, it sought to reassure other military officers that they could act against Noriega without risk of eventual retribution. Instead of acts of violence, the crusade and its opposition predecessors relied on humor and ridicule aimed at Noriega. By its nonpartisan commitments, it sought to enable labor unions, professional associations, and civic groups to join it as formal members. The crusade was a gigantic, cross-class, social movement organization. In turn, its moderate actions and narrow focus on Noriega reassured Panama's elites with regard to its limited intentions: to remove Noriega as the means to advance toward democracy. In short, it sought to create certainties about its future behavior through its conduct of opposition to Noriega.

Much more successful constructions of reliable opposition occurred in the other three countries. Guatemala's Christian Democrats persuaded the army that they were reliable enough to govern. During his presidential campaign, Cerezo also gave public assurances to the military that his government would not bring officers to trial for human rights violations, nor would he curtail the high prerogatives that the army had kept for itself under the constitution and the existing laws. The Christian Democratic Party, moreover, had good prospects for a clear electoral victory, which would enhance the chances of governability. An important military motivation to move toward civilian rule had been to break out of international isolation; victory by the opposition Christian Democrats was an effective way to do that and, in turn, to obtain access to foreign economic and military support.[12]

Violeta Barrios de Chamorro also demonstrated her reliability as an opposition leader by never going into political exile or breaking family relations with those of her children who had become leading Sandinistas and by publishing her daily newspaper, *La Prensa*, under the often unfair conditions and censorship imposed by Sandinista authorities. Her conduct consistently emphasized nonviolence. She agreed to run in the February 1990 elections, accepting the constitution and the laws then in effect though, of course, negotiating over the electoral procedures to guarantee their eventual fairness. Her coalition embraced political parties and social movement organizations across the ideological spectrum; in its very constitution, the National Opposition Union (UNO) reassured many groups and currents of opinion. Perhaps the most visible act of reassurance occurred shortly after it became clear that Chamorro had defeated incumbent Daniel Ortega for the presidency: in a photograph flashed around the world she was portrayed embracing Ortega warmly.

Another example of the construction of a reliable opposition to reduce uncertainties about the future occurred in El Salvador. Rubén Zamora's political party was allied to the revolutionary insurgency during most of the 1980s. Eventually, however, this party decided to participate in the 1989 presidential and the 1991 legislative elections. After the 1991 elections, the ruling conservative party, the Nationalist Republican Alliance (ARENA), and Zamora's Convergencia Democrática on the democratic left agreed to vote for each other's candidates for the assembly's presidency and vice presidency; Zamora was thereby elected vice president. Thus the democratic left reassured the military that the Convergencia could be trusted to be law-abiding and to govern, and it signaled to the insurgents that much could be gained through elections.

The construction of a reliable Salvadoran opposition also encompassed social movement organizations. Having been repressed harshly in the early 1980s, these organizations reemerged during the second half of the decade, though they were deeply divided for various reasons. In the early 1990s, however, several of these social organizations began to form alliances that required them to moderate their demands and their conduct in order to search for an end to the war. Their behavior facilitated the march toward democratic outcomes.

These examples share the intent to create certainty by means of overt behavior. This strategy is consistent with making deals, which is the bread and butter of politics everywhere. In no case, however, does this behavioral strategy logically require a substantive agreement with regard to specific future policies, nor does it bar other procedural or substantive agreements that focus on more general issues. In Panama, the opposition would have liked a deal from regime leaders other than Noriega to remove Noriega, but it could not get one. In Guatemala, Cerezo's deal with the army was articulated publicly but was not part of a wider pact. In Nicaragua, the campaign behavior was the prelude to specific agreements to be reached as part of the transition of power and subsequent government. In El Salvador, the behavior of the democratic left and of social organizations may have paved the way for the complex and comprehensive agreement negotiated between government and insurgency late in 1991, but that behavior did not itself stem from a prior deal. There seems to be, therefore, no clear relationship between the existence of pacts and the movement toward, or the consolidation of, democracy.[13]

Constitutionalizing the Military

These efforts by governments and oppositions sought to create certainty for building democracy prior to a change toward a democratic regime. After a change, the most important step toward consolidating democratic politics was the construction of another certainty: that the armed forces would obey the constitution and that the president would not abuse power by means of the armed forces.

A foundational task of President Chamorro's government was to reestablish civil peace. To that end, her government had to disarm the contras (more formally called the Nicaraguan Resistance), with international assistance under United Nations supervision, and to establish its authority over the armed forces. The latter task had economic implications as well, for her government moved to cut the size of the armed forces by two-thirds and to reduce the military burden on the nation's budget. But in affirming civilian authority over the military, the government also behaved pragmatically, making the first of its many deals with the Sandinistas as they moved toward opposition. President Chamorro agreed to retain former Sandinista commander General Humberto Ortega as chief of the armed forces provided he would sever his partisan links to the FSLN, which he did formally. The Chamorro government, therefore, sought military reduction and constitutionalization, but it also agreed to keep important legal military prerogatives to provide assurances to the officer corps.

This and other subsequent agreements on nonmilitary issues were part of the building of a consensus across forces that disagree on many issues but that are prepared to work jointly, to a limited extent, to make Nicaragua governable. This search for consensus and specific agreements may have become the rule of the game for Nicaragua since 1990, a rule often sorely tested, however. This pattern of sequential agreements also made it possible for the FSLN to change from being the party of the state to being a party in the opposition, though also in critical collaboration with the Chamorro government over some important issues. This outcome was greatly facilitated by the Chamorro government's strong commitment to the democratic values of toleration, respect, participation, dialogue, and keeping agreements.

In Panama, the task was conceptually the same, but the means were different. The U.S. invasion in December 1989 defeated the PDF and made it possible for the new Panamanian government to transform the military into a new and much smaller civilian-controlled police force, the Public Force. The government concluded that it could not afford simply to disband the military, because the thousands of former officers and soldiers would be unemployed, embittered, and armed, posing a permanent threat to public order. Because the new Public Force was smaller, there were substantial savings for the national budget; because of a process of purging and retraining, the force was more likely to be loyal to a democratic regime.[14] Unfortunately, the pacification of Panama was soon dramatically threatened when an unsuccessful coup sought to overthrow the government on December 5, 1990.

Panama's pattern, like Nicaragua's, was to seek military reduction and constitutionalization; the new government gave assurances to the small fraction of officers and soldiers of the former PDF who were hired for the new Public Force. But Panama's attempted reduction of the size of the military and attempted subordination of it to civilian authority goes far beyond anything attempted in Central America outside of Costa Rica. In Panama the new Public Force has none of the constitutional and legal military prerogatives still evident in Nicaragua and Guatemala.

El Salvador's January 1992 agreement focuses centrally on the fate of the armed forces. Consistent with experiences in Nicaragua and Panama, the agreement reduces the size of the armed forces and their burden on the national budget and brings the military clearly under the constitution, the laws, and civilian authority. As in Panama, the Salvadoran agreement calls for a purge of the military but not as extensive as in Panama. The Salvadoran settlement on the military resembles the Nicaraguan case in preserving the armed forces as an institution and in providing guarantees to a substantial number of its personnel. Whether the Salvadoran agreement will be fully implemented remains a question.

Although it shares some commonalities with the others, Guatemala long remained the outlier. President Cerezo did not call out the army to deal with labor strikes or street demonstrations, nor did he invoke state-of-siege provisions to deal with labor unrest. During his presidency, General Héctor Gramajo, the defense minister, sought to communicate to military officers and civilians that the army attempted to remain in its professional role and apart from partisan politics. Many officers had difficulty in adjusting to civilian authority. The size of the army was not reduced as much as in Panama, Nicaragua, or El Salvador, nor was the burden on the nation's budget. The Guatemalan army retained important constitutional and legal prerogatives, including immunity from prosecution for abuse of power, well beyond the region's prevailing norms. (Honduran and Guatemalan civil-military relations resemble each other to some extent, but Guatemala's army has had a greater effect on its society than the armed forces of Honduras have had on theirs.) The December 1996 comprehensive agreements that ended Guatemala's civil war promised, however, to reduce the size of the army and to curtail its prerogatives. Time will tell whether its terms are honored, but other reasons for concern remain.

In Guatemala, the unsuccessful military coups of 1988 and 1989 and, in 1993, President Serrano's failed "self-coup" (which had initial backing from the military high command) present the most serious challenges so far in the region to the constitutionalization of the military. The three attempts show that a significant proportion of officers and troops were ready to overthrow the democratic regime. Defeating the attempts required personal courage and involved serious risks. Most disturbing for democratic consolidation was the weak response to the coup attempts in 1988 and 1989 from President Cerezo and other civilian authorities; even worse was President Serrano's orchestration of the 1993 attempt. In 1988 and 1989 it fell to the army's administrative procedures to punish the plotters, even though the full weight of civilian law should have been applied. Also worrisome was President Cerezo's response to the 1989 coup; it appears as if the president stopped governing eighteen months before the end of his term.

There can be, nevertheless, a more optimistic interpretation of recent Guatemalan history. The coup attempts failed. The Cerezo government was replaced through free and competitive elections by a more conservative government, led by President Serrano, making it less likely that economic elites would support a future coup. Indeed, Guatemala's business leaders opposed the 1993 attempt. Another peaceful transition of the presidency occurred with the election of Alvaro Arzú, a moderate conservative, in January 1996. The Arzú government and the revolutionaries reached a peace accord in December 1996.

In all four countries, progress has been made toward constitutionalizing the military, reducing its size and cost, and reducing the likelihood that the armed forces would be used by the president to abuse power; substantial efforts have been made to construct such certainties in civil-military relations. The greatest changes have been made in Panama because the United States militarily defeated the PDF. The fewest changes have been made thus far in Guatemala, because its army believes that it won the civil war and orchestrated and managed the transition to civilian rule. Intermediate changes have been made in Nicaragua; comparable intermediate changes have been agreed to in El Salvador. In the last two countries the conflicts of the 1980s ended in a tie, at all levels (as in El Salvador) or in ways that balanced each other (in Nicaragua, the Sandinistas prevailed in war but lost in peace).

The Strength of the Electoral Right

"Put in a nutshell," wrote Guillermo O'Donnell and Philippe Schmitter, "parties of the Right-Center and Right must be 'helped' to do well, and parties of the Left-Center and Left should not win by an overwhelming majority." This could even be done, they say, by "rigging the rules—for example, by overrepresenting rural districts or small peripheral constituencies." The reason for this suggestion, they say, is that unless "those partisan forces representing the interests of propertied classes, privileged professions, and entrenched institutions, including the armed forces . . . muster enough votes to stay in the game, they are likely to desert the electoral process in favor of antidemocratic conspiracy and destabilization."[15]

O'Donnell and Schmitter proved right in their political theory, wrong in their electoral sociology. Parties of the right and center-right have received a large proportion of the votes cast everywhere in South America (outside Argentina and Venezuela) and in several countries in southern and Eastern Europe when free and competitive elections have been held. This very strength, as O'Donnell and Schmitter argue, has contributed to keeping the right allegiant to democracy.

So too in Central America and Panama. In El Salvador, the party farthest to the right, ARENA, was "helped" to win the 1989 presidential election by the disarray of the Christian Democrats, by electoral abstention on part of the left, by the left's fragmentation and association with the insurgency, and by the delay of the parties of the democratic left in organizing to contest elections. Nonetheless, there is no doubt that the right is and has been electorally strong in El Salvador. Perhaps precisely because President Alfredo Cristiani is a conservative, he was able to lead the Salvadoran right, including the armed forces, to a negotiated peace agreement with the insurgent left. In the late 1980s and early 1990s, by means of elections and negotiations, the Salvadoran right-wing government protected the interests of its supporters and advanced their economic goals, while it served the nation in the pursuit of a negotiated settlement to the war. ARENA's Armando Calderón Sol won El Salvador's 1994 presidential elections, thereby confirming the right's electoral strength.

Whereas the parties of the extreme right have not done as well in Guatemala as they would have liked, given their historic hold on that country's politics, Guatemala's parties of the right and center-right have done well in national elections, even in 1985 (general) and certainly in 1990 (general), 1994 (congressional), 1995 (presidential, first round), and 1996 (presidential, second round). Guatemala's elected president between 1990 and 1993, Jorge Serrano, was a conservative; his economic cabinet was in the hands of representatives of powerful business groups. The negotiations that his government began with insurgents may have been made possible by this configuration of political forces as well as by the Salvadoran example. In the January 1996 elections, a center-right candidate, Alvaro Arzú, was elected president, demonstrating again the right's electoral clout. As in the case of El Salvador, so too in Guatemala: a center-right president was more capable than a centrist Christian Democrat to make peace with the revolutionaries while, at the same time, retaining the allegiance of the military and the business community.

In Nicaragua, Chamorro won the 1990 presidential election at the head of a broad coalition that spanned the ideological spectrum. Nevertheless, the coalition's center of gravity and its program of government were on the center-right. While the Chamorro government's coalition eventually broke up, the electoral forces of the center-right clearly have held their own.

In Panama, the center-right had an important impact in the 1970s on the policies of the Torrijos regime through the skill and influence of government technocrats. As in Nicaragua, so too in Panama: the opposition to Noriega was a broad coalition that spanned the ideological spectrum. This coalition's center of gravity, too, lay in professional associations and business groups. The organized opposition to Torrijos began with medical doctors and schoolteachers, who were subsequently joined by business and civic organizations. Although Panama's electoral right has lacked the ferocity of pockets of the Salvadoran and Guatemalan right, within Panama's social structure and political style the center-right has done well in elections.

The right in Nicaragua and Panama knew their strength and that they could be influential and win elections; for these reasons, since the 1970s, business and professional groups have pressed for free and competitive elections. The real puzzle, therefore, is why it took the right in El Salvador and Guatemala so long to realize that they could do so well in free and competitive elections. To be sure, the parties of the right have lost elections in the past and will again in the future, but they are likely to have substantial influence in a great many ways. Misinformed about electoral sociology, the right in these two countries indeed believed that they could win only if elections were rigged. Exploring the intellectual and political roots of this belief is not part of this work, but its consequences for Guatemalan and Salvadoran history have been tens of thousands of people killed, countless people injured, the vast destruction of property, and decades of institutional decay and corruption.

Some credit for civilizing the right in El Salvador and Guatemala must go to José Napoleón Duarte and Marco Vinicio Cerezo. They can be criticized for many failures of government, but they respected the integrity of those whom they had defeated in elections. The right began to learn that electoral defeat, albeit unpleasant, was not the end of the world. This recognition began an important change in the conception of power, from "all or nothing," the conceptual parent to coups, repression, and wars, to a pluralistic conception more consistent with democratic norms.

The victories of the parties of the right in Central America and Panama have provided an essential certainty to the propertied and the powerful that democracy is worth the gamble. In Nicaragua and Panama, entrepreneurs need no convincing that they do better under democratic politics than under the rule of revolutionaries or the military. In Guatemala and El Salvador, perhaps to their own surprise, the business elites learned the same lesson in the 1990s.

In all four countries, paradoxically, parties of the right and the center-right were electorally vibrant in the late 1980s and early 1990s because at some earlier moment they lost control of the national government. To regain power, the right had to build a strong conservative party while still in the opposition. Because democracy worked for conservatives to win back the presidency, it is more likely that conservatives will work for democracy in the future.

Statesmanship

Returning to the opening question of why the powerful yield their power, the answer should be clear from the preceding analysis: the costs of suppression, the rational expectation that democratic regimes succeed against insurgencies, the pressures from abroad, economic collapse, and the construction of some certainties. And yet at specific moments real people had to decide to give up power. That is never easy to do, and it is much more difficult to explain.

The Guatemalan army designed a strategy to surrender some of their power. Their analysis was based on rational expectations about the future. Clearly, however, many Guatemalan officers did not want to yield power; that is one reason for the subsequent coup attempts against the Cerezo government. The Guatemalan officers who suppressed those attempts, led by defense minister Héctor Gramajo, showed courage and statesmanship.

The Sandinistas designed a strategy to remain in power. They believed that their leadership of the revolution against the Somoza dynasty gave them the right to rule and that they embodied the nation's spirit in combat against U.S. aggression. On the battlefield, they had prevailed over the contras, but they misjudged their political support and lost the 1990 presidential election. On election night (February 25, 1990) the FSLN National Directorate gathered to analyze the results, which showed a clear victory for the Chamorro-led opposition. The decision to recognize the election results was unanimous. One reason was that the Sandinista commanders had fought against Somoza to enable Nicaraguans to choose freely. The Sandinista commanders who made this decision also showed courage and statesmanship.

Civilian politicians are more accustomed to the democratic rules of the game. Nonetheless, the Christian Democratic Parties of Panama, Guatemala, and El Salvador are especially noteworthy for their contribution to institutional consolidation and respect for rules and for their willingness to give up power once defeated.

A partial explanation for these acts of statesmanship was the gradual creation of new institutions and rules providing some guarantees of personal and collective safety to those about to surrender power. Such rules and institutions may have been the foundations for democratic change. In turn, the cumulative acts of statesmanship have become standard procedure. Though they are no less remarkable, given the region's recent history, they are now commonplace and, as such, have created a new certainty. From the right and the left, from the army in Guatemala to the Sandinistas in Nicaragua, the rhetoric of a quarter century had prepared no one for acts of statesmanship. Not too many years ago the notion that ARENA and the FMLN would have negotiated an agreement to bring a long and bloody war to a civilized end would have been laughed at. These human beings may not have been able to make their history just as they pleased, but at key moments they certainly acted to make their own destiny.

The origin of democratization in Central America and Panama may have been exogenous to normal politics. Democracy in these countries began from the barrel of a gun, and that very origin has limited its scope and may imperil its future. But after such ordeals in the launching of change, the construction of democracy in these four countries depended on the explicit creation of new institutions and new rules to provide formal guarantees to all participants. The construction of democracy also required the conscious action of politicians to demonstrate to the military that they could be trusted to govern as well as to oppose responsibly, thereby making possible the (still imperfect and much delayed) constitutionalization of the armed forces. If politicians of the left and center-left were important, especially in El Salvador and Guatemala, to construct a reliable opposition, politicians of the right were important everywhere to civilize the propertied and the powerful and to make them (and one hopes keep them) allegiant to democracy. Finally, at key moments holders of power chose to give up power in acts of human will that deserve the label of statesmanship. In these ways, the creation of certainty fostered the democratic transition and the eventual consolidation of democracy.

Business, Politics, and Markets

In Central America and Panama the political behavior of organized business is best described around one constant and one variable. At key moments, business has been a force for political liberalization in all four countries, but business has a mixed record with regard to economic liberalization. Neither point is intuitively obvious. On the one hand, some might expect business to support economic liberalization, believing in free markets as the best way to advance its interests and values; some would also observe that business in these countries has been a bastion of authoritarian oligarchical politics and that it is, hence, the least likely group to support political liberalization. My analysis focuses, however, on the effects of business behavior, not necessarily on the intentions of business elites.

Business contributed to political liberalization by opposing clearly and publicly some visible and important policies (typically, economic) of governments that it and others deemed to be authoritarian. In so behaving, business elites helped to open political space. Their criticism of the government legitimized space for freedom of expression and freedom of association in opposition to authoritarian rule. Their use of the press and other mass media to oppose the government furthered this result as well. They forced authoritarian political elites to tolerate opposition on some important issues and, thus, paved the way to toleration of the opposition over other issues later on. The government's response to business opposition would not be murder or imprisonment but respect and conciliation.

Guatemala's business elites played a significant role in persuading the army to break the historical alliance between them, even though it is most unlikely that this outcome was the intention of business elites. In 1985 General Oscar Mejía's government tried unsuccessfully to implement a tax reform package and other economic policies. Despite all the powers of the bayonets, General Mejía could not even raise the cost of an urban bus ticket by one-and-a-half U.S. cents. The military government also enacted a consumer protection law, which business groups, in a well-orchestrated and well-funded mass-media campaign, undermined. This campaign made the military look foolish and ignorant. If the generals were ignorant fools in matters of consumer protection, perhaps they were so on other matters as well; the effect, therefore, was to weaken military self-confidence and embolden opposition action—in both ways favoring political liberalization. Guatemalan business elites probably did not intend to cause widespread

liberalization; but regardless of intentions, that was the result of their behavior.

The response of the Guatemalan army to this business opposition was to
call for a national dialogue, to make concessions, and to strike a deal. The
military concluded from the experience that important economic policy
changes could be implemented only by a government invested with political legitimacy, a legitimacy that a military government could not have. The
army learned to bargain rather than impose, to listen rather than command,
to yield rather than overpower.

In Nicaragua, the contribution of business elites to political liberalization
combined intentions with behaviors. Sandinista leaders acknowledge with
regret some mistakes made in the conduct of policies toward business. Sandinista government policy was resisted not only by wealthy property owners but also by some small-scale merchants and certain sectors of the peas-
antry. Some policies, such as price and purchase controls over grains, had
led to a wave of peasant protest. Merchants, industrialists, and owners of
large landholdings engaged in capital flight and smuggling. One effect of
such action was to make it more difficult for the Sandinista government to
govern, even in its most authoritarian moment. The growth of the economy's informal and black market sectors also made it more difficult for the
Sandinista government to govern. More openly, the peak business confederation (the Superior Private Enterprise Council, COSEP) criticized the Sandinista government's policies over a great many issues, not just economic
policy.

The effect of COSEP's intentional opposition and of business (including
some peasant) behavior that impeded authoritarian policies was to prevent
the consolidation of an authoritarian regime and to sustain political space
for the opposition, thereby favoring political liberalization. At a key juncture the Sandinistas responded by engaging various sectors of the opposition, including business, in the dialogue that led to some political concessions and, eventually, to the February 1990 national elections (which were
won by the opposition).

In El Salvador by the end of the 1980s, important business elites opened
the political space necessary for an eventual settlement of the war, since
continued war was not good for business.[16] Business confederations, such
as the Chamber of Industry and Commerce, spoke publicly in favor of negotiations with the FMLN; in 1990, some representatives from these business associations even had formal discussions with guerrilla leaders. In the
spring of 1991, however, some business sectors linked with sectors in the
armed forces and ARENA launched a massive attack on President Cristiani's strategy of negotiation; this campaign was lavishly carried out in the

mass media and led to the possibility of a military coup. The latter, of course, remains a limitation on the constitutionalization of the military. But even this split in the Salvadoran business community speaks well for the prospects for democracy, making it less likely that homogeneous, oligarchical politics based on a business-military alliance could be reconstructed. Instead, it makes it more likely that cross-class dialogue can occur. The fact that a business executive turned president (Cristiani) led the government and the most conservative party (ARENA) to a successful negotiation augurs well for the politics of conciliation.

In Panama, business opposition to the Torrijos regime began with business attempting to shield some of its leaders from arrest, harassment, and deportation. The government responded by closing the offices of the Association of Business Executives. The business community might for the first time have begun to think about their own stakes in democratizing Panama.[17] In 1980 businessman Roberto Eisenmann was the most important founder of *La Prensa*, the newspaper that would help lead the opposition to Noriega. Years later, business groups and individual executives played a leading role in the campaign against Noriega. In Panama, more than in the other three countries, business groups were the strongest advocates for political liberalization.

In contrast to the nearly uniform effect of business behavior since the 1970s in creating circumstances favorable to political liberalization as the (often unintended) consequence of business opposition to important government policies, business economic behavior has not always favored economic liberalization.

For various reasons, including its reliance on the U.S. dollar and the lack of a central bank, Panama has had the most internationally open economy of the four countries. Nonetheless, in the early 1970s the industrial sector successfully pressured the government for increased protection by means of quotas and tariffs. When Ardito-Barletta became president of Panama, he sought to reduce such levels of protection, with only modest success. This effort to liberalize the market (and especially the proposal for a new value-added tax on services) had the unintended effect of weakening political support for the new president in the business community.

In Nicaragua, the Sandinista government somewhat incoherently coupled its coercive measures toward COSEP and specific business firms with complementary policies in support of particular business firms and sectors. The government gave incentives to agricultural exporters; the financial system was used to subsidize some private firms, which thereby acquired a stake in the economy's continued politicization. In turn, the Chamorro government moved to liberalize the economy; it encountered the opposition of those business firms that had benefited from high tariff protection and sub-sidized credit and from those that had formerly earned oligopoly rents.

In El Salvador, President Cristiani's liberalization of the economy created a complex pattern of winners and losers. For most of the 1980s, El Salva-dor's overvalued exchange rate, high effective rates of tariff protection, and many nontariff barriers such as import quotas were the pillars of import substitution industrialization at the expense of the export sector. The deci-sion to devalue the exchange rate, greatly reduce tariffs and most export taxes, and eliminate most nontariff barriers helped exporters enormously but, by and large, increased pressures on business firms that had gained from the previous import substitution strategy. The results for business, therefore, were variable depending on the position of each firm.

Perhaps Guatemala's business community was the most resistant to free markets and to collective obligations to the nation as a whole. The Cerezo government, led by Finance Minister Rodolfo Paiz, adopted a strategy of economic liberalization. It freed financial interest rates, devalued the cur-rency, and unified exchange rates. It began to dismantle the system that pro-vided high rates of tariff protection and sought to engage Guatemala more freely in international markets. Relying upon its congressional majority, the Cerezo government raised taxes to set the nation's budget on a sound basis and to increase investment in the social sphere. Led by the Chamber of Agri-cultural, Commercial, Industrial and Financial Associations (CACIF), the business community opposed the government over these measures, espe-cially tax reform. However, Guatemala's popularly elected constitutional government had the legitimacy and political support that the military gov-ernment had lacked to enact tax reform. Subsequent to the enactment of tax reform in September 1987, the Christian Democrats won a majority of may-oralties in the April 1988 nationwide municipal elections. In panic, business groups allied with some military sectors to launch the failed May 1988 coup.

At a more modest level, consider the response of some Guatemalan wealthy property owners to tax reform. To simplify administration of the property tax, the Cerezo government and its congressional majority adopted the practice of property value self-assessment. In response, property owners overcame barriers to collective action so that all neighbors in a particular section of a city agreed to undervalue their property to avoid paying higher taxes.

Many business firms generally support—and benefit from—market lib-eralization. This is especially the case for those engaged in the production and export of nontraditional goods. But much of the business community in Central America and Panama behaved in a manner contrary to myth:

business facilitated political liberalization while it has at times impeded economic liberalization.

Mistaken Paths

"The lesson of the third wave [democratization since 1970] seems clear: authoritarian leaders who wanted to stay in power should not have called elections; opposition groups who wanted democracy should not have boycotted the elections authoritarian leaders did call."[18] So too in Central America and Panama. Citizens in these countries have often voted against incumbents in the 1980s and 1990s. Participation in elections, therefore, was likely to pay off for the opposition. It was a serious mistake for El Salvador's democratic left to have delayed as much as it did in reentering the electoral arena, because the parties of the right thus became the only vehicles for the expression of voter disaffection. It was clearly not a mistake for Panama's opposition to participate in the 1989 fraudulent elections; that fraud greatly debilitated the Noriega regime and eventually served to legitimize the government installed after the U.S. invasion. Guatemala's Christian Democrats' entry into the 1985 presidential election and Chamorro's opposition coalition entry into the 1990 presidential election in Nicaragua were clearly sound, for they won.

Another mistake is to govern with insufficient information about one's allies. Ardito-Barletta did not know about much military activity in Panama until after he was forced to step down from the presidency. General Gramajo was surprised by the pusillanimous response of many civilians in the Cerezo government to the May 1988 coup; had Gramajo had more contact with other members of the government of which he was a part, he might have planned more effectively to stop the turmoil in the Guatemalan army in the late 1980s. Rubén Zamora first joined the government of El Salvador in late 1979; at that time he did not even know how to distinguish among military ranks. More serious were abuses of power by the Sandinista government; these actions seemed to stem from a mistaken judgment that the FSLN enjoyed more support than it did.

But the most serious mistake is one of a collective nature: the drop in living standards and the failure to address social questions. The Nicaraguan case is the most dramatic. The Sandinistas made praiseworthy efforts to improve the living conditions of most Nicaraguans; in the years immediately following the 1979 revolution, these efforts made progress, especially in the areas of health and education. By the end of the 1980s, however, the effort had not succeeded: between 1981 and 1990, Nicaragua lost over one-third of the value of its gross domestic product (GDP) per capita (most of this loss occurred after 1984, and a substantial portion of it was related to the war). Although circumstances were less stark in the other three cases, Panama, El Salvador, and Guatemala lost between 13 and 19 percent of their GDP per capita during the same decade. In the early 1990s, Panama's GDP per capita recovered well; El Salvador's performed next best, while Guatemala's recovered more slowly. Nicaragua's decline continued.[19] There is a sense of urgency about the "social debt" that the elites in these countries owe the people and a sense of sadness that so little has been accomplished.

Conclusion

From the region's past, one thing is certain: in the early 1980s no one would have forecast that one-time leaders of the opposition would govern all four of these countries in the early 1990s. No one would have forecast that fair and competitive elections would become routine across the region. No one would have forecast that every military coup attempted since 1984 in this region would fail. No one would have forecast the end of the region's wars. The actions of many, including politicians, army officers, government officials, and academic leaders, have promoted liberalization and democratization in Central America and Panama. Much remains to be done, but much has been accomplished, as well.

3   Constructing Democracies

Parties, Institutions, Market Reforms, the Military, and the International Environment

with Jeanne Kinney Giraldo

While discussing local events, some younger, would-be reformers of Ilhéus (in Jorge Amado's novel, *Gabriela: cravo e canela*) observe that the traditional elites "support a state government that plunders us and then practically ignores us. While our local government does absolutely nothing . . . [and] in fact it actually places obstacles in the way of improvements." The reformers resolve to make changes; as one says to another, "you'll earn twice as much if you get into politics and change the existing situation."[1]

Though Amado wrote this in the 1950s, his themes are still part of the political experience of many ordinary people in Latin America and the Caribbean in the mid-1990s. Government is unresponsive and at times an obstacle, traditional political leaders deserve no support, and political reform is an illusion because those who promise change are likely to change only the beneficiaries of corruption. The record reviewed in this chapter offers much justification for political cynicism and despair.

In the late 1980s and early 1990s, voters in many countries elected to office politicians who promised change but then disappointed them. Elected on platforms committed to change, Fernando Collor de Mello in Brazil and Carlos Andrés Pérez in Venezuela were impeached for corruption and removed from office. Never before had a constitutionally elected president been removed from office in this manner and for this reason in either country.

More generally, the late 1980s and early 1990s was a time of trouble in many Latin American and Caribbean countries, a period when social, economic, and political circumstances were redefined. One sign of disaffection was the pattern of electoral outcomes. In those years, incumbent political parties were defeated at least once in Argentina, Uruguay, Brazil, Bolivia, Peru, Ecuador, Venezuela, Guyana, Barbados, Trinidad and Tobago, Jamaica, Panama, Costa Rica, Nicaragua, El Salvador, Honduras, and Guatemala, as were the incumbent politicians associated with the authoritarian government in Chile in 1989 and in Haiti in 1991.[2] The voters in these countries were unhappy with long-standing rulers and would-be reformers.

Voters have blamed governing parties for the region's prolonged economic crisis. Dire living conditions still prevail years after the great depression that hit this region in the 1980s. By the end of 1994, on average and in real prices, the gross domestic product per capita of the countries of Latin America and the Caribbean had yet to surpass the 1981 level. Among Latin American countries, only Argentina, Chile, Colombia, Costa Rica, the Dominican Republic, Panama, and Uruguay had surpassed the 1981 level. In the Anglophone Caribbean, the record was better: the Bahamas, Belize, Guyana, Jamaica, and the countries that belong to the Organization of Eastern Caribbean States had exceeded the 1981 level.[3] Latin America and the Caribbean, in short, have been battered by the winds of change, anger, hope, and dissatisfaction. One might expect voter apathy and alienation from political parties to rise, politicians and civic leaders to redesign basic national institutions, market reforms to fail, and political regimes to fall.

In this chapter, we advance four propositions that run somewhat counter to these expectations. First, though there is much voter anger, new and many old parties have continued to mobilize support. Several new political parties have become credible opposition contenders even in countries where no "new" party has seriously challenged the political establishment in decades. In other cases, long-established political parties have "reinvented" themselves.

Second, while an orgy of constitutional reform mongering designed to improve democratic governance has occurred, it has had little impact. Attempts have been made to redesign the relationship between executive and legislative branches, improve the performance of the judiciary, and decentralize certain tasks of government, but these attempts have either not gone far enough or have proven counterproductive. In too many countries, the performance of state institutions remains poor and democratic governance is weak.

Third, contrary to the expectations of many in years past, democratic regimes in Latin America have proven more effective at introducing market reforms than had been the case with authoritarian regimes. Even more surprising to certain skeptics, in several cases these governments have used the procedures of democracy to advance and secure such reforms.

And fourth, although the stability of constitutional government in the region is still a matter of concern—especially in view of the coup attempts that took place in the 1990s, some sponsored by constitutionally elected presidents—barriers against *successful* coup attempts have gradually been constructed. Since 1976, outside of Suriname, Haiti, and Peru, all attempts to overthrow a constitutional government chosen through general, fraud-free, elections have failed. Important changes within the armed forces, in the relationships between the armed forces and the rest of the society, and in the international community have decreased the likelihood of successful military coups.

Crises and Opportunities for Representation

Latin American countries are facing a crisis of representation linked to the challenges of two major transitions: from authoritarian to constitutional governments and from statist to more market-oriented economies. This second transition also affects most of the countries of the Anglophone Caribbean. Representative networks were battered by the authoritarian regimes; in some countries, they broke down. In nearly all new democracies, parties face a mass electorate that is larger, more urbanized, more educated, and more exposed to mass media than was the case under past constitutional governments. Moreover, the economic depression of the 1980s and the nearly simultaneous transition toward a more market-oriented economy strained old networks of representation and created demands for new forms of representation. Many parties have reconsidered their long-held adherence to statist ideologies. Labor union power has weakened nearly everywhere, while business and "liberal" ideologies have gathered strength. The cutbacks in government consumer subsidies and in funding for many public services have hurt the poor and weakened the political allegiances of many middle-class sectors.

As a result of these changes, organizations that seek to represent the interests of citizens have been simultaneously destroyed, created, and recreated. Many of these organizations have been political parties, but a wide array of social movements have also been involved, and many parties have drawn strength from such movements.[4]

This section examines four kinds of representational challenges facing countries undergoing the dual transition from authoritarianism and statist economies. In countries where the transition from authoritarian regimes to constitutional governments coincided with the end of civil war, new democracies face the challenge of incorporating parties that have been formed out of guerrilla and paramilitary groups. Second, in countries where parties have historically been strong, democratizing pressures and efforts to undertake economic reform have led to the creation of new parties that challenge the monopolies or oligopolies on representation that one or two parties have long held. In other countries where parties have been historically weak, such as Brazil, the major representational challenge is the construction of more programmatic and responsible parties. And fourth, older political parties in many countries have scrambled to adapt to changed circumstances, with varying degrees of success. On balance, the transformation of old parties and the appearance of new parties may improve the prospects of effective representation in the medium to long term.

Explaining the Defeat of Parties

One manifestation of the crisis of representation is the defeat of parties on election day. The most common reason for the defeat of parties at moments of transition from authoritarian rule has been the perception that they are "tainted." In elections that found a democratic regime, parties associated with, or conciliatory to, an outgoing military regime are punished at the voting booth. With the ambiguous exceptions of Mexico and Paraguay, whose elections in the 1980s and early 1990s were marred by irregularities that protected the incumbents from the full wrath of the voters, the parties most closely identified with an authoritarian regime lost the elections that marked the transition toward constitutional government.[5] This fate befell parties as different as those of the Chilean right, which lost the 1989 elections at the end of the dictatorship of Augusto Pinochet despite an excellent record of economic growth in the late 1980s, and the Sandinistas in Nicaragua in 1990.

In countries where no major parties supported the military regime, voters chose the opposition party most distant from the unpopular incumbents. This was one important reason that in 1983 Argentina's Radical Civic Union (UCR) beat the Peronistas for the first time since the latter political movement was founded in 1946; that in 1980 Fernando Belaúnde beat the APRA Party (American Popular Revolutionary Alliance) in Peru; and that in 1982 Hernán Siles Suazo became President of Bolivia at the head of a leftist political coalition.

Elections have also punished political parties that were elected as the standard-bearers of political reform but that became corrupt once in power. The defeats of the Dominican Revolutionary Party in 1986, the Christian Democrats (PDC) in El Salvador in 1989 and in Guatemala in 1990, APRA in Peru in 1990, and Acción Democrática (AD) in Venezuela in 1993 can be seen at least in part as voter retribution for such perceived failures.

A third source of electoral defeat for parties has been the response to bad economic conditions.[6] This was certainly a factor in the defeat of the Radical Party in Argentina in 1989, as well as in the defeats of the Christian Democrats in El Salvador in 1989 and in Guatemala in 1990, of APRA in Peru in 1990, and of Acción Democrática in Venezuela in 1993. The economic issue weakened every incumbent Brazilian president since the end of military government in 1985, though Itamar Franco's popularity rose at the very end of his presidency thanks partly to the successful inflation containment policies of his finance minister and eventual successor, Fernando Henrique Cardoso. It also weakened Guillermo Endara's presidency in Panama, paving the way for the 1994 election victory of the Democratic Revolutionary Party (PRD) once associated with deposed General Manuel Antonio Noriega.

Given the overlap between these three explanations, which is most important to explain the defeat of parties? We believe that association with authoritarian governments has more explanatory power than the response to bad economic conditions. Except for the two ambiguous cases already noted (Paraguay and Mexico), no incumbent party tainted by association with prolonged authoritarian rule won an election during the transition from such rule. In contrast, some parties associated with incumbent governments have been defeated despite managing the economy well (in Chile and Jamaica in 1989 and in Uruguay and Costa Rica in 1994), and not every government that has mismanaged the economy has been defeated (Acción Democrática retained the presidency in the 1988 elections). Association with authoritarian rule has been punished more systematically than bad economic outcomes, while good economic management has not always been rewarded.

With the evidence available, however, it is more difficult to determine the relative importance of corruption and bad economic conditions. In Argentina in the early 1990s, for example, the positive economic results under President Carlos Saúl Menem meant more in the public opinion polls than the numerous charges of corruption leveled against people in or close to the administration. In Venezuela, in contrast, the positive performance of the economy under President Pérez during the same years did not bolster his popularity as much as Menem's. It did not save him from later impeachment and conviction on the grounds of corruption, nor did it save his party from election defeats that were also caused in part by the economy's eventual downturn.

The defeat of incumbent parties for any of these three reasons is understandable. Indeed, it is the essence of democratic politics that voters should turn out those officeholders whose conduct or performance in office they disapprove. If the reasons these parties have been defeated give cause to worry about the fate of constitutional government in the region, then the way these parties were defeated gives reason for hope that the instruments of constitutionalism can serve the people's needs.

However, another manifestation of the crisis of representation in the 1990s is the decline of electoral participation in the Anglophone Caribbean and Venezuela, countries with well-established constitutional governments in which such participation had been high historically. Citizens find no electoral vehicle that responds to their concerns to bring about meaningful change. From the 1980s to the 1990s, voter turnout declined in ten of the thirteen Anglophone Caribbean countries in which general elections were held. Voter turnout declined as well in Venezuela, a country with a once consistently high voting rate; its abstention rate rose to 44 percent in the 1993 presidential elections, a time of peril for its constitutional life.

Explaining the Birth of New Parties: From Warrior to Peacemaker

By definition, all new parties are born in dissent. Their leaders and followers claim that existing parties no longer represent them. The revolt against established parties has at times begun literally in rebellion. Never before in Latin America's twentieth-century history have so many political parties been spawned by paramilitary or guerrilla organizations. The new parties examined in this section differ in many ways but share one important trait: their founders once used violence to attempt to overthrow the government or dispose of their adversaries. The transformation of military movements into political parties is best explained as a slow, rational process in which exhausted leaders and followers conclude that politics is more cost-effective than war as a way to gain power.

On the left, Venezuela's Movimiento al Socialismo (MAS) traces its origins in part to the Venezuelan Communist Party's decision to abandon the guerrilla warfare conducted against Venezuela's governments in the 1960s, after which some key leaders of that effort founded the MAS. By the 1980s and 1990s, the MAS had won a respected place among Venezuela's political parties, and it played an important role in Rafael Caldera's 1993 presidential election victory.

In Colombia, the M-19 guerrilla group agreed to demobilize in 1989. Its leaders founded Alianza Democrática M-19, which won 12.5 percent of the vote in the 1990 presidential elections, the largest share of the vote for any party of the left in Colombian history. This party went on to win the second largest block of seats in the elections for the Constituent Assembly that met during the first half of 1991, though it had weakened greatly by the time of the 1994 national elections.

Revolutionary victory in Nicaragua in 1979 and the Sandinista defeat in 1990 gradually permitted and eventually required the transformation of the Sandinista Front for National Liberation (FSLN) from a military force into a political party. The FSLN as a party has had a tumultuous history since 1990, but it has remained within the framework of constitutional politics.

In El Salvador, the Farabundo Martí National Liberation Front (FMLN) began its transformation into a political party upon the signing of the peace agreement in 1992; allied with others on the political left, it became the country's second-largest political force in the 1994 elections.

On the right, it is only a slight exaggeration to argue that El Salvador's

Nationalist Republican Alliance (ARENA) was born from a wedding between death squads and a segment of the business community. Roberto D'Aubuisson was the key figure in death squad activities in the late 1970s and early 1980s, and he would become ARENA's leader until his death.

In Argentina, Colonel Aldo Rico led an unsuccessful military mutiny against the constitutional government in April 1987. When national congressional and gubernatorial elections were held in 1991, Rico's Movement for National Dignity and Independence (MODIN) won three seats in the Chamber of Deputies and 10 percent of the votes in the crucial province of Buenos Aires; its subsequent strength has varied but has remained generally modest. Moreover, provincial parties in Chaco, Salta, and Tucumán nominated retired military officers who had served as governors during the previous military government; these candidates won the governorships.

The fate of these parties depends in part on their ability to resolve the often bitter internal debates over electoral strategy that occur frequently among new participants in the democratic process. In Colombia, the M-19's decision to pursue electoral coalitions with traditional parties instead of focusing on party building seems to have backfired; by 1994 its electoral weight was insignificant. In El Salvador, the FMLN split over these issues after the 1994 elections, as did the FSLN in Nicaragua. The importance of the new parties should not be underestimated, however. In the mid-1990s, the MAS was part of the governing coalition in Venezuela. The FSLN and the FMLN remained among the largest political forces in Nicaragua and El Salvador. And ARENA governed El Salvador.

Why did former military combatants lay down their arms to compete in elections? The general reason is not the end of the Cold War, which had nothing to do with the creation of the MAS, ARENA, or MODIN, or the M-19's decision to end the armed struggle. Nonetheless, international factors did affect the costs and benefits of war for both the rebels and the government. The decision of some guerrillas in Venezuela in the late 1960s to abandon the armed struggle was part of a wider international debate within the political left about the proper means to contest power. And the turn away from war by the FMLN and the FSLN was indeed framed by the end of the Cold War in Europe.

Apart from these lesser considerations, a familiar but powerful explanation serves best. Recall Thomas Hobbes's *Leviathan*, in which the terrible experiences of prolonged war lead the combatants to a rational decision to lay down their arms. Through prolonged war, they learn that they cannot win. The end of warfare in Latin America led, however, not to Leviathans but to constitutional governments. In the logic of stalemate, neither side can dictate its preferences to the other. Each settles for the second-best solution:

to contest each other peacefully, so putting something on the negotiating table becomes a more effective route to achieve their goals.[7]

Latin America's warriors-turned-peacemakers stumbled unknowingly onto Robert A. Dahl's axiom that, from the government's perspective, "the more the costs of suppression exceed the costs of toleration, the greater the chance for a competitive regime" (see chap. 2). From the perspective of the armed opposition, the axiom might be rewritten, the more the costs of rebellion exceed the costs of participation, the greater the chance for a competitive regime.[8] Moreover, governments changed their strategies to provide institutional guarantees and other incentives for guerrillas to make peace and participate in politics. Lawful political space expanded; the insurgents responded rationally. Where the terms for peaceful participation remained insufficiently attractive, as for some guerrilla forces in Colombia, the war staggers on.

Explaining the Birth of New Parties: A Protest against Partyarchy and Ideological Betrayal

In recent years, new parties have been more likely to be born and to attract nationwide support when two processes converged: (a) the preexisting party establishment gave signs of seeking to strengthen its ruling monopoly or duopoly, reducing the space for alternative political forces to express themselves within these parties, and (b) the key political party that had received support from the left abandoned its prior policies and veered sharply toward promarket or other right-wing policies, seemingly betraying the public trust and generating a secession on its left. Political entrepreneurs acted when space on the party spectrum was abdicated through ideological betrayal (the pull factor) and when they no longer found room to play a role within the existing parties (the push factor). Facing blocked opportunities to voice dissent, the would-be founders of new parties and their followers exited.[9] The new parties gained electorally as citizens expressed their discontent with the status quo by voting against establishment parties.

Argentina, Mexico, Uruguay, and Venezuela exemplify these trends. In these four cases, the emergence of new parties has been in part a response to what some perceived as the arrogance of the national parties and the predominance within older parties of an apparently self-perpetuating leadership—a classic crisis of representation. Writing about Venezuela, Michael Coppedge uses the word *partyarchy* to describe this phenomenon.[10] In Coppedge's analysis of partyarchy, parties fully penetrate organizations in civil society. We use the term more loosely, to identify countries where the number of parties long perceived as capable of winning a presidential election is only one (Mexico) or two (Argentina, Uruguay, and Venezuela) and where party leaders made use of this monopoly or duopoly to create a cartel of party elites (in Mexico, Uruguay, and Venezuela) or were perceived to be attempting to create such a cartel (in Argentina in 1994). Under partyarchy, party leaders and organizations seek to regulate electoral competition within each party and between the two dominant parties, to enforce party discipline in legislative assemblies and executive posts, and to rely on intra-elite negotiation to address various important issues.[11]

In Uruguay, the constitution was modified in the late 1960s to concentrate greater powers in the presidency and to constrain political rights. Under President Jorge Pacheco Areco, the governing faction of the Colorado Party turned to the right. The government became generally repressive in response to the Tupamaro urban insurgency and began to adopt market-oriented economic policies. Because Uruguay's labor movement had been independent of the traditional parties, it served as a key vehicle to launch a third-party challenge to an entrenched duopoly (the Colorado and Blanco parties) long protected by the electoral law. In 1971 the law-abiding left reorganized into a broad coalition, the Frente Amplio, which captured 18 percent of the national vote, most of it from the city of Montevideo. By the 1994 national election the Frente Amplio had made significant gains in the interior provinces; its share of the national vote rose to just under one-third, in a virtual three-way tie with the Blanco and Colorado parties.

In Argentina, President Menem led the governing Peronista Party toward promarket policies in the 1990s, dismantling the legacy of Juan Perón on which Menem had run for the presidency. Critics responded in various ways. Argentine provincial parties acquired a new lease on life.[12] Historically, they had done well in gubernatorial and legislative elections, but in 1994 they also obtained important representation in the constituent assembly at the expense of both the Peronistas and the Radicals. Support for provincial parties, MODIN, and the left-leaning Frente Grande coalition blossomed in response to the 1994 agreement between President Menem and former President Raúl Alfonsín to modify the constitution, which was widely perceived as an effort to advance their own ambitions. To prevent the continuity of such a duopoly, many voters turned to third parties.

Something similar happened in Mexico, where national elections became much more competitive in the 1980s and 1990s. After 1982, the long-ruling Institutional Revolutionary Party (PRI) abandoned decades of statist policies to shift toward promarket policies, but it was still reluctant to recognize opposition election victories. In response, the center-right National Action Party (PAN) ran on a platform calling for democratization and was able to increase its national appeal beyond its historic bases of support in various states of northern Mexico. Within the PRI, party elites raised the barriers to internal dissent even as they were abandoning decades of statist policies; denied a voice within the party they had called home, dissenters exited to form a new party. The new center-left Party of the Democratic Revolution (PRD), led by Cuauhtémoc Cárdenas, combined these dissidents from the PRI with supporters drawn from other small parties of the left (including Mexico's Communist Party). The PRD considered itself a national party though it obtained disproportionate support from central and southern Mexico.[13] Both the reinvigoration of the PAN and the rise of the Cardenista opposition can be traced to protests against the PRI's monopoly on public office.

In Venezuela in 1989, President Carlos Andrés Pérez shifted away from his populist and statist past toward promarket policies markedly different from those that Acción Democrática had normally espoused. For the most part, the hitherto main opposition party, COPEI, supported the new economic orientation. In the early 1990s, opposition to these economic policies merged with a revolt against partyarchy that had been gathering strength during the previous decade. Opponents felt that they had no choice but to look outside the two long-dominant parties or to abstain; abstention rates in Venezuelan elections, historically very low, rose significantly. A plurality elected former president Rafael Caldera to the presidency in December 1993 after he had denounced the party establishment and its economic policies, broken with COPEI, and founded the National Convergence, which aligned with the MAS and other parties. Another noteworthy result was the explosive growth of Causa R, a new political party that rose from a social and regional base and quickly became a national party. Causa R emerged in the labor movement of the State of Bolívar, led by union leader Andrés Velásquez, who was elected as state governor and served as the party's presidential candidate in 1993. By the 1993 national elections, Causa R had built a strong presence in the Venezuelan labor movement nationwide and drew support from other regions of the country to capture just under a fourth of the votes cast, a virtual tie with Acción Democrática and COPEI.

The combination of partyarchy and doctrinal abandonment set the stage for the rise of new parties. If partyarchy alone were the explanation, similar challenges should have developed in Colombia and Honduras, where the Liberal and Conservative and the Liberal and National parties, respectively, enjoyed duopolies of representation and where party programs did not typically differ much in ideological content. In these countries, however, the question of ideological betrayal never arose. Parties remained reliable: once in office they did not change the behavior displayed in the pre-election campaign.[14] In these countries, despite discontent with the party establishment, no strong new parties emerged in the absence of ideological betrayal.

In the same vein, merely dropping previous programmatic commitments does not suffice to trigger the emergence of a third party seeking to represent interests within civil society. Third parties did not gain much support in Costa Rica in the 1980s, when Liberación Nacional governments under presidents Luis Monge and Oscar Arias veered away from the party's historic statism toward freer market policies but did not seek simultaneously to increase barriers to representation. Court litigation became the channel for dissent from the new economic policies.

In Argentina, Carlos Menem ran for office without hinting that he planned to abandon decades of Peronista commitment to statist economic policies. When he did, the Frente Grande coalition was formed on the left to claim the political space that the Peronistas had ceded, but voting support for the Peronistas (though it declined slightly in 1991 relative to the 1989 elections) remained strong in the two nationwide congressional elections following his policy about-face. The Peronista share of the vote dropped only in response to the Menem-Alfonsín pact to modify the constitution. The Frente Grande had received only 3.6 percent of the votes in 1993 (before the Menem-Alfonsín pact), but it gained 13.6 percent in 1994 (after the pact), when it also carried the capital city of Buenos Aires; the MODIN's share of the vote rose from 6 percent before the pact to 9 percent after it. In the 1995 presidential elections, the Frente Grande joined with others to create the Frente Solidario País (FREPASO). Its candidate, former Peronista senator and governor José Octavio Bordón, won 28 percent of the votes, finishing second to Menem and ahead of the Radicals—the first time in a century that the Radical Civic Union had failed to come in first or second in a presidential election. (The MODIN's share of the votes fell below 2 percent.)

In short, neither a change in economic policy commitments nor the existence of partisan monopolies or duopolies suffices to trigger the emergence of new parties or party coalitions. Together, however, these two factors greatly increase the likelihood that such parties or coalitions will arise and grow.[15] A hypothesis to explore in the future is the following: When parties are formed around groups organized in civil society (Frente Amplio in Uruguay, PAN in Mexico, Causa R in Venezuela), they are more likely to endure and succeed than parties that are formed principally by dissidents who find their paths blocked within existing parties (Convergencia Nacional in Venezuela, FREPASO in Argentina), with Mexico's PRD exhibiting traits of both processes. There is support for this view in the December 1995 gubernatorial elections in Venezuela, in which Causa R received 13 percent of the votes cast, the MAS 10 percent, and Convergencia Nacional less than 9 percent.

Explaining the Birth of New Parties: Constructing Political Society

In other countries, representation has suffered not because of the tight grip of one or two strong parties on public office but because of the predominance of many weak parties. Brazil, for example, has been bereft of "real" political parties. The combination of powerful traditional elites, entrenched regional interests, the incentives created for politicians by the electoral laws, and the norms and habits of politics have left Brazil with weak, incoherent, unprogrammatic, undisciplined, and fractious parties. In contrast, modern parties should be internally democratic, pragmatic, and able to recruit cadres and to respond quickly to problems with well-defined initiatives.

Since the late 1970s, two such parties have been founded in Brazil. The Worker's Party (PT) grew out of the militant unionism developed in the late 1970s in the metallurgical industries of the highly urban state of São Paulo in protest against the ruling military dictatorship and in search of better economic conditions.[16] It has become the largest explicitly socialist party in Latin America, incorporating a variety of small Brazilian left-wing parties and providing a partisan home for many social movements that arose in connection with Roman Catholic ecclesiastical base communities, neighborhood associations, and women's movements. In Brazil's 1990 and 1994 presidential elections, the PT's candidate, Lula (Luis Inácio da Silva), came in second. The PT's formal members have genuine opportunities to engage in internal party life and debate and to choose party programs and policies. The PT has a definite esprit de corps. It is Brazil's first mass political party that does not depend just on the popularity of its leader or the efficacy of a patronage machine.

The second real party is the Brazilian Social Democratic Party (PSDB). Founded in 1988 from a schism in the Brazilian Democratic Movement Party (PMDB)—a classic incoherent combination of traditional clientelism, patronage, and factions—the PSDB sought to formulate a centrist, modern, alternative to other parties, with strong appeal to the urban middle class. The PSDB designed a program for effective democratic governance to which its officeholders were ordinarily bound. In 1994, PSDB founding leader Fernando Henrique Cardoso was elected president of Brazil in large part because of his previous success as finance minister. Like the PT, although to a lesser extent, the PSDB is characterized by programmatic coherence, officeholder discipline, and internal party life.

Since the 1994 elections, then, Brazil for the first time has had real parties in government and in the opposition, in addition to the traditional clientelistic patronage machines. Nonetheless, the strength of those traditional machines was also evident in that election. In order to elect Cardoso to the presidency, the PSDB had to form an alliance with the Liberal Front Party (PFL), a classic patronage party. Thus it remains to be seen how much long-term impact the PT and the PSDB will have on the traditional style of politics in Brazil, especially because skewed electoral laws still limit their representation in Congress.

Explaining the Reinvention of Old Parties

The region's crisis of representation and its economic depression of the 1980s did not overwhelm every preexisting political party, nor was the creation of new parties the sole response to these problems. Many existing parties have made efforts to adapt to changed circumstances—a strategy of re-invention. In most cases, defeat (either of the party or of democracy as a whole) permitted challengers within the party to marginalize discredited factions and leaders, at times relieving them of their power. Defeat also made it easier to reexamine old dogmas and discard failed policies. Defeat alone is insufficient, of course, for the successful reinvention of parties. A reinvented party's programmatic reorientation can be consolidated only if the party is rewarded with electoral victory.

During the 1980s, the Chilean Christian Democrats and the Socialists (including the Socialist offshoot, the Party for Democracy) rebuilt and repositioned themselves and forged an alliance (the Concertación Democrática) to win the 1988 plebiscite that ended the dictatorship. The alliance went on to win the next two presidential elections, in 1989 and 1993. The breakdown of democracy in 1973, the failure of the protests of the mid-1980s to unseat the military government, and the collapse of heterodox economic policies in neighboring countries affected the balance of forces within the parties of the center and the left and, eventually, resulted in the ascendance of new leaders who embraced a market-conforming political platform.

Also during the 1980s, the People's National Party in Jamaica reconstructed its program and renewed its cadres, after the party's failed statist economic policies led to a crushing electoral defeat in 1980. The reinvented party won the parliamentary elections of 1989 and, subsequently, effected a transition of the prime ministership from Michael Manley to P. J. Patterson. The party recognized that its statist economic policies during the 1970s had failed, resulting in its election defeat in 1980.

In Argentina, in response to their 1983 presidential election defeat, the Peronistas reinvented themselves. Founded in the mid-1940s by Juan Perón as a "movement," not a party, the Peronistas (Partido Justicialista) at last held internal party elections in the 1980s to choose candidates for office.

These new internal procedures made it easier to remove many old-time leaders who had lost the support of the rank and file. In the early 1990s, in addition, the Menem government adopted an entirely new profile of economic policies.

In Panama in the early 1990s the PRD successfully recovered from its long cohabitation with General Noriega. After its 1989 defeat the PRD modified its policies toward the United States, dropped its support for reestablishing the armed forces, adopted less confrontational stands toward other political forces, and adopted a market-friendly economic program. It won the 1994 presidential elections.

In Chile, Jamaica, Argentina, and Panama, reinvention of parties rested on a shift from statist to promarket economic policies, a shift made possible by the shock of defeat, which in turn permitted the removal of discredited leaders. In many cases, a comfortable margin of victory for the reinvented parties in a later election facilitated the consolidation of the reinvented party and the policies associated with it. Leaders who changed the historical policy commitments of their party were likely to lose some part of their previous constituency; the larger the victory, the less risky was this change. In Jamaica, the margin of victory of the People's National Party in 1989 meant that the "renovating" leadership did not need to rely on the vote-mobilizing capabilities of the more radical wing of the party. In Chile, the weakening of the Communist Party removed the incentive for leaders of the center-left to back away from their commitment to market-oriented economic policies. In Argentina and Panama, the Peronistas and the PRD, respectively, faced ineffectual opposition parties. In short, a magnificent victory over the opposition was as important to party renewal as the prior defeat of the party itself.

Representational Challenges to the Party System

Many of the new parties under review have been linked to social movements, but the relationship between political and civil society remains problematic in many countries. In Brazil, Chile, Mexico, Nicaragua, and Venezuela, for example, many groups in civil society have sought to increase their autonomy with regard to parties in order to avoid partisan manipulation. In Venezuela and Colombia, new social movements have pressed for the decentralization of the state as a way to weaken central party leaderships, and new local leaders have run for office successfully as independents. Though understandable, these combined trends may well make it more difficult to secure both effective political representation and sustained political cooperation on a nationwide basis.

In addition, there remain important representational voids that not even the new parties have begun to fill sufficiently and that are just as important for effective democratic governance. We call attention to three of them.

First, the representation of indigenous peoples has been woefully inadequate throughout the region. Organized ethnic protest has been emerging since the 1970s in countries with large indigenous populations. In Bolivia, new, small political parties have so far been able to channel these energies and provide some means for representation. But Víctor Hugo Cárdenas, the Aymara leader elected in 1993 as Bolivia's vice president, may be more popular outside Bolivia than in his own country. He can obtain considerable international sympathy and support on behalf of those whom he claims to represent, but his actual backing within Bolivia, even among indigenous peoples, remains modest for a variety of reasons, including the internal diversity of the indigenous community and the limited accomplishments of his administration. Bolivia has also witnessed the phenomenon of "palenquismo"—not organized ethnic protest but populist appeals to indigenous peoples by television and radio personality Carlos Palenque.

In the southern Mexican state of Chiapas, the Zapatista National Liberation Army (EZLN) combines ethnic and regional grievances with a large national program and the disposition to use armed violence to advance its ends. Because of its reliance on violence, this insurgency has been the most worrisome example of ethnic protest.

In Ecuador, the Confederation of Indigenous Nationalities (CONAIE) organized and spearheaded important nationwide protests in the 1990s in opposition to proposed land tenure law changes and other measures that, in its judgment, adversely affected the interests of indigenous peoples. CONAIE also learned to collaborate with some labor unions to organize general strikes. This may well be Latin America's strongest indigenous-based social movement independent of a political party.

Until the 1980s, nationwide political protest by indigenous peoples was extremely rare in Latin America. To understand the change leading to the rise of such protest, four features applied with special force during the 1980s and 1990s: (a) the political opening associated with democratization; (b) the erosion of existing avenues of representation and the increase in material hardship that often accompany the implementation of market-oriented economic policies; (c) the nurturing and enabling effects of institutions such as the changed Roman Catholic Church and other religious communities; and (d) the growth of an international movement of foundations, scholars, and activists to provide support for indigenous organizations in Latin America. There is still the need to explain further, however, why Quechua-speakers in Ecuador organize on behalf of the rights of indigenous peoples who happen to be poor while Quechua-speakers in Peru organize on behalf of the rights of poor people who happen to be indigenous. Why does the likelihood of organized protest on behalf of ethnocultural and linguistic goals vary so much?

A second problem of inadequate representation is evident with regard to gender.[17] Universal suffrage came later to Latin America than to Western Europe and North America, and women's effective participation in politics has continued to lag. In the 1980s and 1990s, some women politicians have emerged on the national sphere, but they are still rare. Some of the new and renovating political parties on the left, such as Brazil's PT, the Chilean Socialists, and Nicaragua's Sandinistas, consciously design their internal rules to attempt, with varying degrees of success, to create an active role for women in discussions and leadership.

A third problem of inadequate representation is the oldest and best known: the question of social class and democratic politics and, more specifically, the compatibility between new, promarket economic policies and the distributive pressures that typically emerge in democratic regimes. Latin American and Caribbean countries have not been good at meeting these goals in the past. The risk of market-oriented reforms is that the prospects for many people are likely to worsen unless there is a conscious commitment to address problems of absolute poverty so that common folk can become true citizens. It is not just the troubles of the powerful, in other words, but the inattention to the troubles of the unempowered that has created a crisis of representation. Effective democratic governance demands that the voiceless be heard.

Reforming State Institutions

In response to the crisis of representation, the legacies of authoritarian rule, and the inefficacy of government economic management in all countries in the early 1980s, government institutions came in for close scrutiny after the demise of authoritarian rule. The result was a widespread and intensive effort to reform the institutions of the state. This section describes the strategies pursued and analyzes their limited success.

We focus on three major areas of attempted institutional redesign. One is the effort to break the gridlock between, and improve the democratic responsiveness of, the executive and the legislature. The second is the effort to reform the administration of justice: to combat crime and corruption, to depoliticize the courts, and to improve access to the court system. And the third is the attempt to bring about territorial decentralization and to devolve responsibilities to subnational governments while seeking to improve their capacity to handle their new duties.

Reshaping Executive-Legislative Relations

With the return of constitutional government in Latin America, scholars and politicians have advanced proposals for institutional reform designed to help solve the problems that they believe contributed to the breakdown of democratic institutions. In many cases, the nature of legislative-executive relations was blamed; in particular, fixed presidential terms and the stalemate between the legislature and the president in presidential systems were seen as crucial factors in democratic breakdown.

The most commonly heard prescription was parliamentarism. Its scholarly advocates believed that incentives for cooperation between the two branches would be increased by tying the legislators' tenure in office to the success of the executive.[18] Legislators who would face the prospect of losing their ballot positions in new elections called by a stymied prime minister would be more likely, the proponents of parliamentarism believed, to organize into disciplined parties and form effective government coalitions. Similarly, executives in parliamentary systems would face votes of no confidence and thus would have more incentives to negotiate with legislators than would a president elected separately from the legislature and unaccountable to it. Despite these arguments, parliamentarism was not adopted in any Latin American country.

In the Anglophone Caribbean, the problems were different. In their existing parliamentary systems, the first-past-the-post electoral system and the small size of parliaments gravely weakened the capacity of the legislature to represent political minorities or to balance the executive. Elections produced large parliamentary majorities, denying even large minority parties adequate representation in parliament. Moreover, parliament was left with few means to check unbridled executive power. Almost one-third of the region's parliament members are also cabinet members. In effect, they are constitutionally debarred from independent and critical stances in relation to the executive because they are also in the executive. These problems remain, for the most part, unsolved.

Although politicians in Latin America and the Caribbean have been unwilling to undertake a wholesale change of state institutions (from presidentialism to parliamentarism, or vice versa), they did make a variety of institutional changes. Argentina (1994), Brazil (1988), Colombia (1991), and Peru (1978 and 1994) convened constituent assemblies to rewrite their basic charter. In Bolivia, Chile, Nicaragua, Paraguay, and Venezuela, legislators undertook constitutional reforms. In Ecuador, a commission of experts drafted a new constitution based on widespread consultation and subsequent submission to a referendum.

There have been two waves of constitutional reforms. The first wave accompanied the transition to democracy and was aimed at solving the problems that were believed to have plagued previous experiences with democracy, especially gridlock and exclusionary practices such as the effective disenfranchisement of large numbers of citizens. Exclusionary practices also came in for sharp criticism in the long-established constitutional polities of Colombia, Venezuela, and the Anglophone Caribbean, where the most widely voiced demand was for an opening of the political system to greater participation (a cry heard also in Mexico). The second wave of constitutional reforms responded to long-standing problems of democratic governance that came to public attention as governments attempted to implement market reforms: corruption, excessive concentration of power in the presidency, and irresponsible behavior by legislators.

The goals for reform advanced by the two waves were broad and potentially contradictory: to break the stalemate between the executive and the legislature, to encourage the democratic responsiveness of the executive by checking its unbridled powers, and to increase the democratic responsiveness of the legislature. This last goal had two aspects: to encourage responsible, programmatic behavior by legislators and to increase the effective representation of voting minorities.

To break the stalemate between the executive and the legislature, several reforms were passed to strengthen the executive. The most widely adopted reform was ballotage, that is, a second round in presidential elections to ensure that the president would be elected by a majority. Since the late 1970s, this has been introduced in Argentina and Nicaragua (where a candidate needs only 45 percent of the votes to avoid a second round) and also in Brazil, Chile, Colombia, the Dominican Republic, Ecuador, El Salvador, Guatemala, and Peru. Another reform was to give special powers to the executive to make macroeconomic policy. Such reforms first occurred in gridlocked democracies: Uruguay in 1967, Colombia in 1968, and Chile in 1970. They would be introduced in Peru in 1979 and 1993, Brazil in 1988, and passed by plebiscite in Ecuador in 1994.

Another reform, introduced in Peru in 1993 and in Argentina in 1994, was to permit the president's immediate reelection, ostensibly to strengthen the incumbent's capacity to govern. The fact that incumbent presidents Fujimori and Menem benefited from the reform, however, led many to see this change as a resurgence of personalism in contexts in which partisan, judicial, and legislative checks on the executive remain weak.

A different approach to breaking stalemates between president and congress focused on the electoral law and the incentives it provides to legislators. The electoral law is often cited as an explanation for the stable governmental coalition in congress in Chile and for unstable coalitions in congress in Brazil. Brazilianists point to electoral law incentives that hinder cooperation, foster party indiscipline and disloyalty, and induce preferential attention to pork barrel politics over policy issues. In contrast, Chile's quite different electoral law of the early 1990s features a bipolar logic that has provided strong incentives for interparty cooperation at the polls and in congress.

To check the president's powers, politicians in various countries have granted greater prerogatives to legislatures. In Colombia, congress was authorized to censure ministers. In Nicaragua in 1994, the national assembly acquired greater authority over tax policy. In Argentina the 1994 constitutional reform created a cabinet chief accountable to the legislature and curbed the president's power to rule by decree. Bans on presidential reelection, already in place in most countries, have been added to several constitutions. In 1994, Nicaragua and the Dominican Republic banned immediate reelection; in 1991, Colombia banned reelection at any time. This strengthening of congressional prerogatives is largely a reaction against the abuse of presidential power that occurred as chief executives attempted to stabilize and reform the economies of these countries. (This happened only to a limited degree in Brazil, where the 1988 constitution increased a great many of the legislature's powers but, at the same time, made the president's decree powers, established in the prior authoritarian constitution, even more arbitrary.)

Meanwhile, some reformers tried to end exclusionary practices and foster the legislature's democratic responsiveness by increasing representational pluralism. In many countries, expansion of the suffrage was expected to provide a constituency for reformist parties of the center and left. The ballotage in Argentina and Colombia was designed to encourage the proliferation of presidential candidates and, consequently, of parties as representative vehicles, by permitting "sincere" voting (in which voters support the candidate they truly prefer) in the first round. Colombia's use of national districts for the election of senators allows voting minorities not concentrated in any region to gain representation in this chamber. Venezuela's shift to voting in part for individual candidates, not just for party slates, seeks to promote greater pluralism and weaken control by party leaders, as well.

The most striking characteristic of these reform processes as a whole, however, is their failure to improve the quality of democratic governance. Constitutional reform has proceeded the least in the Anglophone Caribbean, but Latin Americans also have relatively little to show for their efforts. The greatest disappointments are evident in Brazil, Colombia, Ecuador, and Honduras, where little seems to have changed, and in Chile, where the electoral laws and the standing and structure of Congress remain well below acceptable levels for democratic constitutionalism. In Chile, executive powers are excessive, one-fifth of the senate is unelected, and the electoral law overrepresents conservative rural districts and impedes the effective representation of voting minorities.

How can this failure be explained? Some of the problems are genuinely intractable. Even if leaders knew how to implement reforms and had the power to do so, they would still find it difficult to determine the trade-off between accountability and effectiveness. Thus, the somewhat contradictory goals present early in the reform process were just as evident at the end.

In some cases, the diagnoses and prescriptions advanced by reforming elites turned out to be faulty. Ecuadorian academics expected radical changes, even though the modifications enacted in 1979 were for the most part limited to the extension of the suffrage, party registration, and ballotage and stopping well short of reforming institutional relations between the executive and the legislature. Ecuadorian elites erroneously focused their attention on creating incentives for short-term *electoral* coalitions (such as ballotage), failing to realize that these incentives did not facilitate longer-term *governing* coalitions. Similarly flawed was the exercise in Brazil. Brazilian constitutionalists in 1988 did not address the electoral law's incentives for politicians to focus on pork barrel politics and its disincentives for party discipline. This neglect can be traced to the mistaken notion that fragmented ("pluralist") representation in the legislature and concentrated power in the executive are the best ways to reconcile democratic government and effectiveness. (Although Brazil has long suffered from representational imbalance and electoral fragmentation, the 1988 constitution continued to overrepresent the northeast while failing to establish a minimum vote threshold that parties must meet to win representation in congress.) In both Ecuador and Brazil, constitutional reform did little to solve the problem of governmental gridlock; the president and congress continued to confront each other, the former often resorting to rule by decree.

In many cases, necessary reforms were not passed because they threatened the interests of elites. The first-past-the-post electoral laws common throughout the Anglophone Caribbean protect the interests of the dominant parties best because they exclude third parties from ever gaining significant parliamentary membership. More generally in Latin America, the interests of traditional elites are best served by existing electoral arrangements that reinforce the clientelistic nature of some parties.[19] Clientelistic party systems are characterized by fragmentation, personalism, a patronage or rent-seeking approach to the state and public policy, and a lack of party loyalty on the part of legislators and voters. Party indiscipline is especially evident when politicians desert the parties on whose tickets they ran, as a majority of Brazilian members of congress have done since the restoration of civilian government in 1985 and as a comparable proportion of Ecuadorian members of congress have done since a similar transition in 1979; in both of these countries, as many as a third of the members of the legislature change parties during any one term of office.

In clientelistic party systems, parties fail to articulate the interests of their constituents at a programmatic level, which fuels voter apathy and, in some cases, social violence. Collective action is difficult when power is dispersed among many parties (as in Brazil and Ecuador, for example); even where parties are fewer (as in Colombia and Honduras), internal factionalization and lack of discipline within large parties frequently results in an equally paralyzing de facto multipartyism. Members of congress pursue pork barrel objectives at the expense of legislation or administrative oversight, permitting the excessive concentration of powers in the presidency. Traditional elites can make such conditions work well for them.

In clientelistic systems, presidents can employ patronage to co-opt the opposition, weaken congressional supervision over executive policies, and lull legislators into permitting the use of presidential decree powers. Presidents, too, often prefer the constitutional status quo. For example, Colombian presidents since 1946 have routinely ruled under "state of siege" provisions authorized by the constitution, relying on decrees rather than laws for the governance of the economy.

Traditional elites are less predisposed to respect democratic institutions and processes and more likely to abuse the state for ends that are both antidemocratic and antimarket. The long-standing clientelistic features of party systems in Brazil, Colombia, Ecuador, Guatemala, the Dominican Republic, and Honduras have had the effects summarized above. The two principal parties in Honduras, for example, have offered little effective leadership because their interest is largely directed at meeting the needs of their respective clienteles. Power is rarely exercised to effect a larger vision of the common good. In all such cases, democratic representativeness suffers, and effective constitutional reform to improve governance becomes highly unlikely.

Nevertheless, there have been some modest improvements, especially in countries with little experience of congressional assertiveness or efficacy. Ironically, these improvements have resulted less from constitutional changes than from a more even balance of power between the executive and the legislature. In the 1990s, for the first time ever, the congress of El Salvador plays a role of oversight and legislation, with all of the country's political forces represented. During these same years, the Mexican congress began to question the executive more systematically. Also in the 1990s, albeit after excruciating difficulties, Nicaragua's national assembly began to legislate to address some of the country's ills. After the 1993 national elections, Paraguay found itself with a divided government for the first time in its history; at issue was the capacity of the president and the congress to deepen a still-incipient process of constitutionalizing the government while maintaining acceptable levels of governability.

History also shows the importance of political factors in improving democratic governance. Consider the problem of resolving executive-legislative gridlock. The cases of Costa Rica in the 1950s and El Salvador in the 1990s exemplify the capacity of politicians to learn to cooperate for the purpose of fostering civil peace and establishing constitutional government. In each of those cases, civil wars came to an end and constitutional governments were installed. Venezuela in the 1950s and Chile in the 1990s provide related examples: various parties were able to cooperate to end dictatorship, install constitutional government, and fashion effective relations between president and congress.

Bolivia in the mid-1980s is equally remarkable. Bolivia had a textbook example of a weak, fragmented party system that permitted the military and, later on, drug traffickers to influence the exercise of power. In 1985, Bolivian politicians responded with inventiveness and creativity to a runaway hyperinflation. They formed three kinds of partisan coalitions: one to contest elections; another, in congress, to identify the next president (in the past four elections, the winner of the plurality of votes became president only twice); and a third, also in congress, to fashion reliable congressional governing majorities. The very same parties that brought the country near its grave made possible its resurrection.

These countries were in an epochal transition from economic chaos (Bolivia), civil war (Costa Rica and El Salvador), and dictatorship (Chile and Venezuela). In each case, politicians successfully responded to the problems of their times. These examples suggest that institutional changes are most effective and lasting when they are backed by strong political coalitions and serve the interests of the dominant political forces at a critical juncture.

Reforming the Court System

Judiciaries throughout Latin America are in dire need of reform, but little headway is being made. The problems with the court system occur at nearly every level, for four general reasons: (a) the corruption of judges; (b) the politicization of the courts; (c) the gutting of judicial independence by the president; and (d) the operational incapacities of the court system itself.

In the 1980s and 1990s, reform efforts have attempted to expedite the administration of justice to combat crime and corruption, depoliticize the courts, and improve societal access to the court system. This section looks first at the four explanations for the malperformance of the court system and then turns to reform efforts.

In some countries, especially Bolivia and Colombia, the judiciary has been corrupted by drug traffickers. In Colombia, drug leaders have been convicted infrequently because they have bribed, threatened, or killed judges. In response, the Colombian judicial system acknowledged its incapacity and came to rely on plea bargaining: any person could receive a reduced sentence upon surrendering and confessing one crime. The problem of judicial corruption from drug trafficking has spread to other countries.

Meanwhile, the extent of politicization of judicial appointments by political parties is a threat to impartiality. In Ecuador in 1983 and again in 1993, congressional majorities deeply politicized the appointments to the supreme court, gutting its independence and threatening constitutional order.[20]

The threat to judicial independence comes even more frequently from an executive eager to reduce all obstacles to the implementation of presidential policies. In Argentina in the early 1990s, President Menem increased the size of the supreme court in order to add appointees and, at the same time, reduced the scope of the court's jurisdiction over cases bearing on the "economic emergency." The court's deference to the executive seriously compromised its legitimacy in the eyes of much of the public and the legal community. In other places, such as the Dominican Republic, presidentialist personalism in the appointment of judges is routine and has greatly weakened the independence of the judiciary. Presidents have also meddled with the courts to avert the politically costly prosecution of their allies. In February 1994, President Fujimori used his legislative majority to prevent the Peruvian supreme court from trying military officers accused of extrajudicial executions: the killings of nine students and a professor from La Cantuta national teachers' university.[21] In Argentina, President Menem replaced the independent judges, who were slated to try some of his associates on corruption charges, with more compliant court officers.

Finally, the operation of the courts is itself defective. In Bolivia, for example, the most serious problem facing the judicial system is the non-Spanish-speaking population's lack of access to the courts. By law, all proceedings must be conducted in Spanish, even though this is not the primary language of a substantial proportion of the population. As a result, many people look for justice outside the courts. Operative deficiencies are also apparent in Colombia: in the early 1980s, only one in ten reported crimes ever led to a verdict, and in the early 1990s that figure dropped to one out of twenty. Similar statistics, regrettably, are common throughout the region. In many countries—Panama and Ecuador, for example—the court system is severely underfinanced.

Despite these enduring and serious problems, there are glimmers of reform. In many cases, sustained efforts are under way to allocate greater resources to the courts, to improve the training of judges, and to professionalize their work. Colombia's 1991 constitution created a national prosecutor's office (*fiscalía nacional*), which has the authority to investigate and prosecute cases and to coordinate the activities of all military and civilian agencies gathering evidence on crimes. Thus, the new constitution broke with the Napoleonic Code tradition, in which some judges investigate crimes and others adjudicate them; the reforms freed the court system from investigative responsibilities. During the first two years, the judicial system processed 50 percent more cases than under the old system. This change holds promise for expediting the administration of justice.

Argentina's constitutional reform of 1994 also holds promise. In the so-called Olivos pact between Alfonsín and Menem, a new council was created to nominate all judges prior to their appointment. The constitutional reform created a new general accounting office to audit the government's accounts and, thus, combat corruption. These agreements enhanced the independence and professionalism of the judiciary system, created more effective means to combat corruption, and attempted to depoliticize the judiciary. Parties in El Salvador, Nicaragua, and Paraguay have also reached agreements and appointed balanced supreme courts. The willingness of political actors to compromise raises the hope that one of the root causes of judicial politicization, legislative-executive conflict, might be reduced.

Most ambitious has been Costa Rica's experiment with judicial activism to facilitate societal access to the court system. Since the 1980s, the Fourth, or constitutional, Chamber (Sala IV) of the supreme court has become involved in an ever-expanding number of disputes. Nongovernmental organizations have gone to the Fourth Chamber to challenge the market-oriented economic policies implemented by congress and the executive. The Fourth Chamber has also become involved in tourist, coastal, and national park development projects and in disputes about the rights of indigenous peoples, labor unions, and prisoners. Virtually all important economic interest groups have litigated to oppose the elimination of protection or subsidies. Plaintiffs often try to generate publicity and controversy to provoke the executive to modify its policies. Although effective at channeling discontent in the short run, this approach could lead to the atrophy of legitimate political channels for interest articulation and conflict resolution and a heightened sense of popular cynicism regarding the judiciary.

The Territorial Decentralization of State Powers

In the 1980s and 1990s most Latin American countries placed territorial decentralization on their national agendas.[22] Many see it as a way to unburden the national government by turning over some of its responsibilities to local entities that may understand local conditions better and, reformers hope, may be more effective; at times, it is a way to cut the national budget.

For others, decentralization is widely regarded as a means to increase the participatory nature of regimes, especially in countries, such as Colombia and Venezuela, that began to elect local officials only in the 1980s or 1990s. For many groups in civil society which have had trouble articulating their interests at the national level because of a reluctance to form close ties with political parties, local government holds hope for meaningful participation in community affairs. Parties of the left hope that territorial decentralization will allow their officeholders to prove their competence in government at the local level, paving the way for a claim to national office; Causa R in Venezuela's Bolívar State, the Frente Amplio in the city of Montevideo, and the PT in São Paulo exemplify this strategy. Finally, local governments can provide new participatory opportunities for the informally disenfranchised, including indigenous groups and the poor; their increased participation at the local level might have positive implications for democratization at the national level.

The government and its opposition may have contradictory objectives with regard to decentralization, however. The example of Chiapas illustrates this tension. For the Mexican government, territorial decentralization in Chiapas is a means to pacify the region and co-opt some indigenous elites. For the Zapatistas, who began an insurgency in January 1994, the objective is to establish bases from which to launch wider political challenges, as they did in 1994 and 1995. Despite these high (and somewhat contradictory) hopes, the results are discouraging. In most countries, local governments possess neither the funds nor the technical expertise to assume the new responsibilities assigned to them. Under these circumstances, subnational governments can undermine the efforts of national executives to carry out economic reforms. In Argentina and Brazil, for example, fiscal powers and prerogatives were extended to states and municipalities without corresponding responsibilities; the resulting deficits and debt contracted by subnational governments has hampered the consolidation of economic reforms.

Decentralization can also undermine democratization by reinforcing the power of local elites, their practices of clientelism, and the power of their military or paramilitary allies, as in Brazil, Colombia, El Salvador, and Mexico. Especially in the rural areas, these countries suffer from the inability of the central state to enforce the law equitably throughout its national territory. Instead of increasing the accountability of local elites to civil society, decentralization would decrease even further their accountability to national authority, and it might permit the consolidation of petty tyrannies. Decentralization is also likely to remove certain issues from the national agenda, which has been more likely to be hospitable to initiatives from the political left. Decentralization may some day empower ordinary citizens to take better charge of their government, and permit a wider range of innovation at the local level, but there is still a long way to go before these promises are realized.

Economic Reforms, the Market, and Democratic Consolidation

Free markets and free politics are celebrated throughout much of the region, and thoughtful arguments are advanced about why they "go together" in Latin America and the Caribbean in the 1990s.[23] And yet, many scholars and political activists also argue that the rapid implementation of so-called neoliberal market reforms has disrupted democratic representation, hurt the poor, and increased social conflict.

Market reforms (especially deregulation, privatization, and the termination of business subsidies) can serve the goals of democratic politics. Statist economic arrangements often permit and foster close connections between economic and political elites, reducing the prospects for wider participation and fair contestation. Statist economics privileges business groups whose profits depend on political connections and not necessarily on efficiency or quality. Market reforms can break the ties between political and economic elites, reduce the opportunities for corruption and rent-seeking behavior, and create a level playing field for economic actors. Insertion into international markets provides external actors with the leverage needed to defend constitutional government in the region; such leverage helped to thwart Guatemalan President Jorge Serrano's attempt to overturn the constitution in 1993. In the 1990s, external actors have also used their economic leverage to prevent authoritarian reversals and to widen political openings in the Dominican Republic, Mexico, and Peru.

Some governments—most notably in Argentina, Chile, and Costa Rica—have established partnership between market reforms and nationalism (replacing the historic alliance of populism and nationalism) to consolidate constitutional government with a market economy. In Chile, for example, defenders of constitutionalism and market openings appeal to nationalist sentiments, suggesting that a proud nation would surely wish to meet these standards of "civilized" peoples; similar arguments are made for the integration of the poorest sectors into the national economy.

Democracy, in turn, can help consolidate a market economy. In countries where levels of societal contestation and political instability have been very high and organized opposition forces have been strong, democracy can reduce many transaction costs. There may be fewer disruptions from labor strikes or insurgencies if the would-be supporters of these strategies can find more cost-effective alternatives to advance their interests within democratic politics. In addition, democratic regimes can involve the political opposition in support of a market economy more effectively than can authoritarian regimes. In the 1990s, for example, Argentina's "convertibility law" governing monetary and exchange rate policies and Chile's tax laws resulted from negotiation between the executive and congress. By giving the opposition a voice and a vote in the creation of fundamental, long-term, market-conforming policies, democratic regimes can set the foundations for credible and stable long-term rules. Under these circumstances, rational investors can expect that today's rules will endure tomorrow, even if the opposition wins the general elections. The procedures of democracy help to consolidate the market economy.

But the connection between democracy and the market is complex. Many of the devices designed to maintain fiscal discipline barely meet the test of democracy. For example, a closed and technocratic style of decision making reinforces the unresponsiveness of the state to societal demands—and may well be authoritarian. At times, presidents rule by decree, deliberately bypassing the legislature. These concerns were raised most often in Argentina and Bolivia in the 1990s. Even strong parties such as those in Chile, which have adapted well to the challenges of governance, must still prove their ability to articulate societal interests; there is so much "consensus" in Chile that dissenting interests and values may be neglected.

The turn toward a market opening has coincided with spectacular cases of corruption that led to the impeachments of Presidents Collor in Brazil and Pérez in Venezuela. Concern about corruption also looms in nearly all other countries. During the early stages of the privatization of state enterprises, for example, there are substantial opportunities for government officials to favor certain business groups. Mexico illustrates a related problem: because PRI politicians can no longer rely as much on state resources to pay for their campaigns, they resort to private funds in a political environment in which rules governing campaign financing are weak and often unenforced.[24]

In the short run, moreover, the shift in economic models has contributed to the crisis of representation discussed earlier because parties must over-haul their economic programs and find new ways to gain support from their often surprised constituents. New parties and social movements have arisen to protest these policies, invigorating democratic contestation, to be sure, but also challenging the scope and durability of market reforms. In years past, populist parties and corporatist forms of interest representation had tied labor and other groups to the political system, but in the 1990s these forces have weakened precisely at the moment when public support must help guarantee the stability of economic reforms and constitutional government, especially in Brazil, Mexico, and Venezuela. And, as noted earlier, the rise of indigenous mobilization throughout the hemisphere can be traced in part to grievances exacerbated by market-oriented reforms and left unarticulated by eroded representational networks.

The change in economic models has altered the roles of the political right, the political left, and the traditional elites, shaping the quality of politics and the stability of constitutional government. The political right has increased its participation in party politics in many countries. Parties of the right, or parties with strong support from the right, have proven far stronger than some eminent scholars had, as recently as the early 1980s, thought that they would be.[25] As the 1990s opened, for instance, elected parties or coalitions with strong support from the right governed in every Central American country. This development portends well for the stability of constitutional rule, at least in the short term, because conservative interests (most often those of business) are well represented through the party system.

The marriage between democracy and the market also makes it possible for many economic actors to pledge their allegiance to constitutional gov-ernment. Fewer incentives now exist for business to knock on the barracks door to alter national economic policy. The military is often judged to be too incompetent to manage the economy, given its generally poor record in gov-ernment in the 1970s and early 1980s. Labor unions are weak, and macro-economic policies benefit property owners. Business participates in politics, often supporting parties of the right (though sometimes also other parties), mainly through the deployment of resources at election time (such as pur-chasing television time during campaigns), not through party building. The connection between business and parties may be close in El Salvador (with regard to ARENA) and in Mexico (with regard to the PRI), but it is tactical at best in most countries.

One obstacle to building parties of the right has been the tendency of for-merly populist parties in Argentina, Bolivia, Mexico, and Venezuela to usurp market-oriented economic platforms. One question for these parties is whether they can incorporate the right as leaders and as constituents and still retain the support of the poorer classes. In the mid-1990s, perhaps surprisingly, the answer (except in Venezuela) seemed to be yes—a true feat of partisan skill.

The stability of constitutional government in the short term depends on the representation of the right, but the long-run consolidation of democracy depends on the representation of nonelite interests, often by parties of the left. The development of a social democratic left in Latin America has been encouraged by the same events that have weakened the left in general: authoritarian repression, the collapse of communism, the decline of labor unions, and the narrowing of economic options. Widespread corruption and inattention to social needs have become key issues for these parties. The parties of the social democratic left are very strong in Brazil, the Dominican Republic, Nicaragua, Panama, Uruguay, and Venezuela, and strong in Chile and El Salvador. For them, constitutional government holds the only route to national power in the 1990s. The left's lack of governing experience and the absence of a clear economic alternative are liabilities, however.

Finally, most traditional elites have opposed market reforms because such reforms threaten their control of resources and their access to government policy makers. To the extent that reforms succeed in shifting control over clientelistic resources from traditional elites to the executive, or reduce the salience of such resources by means of privatization and deregulation, the reforms are likely to advance the cause of both freer markets and freer politics. Traditional elites undermine democracy and markets by skewing electoral laws in order to block the emergence of political rivals who articulate mass interests, by placing limits on market and other policy reforms as a condition of their support for constitutional government, and by deforming the mechanisms of political representation with clientelism. These practices have pernicious effects on the extent and effectiveness of democratic governance. The alienation of citizens from the political system and the obstacles to market reforms are greatest where traditional elites are the strongest, as in Brazil, Ecuador, and Guatemala.

In sum, market reforms in many countries have strengthened the right's allegiance to constitutional government (especially evident in the export business sectors), while they have revivified the prospects for parties of the left that can channel some of the discontent aroused by such policies. Traditional elites, in contrast, are the enemies of both markets and democracy.[26]

Empirically, in the mid-1990s voters signaled their preliminary approval of the shift toward a market economy. They abandoned the punitive electoral behavior noted at the beginning of this chapter. They began to reward officeholders who had managed the economy and other fundamental tasks well. Colombia's Liberal party won three consecutive presidential elections in the 1980s and 1990s, in part in response to good economic management. Chile's Concertación Democrática coalition (including Christian Democratic, Socialist, and other parties) won a second consecutive presidential election in 1993, thanks to its consolidation of a transition to a democratic regime and its excellent economic management. El Salvador's ARENA, credited with securing internal peace and reactivating the economy, won a second consecutive presidential election in 1994. Ernesto Zedillo won the fairest-ever Mexican presidential election in 1994 in part because his party, the PRI, was perceived to have rescued Mexico from the economic depression of the 1980s. Fernando Henrique Cardoso was elected Brazil's president in 1994 mainly because of his successful control of inflation during his term as finance minister. Alberto Fujimori was reelected president of Peru in 1995 because he was credited with taming inflation, reactivating the economy, and controlling a virulent insurgency. And Carlos Menem, having presided over the termination of hyperinflation and the revival of economic growth, was reelected president of Argentina in 1995. In these and other instances, rational voters supported new market-oriented policies, thereby wedding the future of constitutional government to the success of the market economy.

For the partnership between democracy and markets to prosper, however, more needs to happen. Poverty must be reduced if citizens are to have the needed resources for effective participation; only with a widespread capacity to participate is democratic consolidation achieved. The reform of social services—their financing, organization, and effectiveness—awaits attention throughout the region.[27] And the capacity of the state to raise revenues to rebuild infrastructure and to improve the quality of health and education requires ongoing effort. Special care must be taken to ensure that privatization decisions and implementation are transparent, not opportunities for corruption. Other issues include the balance between direct and indirect taxation as well as the efforts of middle-class groups to resist reforms that hurt their interests (in Uruguay, most notably to protect and increase middle-class pensions through the use of a plebiscite). The successful defense of past rent-seeking achievements limits the resources available for other urgent needs.

The worry is that the political system will be unable to handle the pent-up demands that are bound to be expressed as the memories of authoritarian governments and hyperinflationary crises recede. Creating the understanding that democracy cannot solve everything is essential for a democratic culture, but it is not sufficient for stability; sooner or later, constitutional government must provide some answers to the material problems of the poor. To justify his authoritarian methods, former Peruvian strongman Manuel

Odría used to argue that people cannot eat democracy. For democracy to be consolidated and for the poor to resist the temptation of authoritarians, democratic polities with market economies must make it possible for the poor to eat.

The Armed Forces and the Consolidation of Democracy

Since the mid-1980s there have been three types of military assault on constitutional government; they are discussed here in increasing order of concern. One, evident in the early 1990s in Haiti, is for the high command of the armed forces to overthrow the government. In the 1980s, this was the principal means to rotate rulers under authoritarian regimes, as in the case of Panama throughout the Noriega years. It was also used to terminate General Alfredo Stroessner's regime in Paraguay. This practice was common in much of South and Central America from the mid-1960s to the early 1980s, but no successful military coup led by the high command has occurred in any of these other countries since 1982 (when a group of Guatemalan military officers overthrew another group). In the 1980s and early 1990s, the less professional the military, the more likely it was that its high command would publicly lead an overthrow of the government, the opposite of the pattern that prevailed in the 1960s and 1970s.[28]

In several countries with professional armed forces, however, there were military mutinies against constitutional governments in the late 1980s and early 1990s. These revolts were led by disgruntled middle-ranking officers in Argentina, Ecuador, Guatemala, Panama, and Venezuela; each of these countries except Panama saw at least two coup attempts in these years.[29] The motivations for the coups varied. In Argentina and Panama, they were related to the downsizing of the security forces; in Argentina they were also related to the prospect of trials for human rights violations. In Argentina, Ecuador, and Venezuela, ambitious and popular officers led the coup effort. In Guatemala, opposition from some business elites to tax and other economic policies played a role. A common aspect of these mutinies was that the military chain of command broke down; the mutinies were aimed at the high command as much as at the constitutional government. Consequently, the capacity to maintain civilian control was shaken because the generals could no longer ensure the loyalty of the lower ranks of the armed forces. Military deprofessionalization was associated with the increased likelihood of coup attempts. All of these attempts failed in the end, because they were opposed by the military high command and because civilian politicians, for the most part, closed ranks in support of constitutional government. But will the high command and the civilians be able to retain control in the future?

Finally, a grave threat to constitutional government may come from a coup led by an elected civilian president supported by the high command of the armed forces against the congress, the courts, political parties, and all vehicles that help civil society seek advocacy and representation for its interests. Pioneered in Uruguay in the early 1930s and repeated in Uruguay in the early 1970s, this pattern is associated in the 1990s with Peru's president Fujimori. Thus far, only Guatemala's president Jorge Serrano has attempted to emulate Fujimori, but without success. In these cases, presidents have claimed that extensive corruption in congress generates gridlock as well as the pursuit of illicit objectives at the expense of the public interest. Presidents thus call on the military to establish a temporary civilian dictatorship; this pattern is particularly worrisome—even if it has succeeded in only one country in recent years—because the problems of corruption and gridlock are real and the disenchantment with the performance of constitutional government has been considerable in many countries.

The aftermath of Fujimori's coup in Peru has made his suspension of constitutional government especially appealing to antidemocrats. The economic reforms initiated in Peru in the early 1990s (before the coup) finally began to bear fruit, while good police work led to the capture of Abimael Guzmán, the founder and longtime leader of the Sendero Luminoso insurgency. Though both outcomes could have occurred without a coup, Fujimori claimed that his decisive anticonstitutional act brought them about. Soon after the coup, the Organization of American States (with strong backing from the U.S. government) pressured Fujimori into calling internationally supervised elections for a constituent assembly (which would double as a parliament) and to agree not to prolong his presidential term without a free election. In April 1995, Fujimori was reelected president by a strong majority. Despite some irregularities, the election was fair enough.

This combination of circumstances recalls the potentially great appeal of a Caesar who proclaims the need for a temporary interruption of constitutional government to save the country and constitutionalism. The problem, of course, is that such interruptions often last for a longer time. Fujimori's economic and military policies, together with his acquiescence to international pressure in returning to the procedures of constitutional government, may have had the paradoxical effect of making a Fujimorazo much more appealing than either Fujimori or the international community ever imagined: he seems to have fulfilled the promise of a short and effective dictatorship.

On balance, however, the barriers against *successful* military coups did rise in Latin America in the 1980s and 1990s and remain high in the Anglophone Caribbean. In general, the "demand" for coups has been constrained by the generally disastrous performance of military rulers in the late 1970s and early 1980s. The economies of Latin American countries collapsed when military presidents governed. The military lost the reputation for competence beyond its specific professional sphere, though the Pinochet government in Chile regained such a reputation during the second half of the 1980s. The demand for coups has also been reduced by the strength of parties of the right, as noted above; many business elites no longer rely on military coups to advance their objectives, because civilian rule delivers their objectives. The "supply" of coup makers has also been limited because military officers recall their frustration, their unpreparedness, and the loss of their own military professionalism when they attempted to run the government. If the memories of military misgovernment fade and the performance of constitutional governments remains weak, however, the prospects for such coups might increase again.

Another reason for the decline in the frequency of coups is that, in many cases, the armed forces can have their demands met without resorting to such tactics. The military retains significant prerogatives in countries as different as Chile and Nicaragua, Cuba and Honduras, Brazil and Peru, Colombia and Guatemala. Military courts defy civilian jurisdiction over the criminal activities of some military personnel. The military continues to control police forces and intelligence agencies in a great many countries, without significant civilian oversight. Military officers (both active and retired) continue, directly or indirectly, to control important state enterprises; in Chile, for example, a portion of earnings from copper exports is explicitly reserved for military use. In these ways, the armed forces in many countries retain an independent source of revenue to shield them from budget austerity. In some countries, military commanders also maintain significant subnational influence through their alliance with local power elites. In countries where civil violence is particularly high, the armed forces exercise even greater power; despite transitions to constitutional government and despite elections, much of Colombia, Guatemala, and Peru has remained under direct military rule. For the rural citizens of these countries, no democratic transition has taken place. Such military prerogatives remain important obstacles to the realization of democratic practice.[30]

There is considerable debate about the appropriate roles of the armed forces in contemporary Latin America. In Argentina and Uruguay, civilian governments have eagerly promoted military participation in international peacekeeping and peace-enforcing operations under the auspices of the United Nations in order to focus the armed forces on these new professional tasks. The hope is that the military will be less likely to interfere in domestic politics if so occupied.

One persistent concern about any military operation, including military involvement in combating drug trafficking, is the need for effective means of civilian control. For the most part, such mechanisms remain insufficiently developed, and in some countries they have yet to exist because too many civilian "defense experts" have been specialists not in controlling the military but in aligning with them to make coups.

There is a related concern about military involvement in the development of infrastructure or the improvement of public health. Such normally praiseworthy activities may blur civilian and military lines of authority, reviving the notion (proven false during the economic crises of the late 1970s and early 1980s) that military officers can handle the routine affairs of government more effectively than civilians. In short, the task of establishing civilian supremacy over the military remains daunting, and the likelihood of coup attempts remains high. Nonetheless, the prospects for continued constitutional government are better than at any time since the Great Depression of the 1930s.

International Defense and Promotion of Democracy

Never before has there been such a strong international commitment to the defense and promotion of constitutional government in Latin America and the Caribbean. Such a new commitment is yet another barrier to successful coup attempts. Propelling international activity on behalf of constitutional government is a change in Latin American governments' attitudes toward intervention. This shift is best exemplified by Resolution 1080 of the Organization of American States (OAS), enacted in Santiago, Chile, in June 1991; the resolution requires OAS member governments to address the interruption of constitutional government, should it occur.

There is also a marked change in the behavior of the U.S. government. Twice since the end of the Cold War in Europe, the United States has deployed tens of thousands of troops to a near neighbor, motivated at least in part by the need to establish or restore viable constitutional government. In Panama, international observers found that Guillermo Endara won the 1989 presidential elections but was prevented from taking office because the military government stopped counting the ballots when it became evident that its candidate would lose. In Haiti, Jean-Bertrand Aristide was duly elected president and took office, but was subsequently overthrown.[31] In Panama in 1989 and in Haiti in 1994, U.S. troops deposed the military ruler and installed a civilian president, Endara and Aristide, respectively. While the renewed commitment to constitutional government is encouraging, the lowering of barriers to the use of force across international boundaries is a source of concern.

The U.S. and other governments in Latin America, the Caribbean, Canada, and Western Europe, as well as the United Nations and the OAS, have also played valuable roles in ending wars in Nicaragua, El Salvador, and Suriname, making possible a transition toward more open politics. Through election observation, moreover, foreign governments and transnational nongovernmental organizations have fostered a climate for freer elections in those three countries and also in the Dominican Republic, Guyana, Paraguay, Peru, and Mexico. These international actors have supported trends away from electoral abuse and fraud, assisted by the logistics that permit freer and fairer elections, and have denounced violations of the electoral process where they occurred. In Guatemala in 1993, the international community played a decisive role in foiling President Jorge Serrano's attempted coup against constitutional government. In Paraguay, an attempted military coup was defeated in 1996, thanks to citizen protests and the active intervention of the governments of Argentina, Brazil, Uruguay, and the United States, as well as the OAS secretary-general, César Gaviria. And in the early to mid-1990s, the international community, including the Clinton administration, helped advance peace and constitutionalism in Guatemala, El Salvador, and Nicaragua, as well as defending constitutional government in Venezuela.

The defense of constitutional government has had some noteworthy limitations. Transition to civilian rule in Haiti was not accomplished without military force. And Peruvian president Fujimori's coup against constitutional government was not reversed; its thrust was mitigated through international pressure and negotiation in ways that, inadvertently, may have increased its appeal. On balance, however, the international community has had a good record defending constitutional government in the 1990s.

There is also the hope that some countries' increased international engagement will promote constitutional government at home. Mexico's participation in the North American Free Trade Agreement (NAFTA) may help consolidate the economic reforms enacted in the late 1980s and early 1990s, assist the country's recovery from the late 1994 and early 1995 currency devaluation shock, and foster a more open political climate. The administrations of Presidents Carlos Salinas and Ernesto Zedillo were required to change many undemocratic political practices in order to safeguard Mexico's participation in NAFTA. Under international scrutiny, Mexico created mechanisms to protect human rights, reduce the likelihood of election fraud, and recognize opposition victories for subnational offices. Similarly, Paraguay's engagement in international trade and other economic relations through MERCOSUR (with Argentina, Brazil, and Uruguay) has further opened the political system years after the end of Alfredo Stroessner's dictatorship and, as noted, helped foil a coup attempt. Freer markets in the global economy, as in domestic economies, may contribute to the consolidation of freer politics in the long run.

By the same token, however, international factors may also create pressures that destabilize domestic politics. NAFTA, for example, is making it very difficult for Mexican maize producers to compete with imports from the United States, fueling discontent in already volatile rural areas and giving credence to enemies of NAFTA (and of the government) within Mexico.

These perspectives offer a window into the future of Cuba: Will it be like the past in Panama in the 1980s and Haiti in the early 1990s, where massive U.S. military intervention occurred after unarticulated civil societies and weak and fragmented opposition movements within and outside the country were unable to launch a successful process of democratization? Will it be like Nicaragua and El Salvador in the 1980s, where extensive civil war with external participation lingered for years? Or will it be like the 1980s and 1990s in much of Central America, Mexico, and Paraguay, where an engaged international community aided a peaceful transition toward more open politics? The third scenario would require, of course, that Cuban leaders be more willing than they have been in the past to negotiate rules of governance with the domestic opposition. From the perspective of democratization, the prospects are not good; the current political regime seems likely to endure, though it has already become much friendlier to international market forces. We believe that the third scenario has the better chance of achieving Cuba's successful transition to democracy because it would impose the lowest costs on its people and its neighbors.

Conclusion

"Like all men in Babylon," Jorge Luis Borges wrote, "I have been a proconsul; like all, a slave. I have also known omnipotence, opprobrium, imprisonment."[32] In many ways, this characterizes the experience of many prominent Latin American politicians in the 1990s. Some, like Argentina's president Carlos Saúl Menem, spent years in prison under military government. Others, like Brazil's president Fernando Henrique Cardoso, spent years under official opprobrium and exile during his country's period of military rule. As Latin America and the Caribbean approach a new millennium, the task is to banish forever slavery, opprobrium, and imprisonment without succumbing to the temptations of the omnipotent proconsul. The power of presidents and ministers to govern is at times vast and injurious to democratic practice, for it falsely presumes that the executive alone has been elected by the people.

In this chapter, we call attention to the importance of institutions and procedures that remain fundamental for democratic practice, in particular, parties and their key role as bridges between state and society. And we ponder the issues and concerns that arise within governments regarding executive, legislative, judicial, and military institutions. These institutions and relationships are at the heart of the future of constitutional government in the Americas. With regard to the prospects for military intervention in politics, we echo the alarm of others and note the extent to which the military may remain involved in politics short of staging a coup. Nonetheless, we are heartened by the decreased frequency of successful overthrows of constitutional government.

Thus, the task at hand is to improve effective democratic governance. We are encouraged by the capacity of many to organize peacefully to participate in political life. But we are discouraged by continuing evidence that the design and redesign of the institutions of constitutional government have fallen short of the needs of these countries. Between these two trends lies the future of democracy in the region.

Ideas and Leaders in Freeing Politics
and Markets in Latin America in the 1990s

"Men make their own history," Karl Marx wrote in 1852, "but they do not make it just as they please."[1] Scholars of Latin America have spent much energy understanding the second half of that sentence, namely, the importance of structures and their legacies. In this chapter, I am mindful of that second half but call attention to its first half: the conscious choices made by some political actors in the 1980s and the 1990s in Latin America to foster freer politics and freer markets and, in that way, to reinvent Latin American history.

I do so not only to record that the ideas, styles, and wisdom of specific leaders make a difference but also to show that these leaders used strategies and tactics that are not only personal or idiosyncratic but also potentially universal in their applicability. Some constraints can be overcome, others cannot. In this work, I am especially interested in how technopols employ some constraints that are difficult to overcome in order to help foster a national consensus on desirable policies to modify the impact of such constraints in the long term. The approach of these technopols to politics and economics is portable—leaders in other countries can learn from their successes and failures.[2]

In the first half of the 1990s, Argentina, Brazil, Chile, and Mexico each had a more pluralistic political system, a more market-oriented economy, and a more intense and competitive insertion into international markets than had been the case as recently as the mid-1970s. In each, there has been a simultaneous effort to address major economic and political questions. For the first time perhaps since the 1930s, each of these countries is engaged in a far-reaching national project to reshape its future. As the case of Mexico shows, however, market-oriented reforms can be implemented in a nondemocratic political system; and Mexico's December 1994 financial crisis also indicates that the success of economic reforms is by no means guaranteed. Even in the wake of this crisis, however, the extent and significance of the changes enacted during the first half of the decade remain impressive.

And just as impressive is the persistence of these countries, including Mexico, on the path of reform.

In this chapter, I seek to understand the relationship between ideas and leaders, on one side, and democratic politics and market-oriented government policies, on the other. I focus on five political leaders who have taken ideas seriously and who have acted in politics and government based in part on these ideas. They are Argentina's economy minister Domingo Cavallo; Mexico's finance minister Pedro Aspe; Brazil's senator, foreign minister, finance minister, and president Fernando Henrique Cardoso; Chile's deputy Evelyn Matthei; and Chile's finance minister Alejandro Foxley.

Four of the five have been finance ministers, though none serves in that post now. Matthei was chosen for this study to focus on a younger, technically trained leader who was, at the time the study began, a rising star in her nation's politics, playing a role in the opposition that recalled aspects of the early political careers of Cavallo, Cardoso, and Foxley. All five have been or, in my judgment, are likely to be candidates for the presidency, and Cardoso is president. These five leaders personify the ideas and behavior that concern this analysis. Their actions have made a major difference already. This biographic approach to the subject, therefore, focuses on the principal agents of change. I call them technopols.

They differ along several dimensions. One is their relationship to democracy. Aspe, Cavallo, and Matthei worked at some point for nondemocratic governments, but Cavallo and Matthei were also able to become prominent political figures under democratic regimes.[3] Cardoso and Foxley never worked for nondemocratic governments. Another dimension of variation at the outset of this project was that three were finance ministers but two (Cardoso and Matthei) were only prominent leaders of the opposition in congress. Finally, they differ as well in their ability to accomplish the goals they set for themselves; on this account, Aspe and Matthei were less successful than the others.

This chapter addresses three general questions: Where do ideas that become economic policy come from, and how and why do those ideas become policy? What do these ideas imply about the role of the state in the context of a market economy? And what is the relation between technically trained, politically engaged public figures (technopols) and the practices and prospects for democracy? I argue that those under study have taken ideas seriously in their professional careers. The ideas on which they have focused are cosmopolitan and meet normal international professional standards. Moreover, most of these people have themselves contributed to the formulation of the ideas that they eventually came to implement.

What makes some technopols successful at reaching the goals they set for themselves? Those under study are not "mere" technical economists invested with power by politicians.[4] Instead, successful technopols have made economics "political" and, in so doing, have created their own power and have enabled their politician allies to govern more effectively. Technopols have made economic policies acceptable to the public at large in democratic or authoritarian settings. More important, technopols have fashioned economic policies guided by their political analysis of the circumstances of their respective countries at given historical junctures; economic policies must meet requirements that originate in the political sphere.

Thus technopols often act in ways that are unfamiliar to many professional economists.[5] Technopols design economic policies by understanding their nations' politics first: the forces of politics are harnessed to fashion economic programs. The unsuccessful cases feature "technos" who consciously choose not to be "pols" or who are not allowed by their presidents to behave openly as pols (as appears to have happened to Aspe). They disdain political work; they may cherish econometrics but not the rough and tumble of partisanship. In the apt phrasing of Catherine Conaghan and James Malloy, such economists wear a "mental shield" to keep out the messiness of politics.[6] In contrast, successful technopols are not mere cooks reproducing the recipes of their foreign instructors, nor mere photocopiers of the economic dogmas of other countries. Their discovery of the necessity of politics for the making and the selling of sound economic policy in the real contexts of real countries is what makes them pols.[7]

For technopols to be successful in either democratic or authoritarian political systems, they must also build their own teams and institutional bases to provide them with ideas, cadres, and bases of support for their work. They must also create their own independent power, connected to but not fully representative of the societal actors targeted for reform, from which they can contribute to a wider political coalition and the construction of change. The strategies chosen by technopols help to shape the extent of their influence.[8] They are not the marionettes of other politicians.

There may be an empirical limit to the replicability or portability of this argument beyond these cases, however. The political and economic crises in these four Latin American countries in the 1970s and 1980s, in the end, opened the way for democratic technopols in Argentina, Brazil, and Chile and contributed to political and economic change in Mexico. The rise of these technopols had a structural origin but a voluntarist outcome. It remains for subsequent research to determine whether successful technopols can arise in contexts with less traumatic economic and political antecedents.

What is the relationship between technopols and democratic politics? Worldwide, democracies have been consolidated only in countries with market economies. In the long run, the market has been good for democracy, although markets flourish in many nondemocratic countries, too. In addition, in the late twentieth century substantially pluralist, and preferably fully democratic politics, best addressed the problem of how to shape long-run rational expectations concerning the economies of Latin American countries. Pluralist regimes give more credible assurances that today's competent but less intrusive state and its market-oriented economic policies will endure tomorrow. In Latin America's present and likely future circumstances, democracy is good for markets, although it had not always been so in the past.

Better than many of their predecessors, the technopols under study understand that there may be, in the long run, an elective affinity between freer politics and freer markets. And, where there has been a democratic deficit, as in Mexico in 1994, the weakness of democratic practices—lack of effective procedures to compel the executive to listen to critics—helps, in part, to explain the eventual failure of economic policy.

Technopols and Technocrats

Technocrats have received much attention in scholarly, policy, and journalistic writings. A familiar definition of technocrats is "individuals with a high level of specialized academic training which serves as a principal criterion on the basis of which they are selected to occupy key decision-making or advisory roles in large complex organizations—both public and private."[9]

In the 1970s, important scholars associated the rise and diffusion of technocrats with the rise and consolidation of authoritarian regimes. In perhaps the most important book published in that decade, Guillermo O'Donnell argued that technocrats believe that "the ambiguities of bargaining and politics are hindrances to 'rational' solutions." Technocrats, O'Donnell argued, often studied abroad but could not operate effectively back home until they "constitute[d] the core of the coalition that [would] attempt the establishment of an authoritarian, 'excluding' political system. The usual verbal allegiance to political democracy is apparently the weakest component in their [foreign] role models. It is easily abandoned to promote an authoritarian political system that will (it is believed) facilitate more effective performance by the [technocratic] role incumbents."[10] Scholars have long understood the centrality of ideas for such roles, but have asserted that the ideas are likely to be antidemocratic.[11]

I differ from the authors of these definitions and arguments. I do not assume that technocrats must always be appointed or selected; some highly trained individuals could be elected to public office. Similarly, an opposition leader could become a shaper of the parameters of fundamental policies. More important, technocrats can and have served under very different political regimes. They can operate in market economies as well as in those that were once centrally planned. They need not be beholden to any one substantive ideology, nor are they inherently "democratic" or "authoritarian." Rather, technocrats offer a methodology to understand social problems that rests on a belief in the ability to arrive at the optimal answer to any problem. Their key criteria for action are realism and efficiency. Their legitimacy, they believe, comes from their appeal to rationality and science in their methodology.[12] Though technocrats are often economists, other social scientists (Cardoso) may qualify as well.

Technopols are a variant of technocrats. In addition to being technocrats as just defined, technopols are political leaders (a) at or near the top of their country's government and political life (including opposition political parties) who (b) go beyond their specialized expertise to draw on various different streams of knowledge and who (c) vigorously participate in the nation's political life (d) for the purpose of affecting politics well beyond the economic realm and who may, at times, be associated with an effort to "remake" their country's politics, economics, and society. Technopols so defined may operate in either authoritarian or democratic regimes. Whereas technocrats often rise through bureaucratic ranks (as do some technopols), technopols may have also been outsiders to the bureaucracy: successful economic consultants, prominent academics, or leading opposition figures. Technopols fear politics much less than technocrats because technopols define the "rational" somewhat differently from technocrats; for technopols, a rational policy is not only technically correct but also politically enduring. Rationality thus defined can be achieved only through politics. Technocrats are not new. Authoritarian technopols are not new. Technopols in democratic or democratizing politics are relatively new, however.[13] It is to them that this chapter devotes the bulk of its attention.

Cautionary Tales: The Stories of Joseph and Turgot

In order to assess the significance of the cases under discussion, recall aspects of the subject that are as ancient as political systems. This section considers two historical cases to set a baseline from which to make comparisons, looking well into the past and outside of Latin America to make the point that the question of technocrats or technopols is timeless and crosscultural.

The Book of Genesis (chapters 39–41) describes one of the first technopols, Joseph, who rose to become Pharaoh's chief minister. Joseph demonstrated great professional skill and administrative competence in governing Egypt. (Joseph does not fully qualify as a technocrat or technopol, however,

because his initial specialized knowledge—divining Pharaoh's dreams—
came from God, not from specialized education). What made Joseph a technopol, rather than a mere technician, was his ability to connect his evolving
practical knowledge and skill to the power of the state. Joseph was an effective forecaster and planner who designed successful programs to store food
during seven years of plenty in order to survive through seven years of
famine. He applied specialized knowledge to empirical analysis, implemented actions, and sorted through effects well into the future. He combined ideas and implementation with a long time horizon. Joseph was not
a populist. He smoothed out the economic cycle at a time of plenty by means
of forced savings for the time of famine.

Joseph operated in a constrained international environment. Egypt's survival and power depended on his technocratic success while his authority
derived from his superior. Joseph was not simply a captive of these constraints, however; he acted to enlarge his freedom of action. His performance centralized political power in two ways. One was procedural: "I am
Pharaoh; without your command no one shall move hand or foot in the
whole land of Egypt" (Gen. 41:44). The second was substantive. Joseph's
policies centralized the economy and weakened citizen rights: "Joseph,
therefore, bought all the land of Egypt for Pharaoh, for every one of the
Egyptians sold his field because the famine was unbearable for them. Thus
the land became Pharaoh's, and from one end of Egypt to the other Joseph
made the people slaves" (Gen. 48:20–21). Joseph was an authoritarian technopol. He was not a mere economist but a master of the expertise necessary
to reshape an economy, a society, and a polity to serve centralized authority. Joseph foreshadowed the state-aggrandizing economic policies evident
in Brazil during much of the 1970s; not every technopol has believed in free
markets, and certainly not in free politics.

Many technopols, however, have believed in freer markets and have acted
to make them a reality. In 1774, France's Louis XVI recalled the parlements
(sovereign law courts) abolished in earlier decades and appointed a reform
government, headed by Turgot, a philosophe and widely respected government administrator. Turgot deregulated the economy by suppressing the
guilds, which were privileged monopolies in various trades. He liberalized
domestic trade in grain. He took steps to "shrink the state"; he moved to
abolish the corvée, the annual compulsory peasant labor on France's roads.
He launched a tax reform process. He favored legal toleration for Protes-
tants. However, the Parlement of Paris, supported by provincial estates and
the Roman Catholic Church, opposed him, and in 1776, Turgot resigned.

More clearly than in Joseph's case, Turgot's education and specialized
training were his merits. He combined ideas and implementation. His skills

were conceptual as well as administrative. He, too, planned ahead in a constrained international environment, as France prepared for war. As with Joseph, Turgot's authority came from the monarch; as with Joseph, Turgot was no mere economist; he was also a philosophe. Turgot had a broad agenda to reshape France, even extending to religious toleration. Turgot, too, was an authoritarian technopol, commanding on the king's behalf. But he believed in freeing markets—in a mixture of authoritarian rule and market-oriented policies not unlike those that prevailed in Argentina and Chile in the 1970s.

The stories of Turgot and Joseph illustrate why scholars have been skeptical that technocrats or technopols could foster liberal democracy. To save Egypt, Joseph reduced its citizens to slavery, a metaphor heard at times in southern South America in the 1970s. Turgot's economic reform program was defeated in court, challenging his claim to superior wisdom and showing that constitutional procedures can come in the way of market reforms. These examples suggest why technopols and technocrats have worked for authoritarian regimes: such regimes may seem more capable of adopting "sound policies" than governments that operate under constitutional restraints. Authoritarian Egypt managed well the transition from plenty to famine; independent sovereign law courts in France blocked efficient economic reforms and liberalizing political changes.

And yet, Joseph and Turgot are not alike. There have always been differences among technopols. Joseph was an intentional centralizer. Turgot centralized power to accomplish reform, but many of his policies, if successful, would have devolved state power to the society and the economy (deregulation of business relationships, freer labor, wider religious toleration). If technopols are to work for democratic regimes, there must be a large political coalition to empower them to act, to keep them in power, and to keep them accountable to the principle of eventual devolution of power to those outside the state apparatus.

The Tensions within the Role of Technopol

Technocrats combine aspects of other professional vocations: scholar and administrator. Technopols add a third: politician. Democratic technopols must also operate within two constraints of procedural democracy: unlike Joseph, they must face rules and structures that prevent them from reducing the autonomy of civil society, and unlike Joseph and Turgot, they must work through constitutional government. These roles and constraints pose many difficulties, however. Max Weber has shed some light on the tensions inherent in the role of technopol.[14] I turn to him to show the universality of the concern with such public roles well beyond contemporary Latin America and the tensions that technopols must resolve.

For Weber, three qualities matter in a politician: passion, a feeling of responsibility, and a sense of proportion. "Passion" means devotion to a cause outside of the self. "Responsibility" need not, for Weber, have a democratic component; it is not whether the politician is responsible before the voters but whether the politician is responsible to the cause and makes it the "guiding star of action." "Sense of proportion" is often called pragmatism: the "ability to let realities work upon him with inner concentration and calmness."[15] Politics is born in the heart but is made in the head. Politics seeks power, that is, the means to influence others and shape their behavior.

Scholarship, in contrast, seeks its own undermining: "the very meaning of scientific work . . . raises new questions; it asks to be surpassed and outdated." In that same spirit, scholarship must be nonpartisan: "The primary task of a useful teacher is to teach his students to recognize . . . facts that are inconvenient for their party opinions."[16] Weber therefore doubted that scholars could be political leaders and remain scholars.

The bureaucrat is different yet again. Office holding requires a "firmly prescribed course of training, which . . . [takes] a long period of time."[17] In this "duty," the relationship to others is impersonal; there is no loyalty to any one person but to the procedures of science. Officials should have independence from their superiors and the electorate. Bureaucracy provides for a "rationalist way of life" that has, at best, an ambiguous relationship to democracy.

Weber would doubt that a technopol could exist, because the requirements of passion in politics and the responsibility to advance a cause require a faith that is at odds with the perpetual questioning of the scholar and the nonpartisan rationalism of the bureaucrat. Weber would doubt that technopols could build partisan teams and still meet the standards of high technical expertise. A technopol's claim to scientific legitimacy would be flawed because officials could not meet fundamental tests of scholarship: they have too much passion, they are too responsible, and they are too partisan.

Weber's approach sheds light on the dilemmas faced by authoritarian technopols. The authoritarian technopol acts on a passion to create technocratic policy dogmas to be applied relentlessly through economic policy making independent of popular constraint. Such an official, however, would be likely to lose a sense of proportion and would, in the end, be equally ineffective as politician and bureaucrat: the proposed "efficient reforms" would not be consolidated because the governed would not have consented. This helps to explain the inherent weaknesses in the economic policies adopted in Argentina and Chile in the 1970s and some of the problems faced in Mexico in the mid-1990s.

The democratic technopol is more likely to retain the "sense of proportion" necessary to shift policies in response to practical circumstances, not necessarily from personal virtues, but because the procedures of democracy require such prudence from politicians who seek to be effective. The commitment to a sense of proportion and the readiness to change policies explain the policy corrections and adjustments evident in several of the cases under study: a principled pragmatism, not wedded to dogma but also not volatile or capricious. Thus democratic technopols may combine the roles of politician, scholar, and bureaucrat more successfully than do authoritarian technopols. Some democratic technopols may behave as "teachers to the nation," that is, bearers of a more impersonal loyalty to a democratic regime, committed to educate the public about facts that are inconvenient for their party opinions. Such a technopol is well suited to the politics of opposition, as Cardoso, Foxley, Matthei, and Cavallo have demonstrated at various times.[18]

The Choices of Democratic Technopols in Latin America in the 1990s

Democratic politics in Latin America has been marked in recent decades by instability, policy ineptitude, corruption, and countless other ills. And yet, authoritarian politics in Latin America over roughly the same time period has also been characterized by instability, policy ineptitude, corruption, and countless other ills. No doubt, in 1976, many Argentines viewed the democratically elected Peronist government then in power as the worst in Argentine history, only to realize a few years later that a military government could perform even worse. Likewise, in Mexico, it was an authoritarian Mexican political system that plunged the country into the economic collapse of the early 1980s. No doubt, democratic Costa Rica's economy suffered a severe decline in its gross domestic product (GDP) at the birth of the so-called debt crisis in 1982, but General Augusto Pinochet's authoritarian government in Chile had an even more severe economic collapse that year. By 1984, democratic Costa Rica had surpassed the level of its 1981 GDP (in 1988 constant dollars); authoritarian Chile surpassed its 1981 GDP level only in 1987.[19]

In the 1990s, democracy, Latin Americans knew, was no cure-all for their ills, but their own experience had led them to distrust the claims of would-be authoritarians. Many Latin American democratic regimes remained partial, fragile, and in many ways incapable of delivering on the promise of democracy. But for a significant portion of technopols and the public at large, the logic of democracy had gained much ground over the logic of authoritarianism.

The influence of technopols in Latin America in the 1990s stems less from the presence of the technically skilled at the apex of the state and more from the belated recognition that there may be, in Weberian terms, an "elective affinity" between freer markets and freer politics. By this expression Weber did not mean a mechanistic or deterministic connection; he meant, instead, a correspondence ("affinity") of choices ("elective") and institutions in the areas of politics and economics similar to what is highlighted in this chapter: deliberate political entrepreneurship and institutional design can draw upon markets and democracy to reinforce one another.[20]

Democratic technopols in Latin America in the 1990s chose freer markets for both political and economic reasons. In economic terms, freer markets are typically a part of the professional training of most technopols; that has changed little.[21] In politics, democratic technopols have come to appreciate that freer markets permit less room for arbitrary state actions such as those that gripped much of the region from the mid-1960s to the late 1980s. Markets do not ensure civil society against an authoritarian state, but markets can be one important check on the abuse of state power. Markets may not disperse power enough, and in Latin America's small economies market power is often highly concentrated, but markets disperse power more than if it were centralized in the hands of state decision makers.

Democratic technopols in Latin America in the 1990s chose a competent state (in contrast to the vanishing state in some neoliberal prescriptions) in order to foster consultation with business and labor to create and maintain stable and clear rules by means of the exchange of information and points of view; in that way, they sought to reduce market instability. Democratic technopols also chose the competent state to invest in education and health (human capital) both because they considered it ethically right and because it contributes to market efficiency. The competent state can also more readily address market failures and, in particular, can channel resources to enable the poor to overcome their condition.

In the long run, I wish to suggest, the logic of democracy best promises to set the parameters that may ensure the success of the market. That is, a democratic political system committed to a market economy, and capable of delivering on that commitment, is the more effective and stable long-term political response to the problems posed by the rational expectations of economic actors. Rational economic actors look for rules and institutions that endure even as presidents, ministers, and economic cabinets change; authoritarian regimes can provide certain assurances to economic actors for some time, but democratic regimes can also provide long-run assurances, provided government and opposition are committed to the same broad framework of a market economy. In this sense, the opposition gives the most effective long-term guarantees about the continuity of a market economy; when the opposition supports the basic principles and rules of a market economy, then economic actors rationally can expect that a change of government leaders will not imply the overthrow of a market economy. And only democratic political systems embody the compromises and commitments that may freely bind government and opposition to the same framework of a market economy.

To be sure, in a number of East Asian countries authoritarian regimes have managed the economy exceedingly well for several decades. In this book, however, I analyze societies in which the extent of political contestation and political participation are already intense and widespread and in which military governments were quite unstable. For countries with these political structures, the logic of democracy surpasses the logic of authoritarianism.

Democracy's procedures can restrain the passionate extremism of government officials while permitting more circumscribed forms of commitment. In democratic political systems, moreover, elections provide routinized means for sweeping away failed policies and politicians and starting afresh, which can contribute to the credibility of new, sounder economic policies. Authoritarian regimes cannot get rid of mistaken policies or wrongheaded leaders so readily.[22] In the logic of democracy, to be sure, leaders must elicit the consent of the governed and are thus more likely to consolidate efficient economic reforms for the long run, setting and signaling clear and stable political and economic policy rules that help to shape the rational expectations of economic actors. That has been the long-term experience of Western Europe, North America, and Japan.

Latin America's democratic technopols are also keenly aware of the sorry economic record of democracy in Argentina, Brazil, and Chile at various key junctures during the third quarter of the twentieth century. In these countries, various democratic regimes failed to deliver on the promise of the logic of democracy for markets. The task of democratic technopols in the 1990s became, therefore, to make the logic of democracy work for its own sake and for the consolidation of market economies in these same countries.

Latin America's democratic technopols in the 1990s sought to turn democracy's capacity to elicit the consent of the governed into an effective instrument for political and economic reform. A broad democratic consensus would help to make and consolidate changes; that consensus would contribute to the credibility of the reforms in the eyes of economic actors precisely because the changes would have been made with the opposition's consent. This was the essence of the strategy followed by Foxley, Cavallo, and Cardoso. In a nondemocratic political system, Aspe, too, widened the scope of consultations with societal leaders.

Today's economic policies, economic actors in Argentina, Chile, Mexico, and perhaps Brazil have reason to expect, will endure tomorrow even if the largest opposition party were to win. Today's market-based policies made in a democratic or in a democratizing regime (as in Mexico in the late 1990s), citizens have reason to expect, will make it less likely that dictators or demagogues could imperil citizens' lives and liberties or, in the future, those of their children. That is the hope in all four countries and is certainly the intention of all those under study in this chapter.

The Making of Technopols

Technopols are made in school, in religious and secular faiths, in teams, on the world stage, and in specific national contexts. These five factors identify their commitment to high standards, their passionate convictions, their mode of professional work, their cosmopolitan vision, and their devotion to their homeland. Together, these factors point to the sources of the ideas and the means of their implementation.

Pedro Aspe's early education was forged in the rigor of a fine Jesuit school, Alejandro Foxley's in a similar Franciscan school. Early on, both combined a Roman Catholic faith with a commitment to academic excellence. Evelyn Matthei's education at a Roman Catholic University resembled the religious schooling of Aspe and Foxley. A more decisive combination of schooling and secular faith developed during their respective university educations.

Even as an undergraduate in Mexico's Autonomous Institute of Technology (Instituto Tecnológico Autónomo de México, or ITAM), Aspe became part of a team that embodied a secular faith: the training of technically skilled young economists who would eventually reshape the nation's economic policy. Overt mentoring and team construction (by Antonio Bassols, Javier Beristain, and Francisco Gil Díaz) were an integral goal of the ITAM Economics Department. The same pattern recurred as Aspe studied at MIT, where Rudiger Dornbusch instilled in him the "passions" for technical sophistication, cosmopolitan breadth, and policy relevance.

A comparable pattern marked Fernando Henrique Cardoso's university life. He, too, became part of a team that embodied a comparable secular faith: the development of sociology as a science with the same rigor as that of the natural sciences. Overt mentoring and team construction (by Florestan Fernandes at the University of São Paulo) were also integral goals. The sociology Fernandes taught to Cardoso was a tropical transplant of what Fernandes had learned at the University of Chicago; thus while remaining in Brazil, Cardoso's early intellectual training acquired a cosmopolitan dimension that would be reinforced by his subsequent work and residence in other countries.

Foxley and Cavallo followed a path similar to that taken by Aspe, studying economics in the United States (Foxley at the University of Wisconsin at Madison and Cavallo at Harvard), while Matthei's path is closer to that of Cardoso; she studied economics at the Universidad Católica in Santiago, an institution that had come to replicate and adapt the University of Chicago's Economics Department.

The cosmopolitanism of this training would be crucial for their subsequent work. None of these technopols is intellectually or personally parochial. None fell into the trap of believing that "my" country is so different that the international norms of technical analysis should not apply or that "no foreigner can teach me about my homeland." All were concerned about universal questions; all addressed their work as professionals whose standards and tools are worldwide and universalistic. Cardoso's early studies of race relations, for example, were funded by a grant from UNESCO and addressed universal concerns in the sociology, economics, and politics of race. Aspe, Cardoso, and Foxley wrote doctoral dissertations in economics and sociology on topics, and with tools, that were consistent with standard norms in their disciplines. Cosmopolitan ideas, understood, applied, and developed according to universalistic professional standards, became parts of their selves.

When these young adults were in school, this cosmopolitan trajectory entailed some professional risks. Two of Latin America's best-known economists of the 1950s and 1960s, for example, denounced this trajectory: "The majority of young economists who go to industrialized countries for training return to their home environment with theoretical schemes that are to a greater or lesser extent divorced from objective reality and from the economic problems of their own countries, and often with research methodologies that have no possibility of being usefully applied." They bemoaned the practice of "copying painfully and without critical adaptations whatever emanates from Harvard" and other such universities. "It would be unfortunate," they said, "if these new professionals should assume" government posts "with ideas, attitudes, and analytical equipment that are entirely inapplicable and lacking in realism."[23]

Perhaps in tacit reply to this concern, the three who got their doctorates in economics in the United States—Aspe, Cavallo, and Foxley—wrote their dissertations on topics bearing directly on their respective countries. Foxley, for example, did not eschew complex mathematical models but he developed one for the Chilean economy. Aspe may have reached the furthest in the attempt to creolize economics by studying the history of Mexico with Harvard's historian John Womack Jr. More important, their cosmopolitan ideas and skills along with their concern with their homelands gave them the professional autonomy needed to challenge prevailing orthodoxies back home. Cavallo's doctoral dissertation, for example, took issue not only with structuralist and dependency analyses of Argentina's economy but also with the monetarist ideas that informed Argentine government policy in the mid-1970s. Cardoso's work on race relations helped to puncture the prevailing myth of Brazil as a racial paradise.

Equally noteworthy, cosmopolitan team building in a national context became an essential task for these would-be technopols early in their respective professional careers. Their professional autonomy and eventual political clout would be buttressed by creating analytic and policy teams. The teams would have links to government and business but would retain their distance from both. The connections helped to generate information and build trust; the distance enabled the teams to formulate their own ideas and recommendations, which were at times contrary to the wishes of economic, societal, or governmental actors. These teams would embody the secular faith in social science; their missionary behavior would lead its adherents to spread the faith.

Soon after Aspe's return from MIT to his intellectual birthplace at ITAM, he became its Economics Department's chair. As the critics of the practice of training Latin American economists in the United States would suspect, Aspe realized that the theoretical models and empirical cases that he had studied suggested that Mexico's economic policies in the late 1970s were gravely mistaken. To change them became a professional mission; to do so required training a new generation of economists. Aspe reshaped the ITAM economics curriculum and raised academic standards, all the while creating a team of economists that would in due course follow him into government office. He continued to send a steady flow of students to U.S. universities. Aspe, his former students, and his eventual ministerial staff members similarly describe their "shared vision" and Aspe's role in defining that vision; all agree that this common faith made their team effective. During the Salinas presidency, Aspe's people colonized ministries beyond Aspe's portfolio in finance, filling senior posts in agriculture, social development, the central bank, and education; others became state governors and members of congress. The ideas shaped the team, and the latter, in turn, became the collective carrier of those ideas into universities and government agencies.

Cavallo returned to Argentina and founded his own think tank, the Institute for Economic Studies of the Argentine Reality (Instituto de Estudios Económicos sobre la Realidad Argentina, or IEERAL); he eventually gained the full support of the Fundación Mediterránea, with which he has remained associated.[24] Cavallo, too, recruited young, highly trained, internationally oriented economists. They shared Weber's "passion" to reduce the weight of the state on the nation's economy and the "responsibility" to foster policies to that end; they also became loyal to Cavallo. Diagnosis, analysis, and prescription, built around a faith in a market economy and in the universalistic tools of economics, were at this team's core. When Cavallo became Argentina's minister of economy, virtually the entire staff of IEERAL was appointed to key positions in the ministry; nearly three hundred had worked at the institute or were otherwise connected to its staff. The ideas shaped the team, and the team became the collective carrier of the ideas.

A similar story is evident in Foxley's case. Foxley returned to Chile to work in the National Ministry of Planning in President Eduardo Frei's Christian Democratic government in the late 1960s. Upon the defeat of the Christian Democrats in the 1970 presidential elections, Foxley left the government to found an economic think tank that would eventually be known as CIEPLAN (Corporación de Investigaciones Económicas para América Latina [Economic Research Enterprise for Latin America]).

As with Cavallo's IEERAL, Foxley's CIEPLAN gave a technical voice to the opposition. CIEPLAN's "passion" was for the market in a democracy; its "responsibility" was to advance both. Its associates needed to demonstrate their command of technical economics, just as good and preferably better than that of the economic team (commonly known as the Chicago Boys) that worked for General Pinochet's government. CIEPLAN criticized the government's dogmatic refusal to address the costs of opening Chile's economy to international markets as well as the government's technically misguided exchange rate policies of the late 1970s and early 1980s. When Chile's economy crashed in 1981, Foxley and CIEPLAN's scientific credentials were vindicated. As in the cases of Cavallo and Aspe, CIEPLAN staff followed Foxley in 1990 into the Christian Democratic government of President Patricio Aylwin, colonizing various Chilean government agencies, in which they assumed senior posts.

Cardoso's path is consistent with this analysis. In April 1969, Cardoso and his colleagues founded CEBRAP (Centro Brasileiro de Análise e Planejamento [Brazilian Center for Analysis and Planning]); he served as its president and senior researcher until 1982. CEBRAP became a refuge for the intellectual opposition to the military government that had come to power in Brazil in 1964. It became as well a leading research institute on social, economic, and public policy issues. Like CIEPLAN, CEBRAP was motivated by its passion for democracy and its commitment to research excellence. CEBRAP's role as a source of government officials awaited the return to civilian government in 1985. When Cardoso was appointed finance minister in May 1993, several former CEBRAP scholars became senior government officials in various ministries; months later, upon Cardoso's election to the presidency, many of these colleagues were promoted as well.

Although Matthei did not found or participate in a research-based institution herself, at the Catholic University of Chile she was recruited into a team committed to the vision of economic transformation associated with the Pinochet government in the 1970s and 1980s. She demonstrated impressive intellectual talent and effectively mastered the tools of economics. Miguel Kast was the mentor; the Chicago Boy ideas were the faith. She was schooled in perhaps the best organized and orthodox economic team seen to date in any Latin American country. Matthei never forged, however, a formal institutional tie beyond her government service with the founders of this model in Chile. Unlike others in this chapter, Matthei entered political life as a somewhat isolated player. This lack of experience with a team and the absence of an institutional base in her own political party from which to inform her ideas and forge alliances may have hurt her political career. Institutional founders, therefore, were more likely to become successful technopols; Matthei's different career trajectory may have left her insufficiently prepared for the top of Chilean politics.

All technopols began their careers, therefore, with early experiences that emphasized academic excellence, faith in a cause (religious or secular), the centrality of a cosmopolitan vision anchored in professional competence that met universalistic standards, and a deep immersion in each nation's historical context. At the political level, the four more successful technopols founded teams and institutions in opposition to the government policies of the time. The politics of opposition would become "scientific" in response to governments that claimed that their policies were based on economic science. Incumbents would be challenged in the same rational terms on which incumbents wished to be judged: authoritarians would be challenged in terms of their economic policies, democrats in terms of their occasional willingness to resort to rule by decree.

Those teams and institutions would become the eventual vehicles to articulate, develop, and transmit key ideas and to colonize state agencies through the appointments of team members to various ministries. There was a "passion" for a set of ideas and a shared responsibility to seek to implement them. Even before they reached power, these technopols differed from Weber's notion of scholarship: these were politically engaged intellectuals, "partisans" of their ideas through their teams.[25]

The Making of Democratic Technopols: Ideas, Institutions, and Opposition Parties

Democratic technopols are made in their opposition to the government of the moment. They build up a political party as well as a program of government consistent with the ideas they wish to implement once in power. As seen in the previous section, their initial location in the opposition fosters the team's cohesion and induces a sharpening of their technical skills, thus enabling them to advance their ideas in public debate.

Cardoso spent much of his adult life understanding and seeking to change Brazil's political and social conditions. Cardoso published a wide array of books and articles in which he developed, refined, and modified his views on democracy, equality, participation, the role of the state, and the place of Brazil in the world. To turn those ideas into reality, institutions were needed beyond CEBRAP: a political party had to embody and carry forward these ideas. In the early 1970s, Cardoso joined the only legally permitted opposition party, the Brazilian Democratic Movement (Movimento Democrático Brasileiro, or MDB), and attempted to turn it from mere reliance on clientelism into a programmatic party. In 1988, Cardoso and his associates founded a new party, the Brazilian Social Democratic Party (Partido da Social Democracia Brasileira, or PSDB); Cardoso became the party's leading intellectual spokesman. Cardoso and the PSDB pressed the new civilian government to move more firmly to install democratic practices and to combat corruption. They advocated replacing Brazil's presidential system with a parliamentary system. The PSDB adopted internal democratic practices to set an example.

The massive abuses committed by the Brazilian authoritarian regime, and the subsequent failures of the state's economic policies, turned Cardoso and his party toward a wider role for the market than had been the case in their earlier thought and experience: the stronger the market and the more constrained the state, the less likely that the state could exercise arbitrary power or hurt the economy. Cardoso and the PSDB sharply criticized the large, cumbersome, arbitrary, and excessively intrusive Brazilian state but also insisted that the state has an important role in protecting the poor and leading the nation through a viable industrial economic strategy. Both Cardoso and his party differ substantially from socialist programs well to their political left in contemporary Brazil; in particular, Cardoso and his party differ from the Workers' Party (Partido dos Trabalhadores, or PT) in their critique of the state. Nonetheless, the commitment to redress the "social deficit" in education and health and to reduce widespread inequalities remains a centerpiece of their thought.[26]

Cardoso's task, to turn ideas into practice, was made unusually difficult by the nonprogrammatic nature of Brazil's political parties, by their lack of internal discipline, and by the fluidity of party and factional alliances.[27] Much of his energy was invested in constructing vehicles to advance the notions of democracy that flowed from his Brazilianist and cosmopolitan commitments. It was also invested in constructing political coalitions in congress to the same end. For this technopol, democracy has always been at the center of his thought and political action. His training and his values have been linked from the very beginning.

Foxley's political trajectory is somewhat different. From his youth, he has been a member of Chile's Christian Democratic party and, as such, has been committed to making democratic politics work in Chile. Unlike Cardoso, Foxley did not have to build a democratic party, because one already existed; the task was to wed Christian Democracy to market-oriented policies and to do so within a wider political coalition to defeat the dictatorship and return Chile to a democratic regime. This was not merely a tactical concern. Foxley believed that just as the free market was inadequate to the task of managing the transformation of the economy, so too the political free market was unsuitable to reconstructing democracy. In economics, Foxley believed in greater cooperation among government, business, and labor as well as in state action to address severe social ills. In politics, Foxley believed that only through concerted actions could agreed-upon limits be set to prevent the polarization that in the early 1970s had destroyed Chilean democracy.

In the 1980s, Foxley labored much of the time to reconstruct Chilean democracy and to retain a largely market-oriented economy. The key effort was to build a political and programmatic alliance between the democratic left and center, mainly between the Christian Democrats and the various democratic socialist parties. One of Foxley's important goals was to fashion both an electoral and a governing coalition, that is, a political coalition that would win the election and remain together to implement an agreed upon program of government. In so doing, Foxley and CIEPLAN changed some of the substance of their views and the specific content of some of their critiques of government policy. By 1987, Foxley realized that Chile had successfully transited out of a strategy of import substitution industrialization (which he had long criticized) and toward an export-oriented strategy and that many entrepreneurs were behaving consistently with the new economic model. Thus, the new task was not only to criticize implementation but also to consolidate Chile's insertion in the international market and to protect the gains in economic efficiency while seeking to add new protections for the weak and the poor. To do so, Foxley the politician assertively led his party and its allies to adopt views more favorable to freer markets than those toward which the parties had been inclined.

Better than the Chicago Boys and the Pinochet government, Foxley and CIEPLAN anticipated the international ideas that came to prevail by the end of the 1980s and the early 1990s: that markets should foster growth with equity. They contributed impressively to the creation of a victorious coalition committed to markets in a democracy that would receive international backing. Indeed, Foxley had warned the Chilean right nearly a decade before its electoral defeat that it had forgotten its own ideological roots: "In the political sphere, [the Chilean government's] model has not been able to solve the inherent contradiction between economic freedom, a basic objective of the model and of [Milton Friedman's] 'ideary', and the political authoritarianism which accompanies it. After all, facing the dilemma, it seems that the Chilean model has certainly chosen capitalism, but has forgotten all about freedom."[28] Sooner than the political right, Foxley understood the power of combining freer politics and freer markets. His party's 1989 electoral victory rewarded the commitment to markets and democracy on which he had built his professional life.

Matthei illustrates the same principle at a different moment. For her, the key political question was how to salvage the parties of the right for democracy and how to ensure that the nation's market orientation would continue. Matthei offered and fashioned a new face for Chile's right. After Patricio Aylwin's inauguration as president in March 1990, the right moved to the opposition for the first time since the early 1970s. There were two tasks for a democrat of the right. The first was to ensure that the parties of the right would remain within the rules of the new democratic regime. The second was to position these parties to do well in elections and eventually to win back power democratically.

Matthei undertook both tasks with clarity and effectiveness. She played an important role in the negotiations over tax reform between her party, National Renovation (Renovación Nacional, or RN), and the government. In so doing, she demonstrated to RN and to the government that civilized politics was possible and that RN was loyal to the democratic regime, though from the political opposition. Toward the longer term, Matthei fashioned a political strategy that emphasized social issues to win cross-class political support. Common crime, the regulation of organ transplants, the defense of the family, the modification of divorce laws, the rights of the unborn, and the improvement of education and curricular change were issues to which she devoted political attention. Her political strategy was to diversify the portfolio of issues on which the parties of the right could win elections, beyond her and her party's long-standing belief in the virtues and utility of the market economy.

Matthei combined this political strategy with impressive communications skills. Her abilities to articulate her party's position and to project sincerity and caring for ordinary human beings were noteworthy political assets. Much more than any of the other trained economists discussed in this chapter, Matthei was able to move her attention successfully to topics and concerns beyond those of the economics profession. Her work toward the transformation of the ideas, practice, and appeal of her party, while keeping her early faith in markets, contributed to the consolidation of Chilean democracy and has earned her a place among the democratic technopols.

Cavallo came to democratic politics later in life than Cardoso, Foxley, and Matthei. Under the military government, he served as undersecretary for internal affairs in 1981 and as president of the central bank in 1982; the sum total of his government service in these two posts was ten weeks. Cavallo's IEERAL, however, was typically a critic of many of the economic policies of both military and civilian governments, a classic role of the opposition. Like Cardoso and Foxley, however, Cavallo soon discovered that more than a think tank was needed to make political change happen. In 1987, Cavallo chose to run for congress as a Peronist candidate, in opposition to the governing Radical Party rather than wait for someone to name him again to appointive office.

Aspe's career in the technical niches of Mexico's government foreclosed a role in the democratic opposition, though, as shown earlier, Aspe's professional career began in the "technical" opposition to Mexican economic policies in the late 1970s. Nor did this career pattern enable him to contribute to Mexico's very gradual political opening.

At the outset, these technopols differed in the relative importance that they accorded to the market and to democratic ideas. Democracy was a particularly high value for Foxley and CIEPLAN and for Cardoso and CEBRAP. They would not succumb to the temptations of Joseph or Turgot. Democracy was not a predominant concern for Aspe and his team at ITAM, or for Cavallo and Matthei while they served in military governments. Belief in the market was also a high value for all but Cardoso and CEBRAP, and even these Brazilians gradually moved to embrace markets, just as Cavallo and IEERAL—and Matthei—moved to embrace democracy. By the early 1990s, the views of these technopols (though least so in the case of Aspe) had converged to uphold both democracy and markets.

The making of democratic technopols begins in the opposition. The technically talented must engage in persuasion to secure funding and to spread their ideas; they must look for allies to advance their cause. In the opposition, they hone their technical skills to improve the efficacy of the presentation of ideas, but to be truly effective in the long term, they must link up with a political party and work to build or to reshape such a party. They learn the utility of democratic behavior to advance their technical ideas, and they learn the need to refashion their technical ideas to serve democratic goals.

Much of the professional careers of Cardoso, Foxley, and Matthei was spent in this fashion; at a later time, similar behavior would become evident in Cavallo's career. Cardoso from the left, Foxley from the center, and Matthei from the right moved their associates from their early policy predilections. Cardoso struggled against the Brazilian left's love affair with the state. Matthei fought the Chilean right's Olympian forgetfulness of the politics of daily life. Foxley moved allied politicians toward positions supportive of freer markets while ensuring the bases for political and economic agreement in a fragmented party system. Cavallo, too, struggled against Peronist nostalgia for economic autarchy. As Max Weber's scholars should, all four made a case that was at the time inconvenient for their respective party's opinions. Each sought to combine democracy and markets to varying degrees and in different forms, and each was an effective political entrepreneur in so doing. They helped their countries to consolidate or to approach politics consistent with their ideas.

These technopols came to recognize that political pluralism and markets work best if the effort is made to make them work together. The full flowering of these technopols, therefore, occurred (Mexico excepted) in the context of both democracies and markets, in response to the economic catastrophes that befell these four countries and to the harsh dictatorships suffered in the three South American cases.

The Critical Juncture

The historical moment for the technopols under study came when the pillars of the old order crumbled. There was a structural origin to the economic and political changes evident in these countries by the early 1990s, but there was also a voluntarist resolution. The structural crisis helped to provide the opening for the actions of technopols.

These technopols rose to influence in their respective countries at a specific historical moment, typically when five factors converged.

An economic crisis unprecedented in its severity since the Great Depression of the 1930s gripped these countries in the early 1980s (in Chile, a severe economic breakdown had also occurred in 1973).

When the crisis broke, authoritarian regimes of varying harshness held power in each of the four countries; incumbents were blamed for the economic crisis to varying degrees, which blame helped to discredit authoritarian approaches or at least weaken support for them.[29] Cavallo, in particular, learned that military governments were unlikely to generate or sustain sound and politically viable economic policies.

Authoritarian technocrats and technopols held positions of power in each of the four countries, and to some degree they and their style of governing were discredited or challenged.

For diverse reasons, including the economic crisis, the political process opened up, though to varying degrees, in each of these countries during the 1980s, first accelerating the circulation of elites at the top of the government and, eventually, leading toward democratic regimes in Argentina, Brazil, and Chile and toward a further easing of Mexico's always less severe authoritarian regime.

Democratic governments pursuing statist economic policies at first proved incapable of resolving severe economic crises in Argentina under President Raúl Alfonsín, Brazil under President José Sarney, and Chile, earlier, under President Salvador Allende, thereby increasing political support for more market-oriented alternatives. The failures of statist policies pursued to varying degrees by the Alfonsín, Sarney, and Allende governments impressed Aspe, Cardoso, Cavallo, Foxley, and Matthei.

In 1982, Latin America's foreign debt crisis erupted, announcing the birth of economic trauma. In that year, Chile's GDP per capita fell 14.5 percent, Argentina's 7.2 percent, Mexico's 3 percent, and Brazil 1.6 percent; in 1983, Brazil and Mexico each lost an additional 6 percent of GDP per capita. From 1981 through 1989, GDP per capita fell by over 9 percent in Mexico and by over 23 percent in Argentina; Brazil ended the decade at the same GDP per capita as when it began, while Chile's economic recovery during the second half of the 1980s erased the losses of the early 1980s and led to a meager net cumulative gain (1981–89) of just under 10 percent. From the early to the late 1980s, real average wages plummeted in the four countries. During the 1980s, Mexico, accustomed to low inflation rates, suffered from rapidly accelerating inflation. From 1983 through 1989, Argentina and Brazil had annual triple-digit consumer price inflation every year but 1986; both countries had annual four-digit price inflation in 1989 and 1990.[30]

At the moment of economic crisis, there was available an international pool of theoretical and empirical ideas that emphasized the utility of markets; these ideas had become dominant in the industrial countries during the 1970s and the 1980s, precisely when these technopols-in-the-making lived there. These market-oriented international ideas were nested in economics departments, in international financial institutions, and in major private foundations, which fostered and funded the spread of these ideas through the think tanks and teams founded by these technopols.[31] The international context was favorable as well because these ideas were supported by the U.S. government, its major allies, and public and private international financial institutions. They "demanded" competence from the economic policy makers of Latin American countries. Technically trained leaders, therefore, would help to generate international and eventually domestic political legitimacy: they knew how to act in accord with "universal" and "scientific" requirements.[32]

The economic crisis alone did not "cause" the opening of politics, but it facilitated such an opening. The economic crisis permitted technically qualified opposition leaders to criticize authoritarian technocrats on their own terms. The technical criticism of failed economic policies opened a wedge for political liberalization at the elite level, complementing mass protests against prevailing policies. In this fashion, technically qualified people in the opposition derived political legitimacy from the international community to challenge the government and, because they were competent to do so, garnered support for themselves within the opposition and for the opposition in the wider public.

Beginning in the late 1970s, another international pool of ideas became available. It asserted the centrality of democracy as the way to govern and the importance of respect for human rights in the relationship between state and society. The support for democracy and human rights became a part of the programs of the worldwide federations of Christian democratic, social democratic, and liberal parties of special pertinence in Western Europe. The international action of many leaders and parties in the industrial democracies helped to weaken international backing for authoritarian rule in Latin America. In the United States, this idea first reached policy salience during Jimmy Carter's presidency. Though nearly discarded during Ronald Reagan's first term, the centrality of democracy as an organizing principle for U.S. foreign policy gathered support during Reagan's second term and especially during the Bush and Clinton presidencies. The U.S. government and the European Union also came to "demand" democratic leadership in Latin America. Cardoso and Foxley gained personally from their international standing as democrats. In Latin America, moreover, normative commitments to democracy have been especially noteworthy among intellectuals and politicians in the 1980s and 1990s.[33] Most cosmopolitan technopols gradually came to incorporate the two international pools of ideas, one favorable to markets, the other to democracy.

The availability of international pools of ideas that emphasize the utility of markets and democracy does not, of course, explain the policy choices and value commitments of the technopols under study. As shown in the previous section, these technopols came to these ideas on their own, in part by "swimming" in these pools of ideas during their time abroad; Cardoso and Foxley, for example, strongly believed in democracy well in advance of the Reagan administration's embrace of democratic ideas in the second half of the 1980s. Having made their own choices to foster markets and democracy, however, several of these technopols at first were not listened to by their fellow citizens.

The structural crisis in state and economy opened the wedge for these technopols to be heard and to enter government as carriers of their own ideas. By the early 1990s, these ideas were at last legitimized and reinforced by the changed international intellectual and political climate. (In Mexico, it took a second economic crisis in 1994–95 to make way for a democratizing political system.) Would-be technopols had learned as well as generated ideas of interest to the international community and to their fellow citizens. Technical skills had become widespread and respected enough to legitimize the importance and validity of the teams that these technopols had founded. These technopols and their teams stood ready to fashion government programs to respond to the crisis by means of new ideas and their teams' staffing of the national government, especially in the wake of the economic policy failures of preceding civilian governments in Argentina, Brazil, and Mexico. They were the idea makers who were about to become idea carriers and policy makers.[34] Unlike technocrats in the past, democratic technopols joined opposition political parties to ride into government power (Mexico, again, being an exception). All five technopols gained power thanks to their association with political parties.

These technopols linked a wide vision, universalistic ideas about markets and politics, and technical skills with a strong commitment to their homelands and to political pluralism.[35] In their careers, they falsified the proposition that those trained abroad, or trained "abroad at home," could not operate sensibly and effectively in government office. They would act to open up markets and politics and, in so doing, remain faithful to the twin cosmopolitan ideas of the age. To the parochialism of some in the past, they responded with an effort to install a patriotic cosmopolitanism, grounding international experience in the empirical context of each country. In such fashion, the structural crises facilitated the voluntarist resolution in favor of markets and democracy.

The Actions of Technopols: From the Fat to the Fit State

A central concern of these technopols has been to recraft the state. In so doing, they demonstrate that they are not neoliberals (the usual label—applied even, in the mid-1990s, to Cardoso), if by neoliberal one means the strategies associated with Ronald Reagan or Margaret Thatcher. These technopols sought not to kill the state but to save it, to force the state to shed its "fat" but to ensure that the state will be "fit" to govern and to elicit the consent of citizens. In each case, these technopols sought to cut back the state's reach into the society and the economy, but they also sought to increase government revenues and improve the delivery of government services. In several cases, they sought to redirect the savings from cutting back on certain state actions to redress inequalities or improve support for the poor.

For Matthei, there have been fewer opportunities to recraft the state, because she has not wielded top executive power. In the 1970s and 1980s, Matthei supported the Chilean government policies of privatization of state enterprises, and in the 1990s, she advocated the privatization of several enterprises that remained in the state's hands. But state shrinking does not, in fact, characterize her position. The social policies that she advocated would expand certain areas of state activity. Most important, she was the government's key ally from the opposition, helping to obtain broad enough support in congress for a tax reform to raise revenues to pay for new social expenditures. Matthei's political career exemplifies how even certain politicians from the right support the competent state: fit, but not fat.

From congress and the center-left, Cardoso argued strongly against the bloated and ineffective state while also seeking to deconcentrate power in the presidency by means of a constitutional shift to a parliamentary regime. Among these technopols, Cardoso is also the strongest advocate of government services for the poor and the weak. For Cardoso, the arbitrary state was democracy's worst enemy, and the fat state was the main source of corruption, evident most tragically in 1992 with the impeachment and subsequent resignation of Brazil's first directly elected president in three decades, Fernando Collor de Mello. As finance minister, Cardoso raised revenues and protected government services for the poor even as he sought to limit the state's intrusion into society and economy.

Finance Minister Alejandro Foxley sought to retain and foster Chile's integration into the international economy, to stabilize the economy from its inflationary bout at the end of the Pinochet regime, and to foster social equity. Minister Foxley fostered freer trade agreements while resisting calls for trade protectionism. By institutionalizing free trade, the nation would set clear and stable rules for the future. On the other hand, Foxley under-

stood the need for the regulation of financial markets to prevent the reck-
less inflow of funds that unraveled Chilean economic policies in the late
1970s and early 1980s. But perhaps Foxley's most important accomplishment was his management of macroeconomic policies and the social deficit.

Could Chilean democrats manage the economy? The authoritarian regime's claim to fame had been its ability at last to foster real economic
growth by the second half of the 1980s. Nonetheless, rational investors
would expect a continued high political risk from operations in Chile because there was reason for uncertainty about future government policies:
Could the economic policies of an authoritarian regime elicit enough consent from the governed to endure? If parties of the center and the left were
to replace the dictatorship, what economic policies might they follow?

Chile's Chicago Boys in their various incarnations could never successfully address this problem of rational expectations as long as the Pinochet
regime continued. This rational expectations problem could best be addressed in a democracy in which either the renovated right would receive
popular endorsement or the center and the left would govern through
market-oriented and stable macroeconomic policies. From the perspective
of the rational investor, paradoxically, the second of these options would
best ensure the future, for it would signal a truly comprehensive consensus
on the wisdom of Chile's new economic trajectory: only when there is a
democracy committed to markets and governed by the center-left could the
rational investor be certain that market norms would prevail, no matter
which party governed. (Sociologically, of course, most investors typically
do not behave this way; they tend to prefer center-right governments. They
understand the utility of market-oriented center-left governments only after
markets and democracy are consolidated without their active support.)

Foxley understood the utility of democracy for markets and the utility of
markets for democracy. Democracy would address the problem of rational
economic expectations; markets would generate the growth to consolidate
democracy and would provide the funds to address the social agenda. This
technopol exemplifies the long-term elective affinity between markets and
democracy.

Foxley's opening economic policies were austere; public spending was
sharply restrained in order to break the late Pinochet regime's inflationary
spiral and to stabilize public finances even at the cost of slow economic
growth in the short term. These policies set the basis for spectacular nonin-
flationary economic growth in 1991 and 1992 and for continuing good economic growth rates thereafter. To address genuine problematic social legacies of the Pinochet regime, Foxley led the government to negotiate with the
right-wing party National Renovation (prominently including Deputy Eve-

lyn Matthei) over a tax reform whose revenue proceeds would fund government initiatives, especially in health and education. Through these technically competent policies, Foxley demonstrated that growth with equity was not just a slogan but a feasible policy goal. Foxley also demonstrated that the parties of the center and the center-left had no wish to resurrect the fat state but were more competent to recraft the fit state to address the nation's needs and hopes.

Economy Minister Domingo Cavallo faced a different problem of rational expectations as he sought to govern under President Carlos Menem and the Peronist party. There was "certainty" that Argentina was ungovernable, that the state apparatus was inept, and that the economy would repeat the cycles of decline and decline that had marked it for decades, the best example of a country that had succeeded at becoming "underdeveloped" in the twentieth century. There was a related rational expectation: the "certainty" that the Peronists, given their past record in government, were closet populists and incompetent rulers.

If Foxley's opening policy package had to combine a progressive social policy with an austere fiscal policy to become credible, Cavallo's had to be shocking but democratic, for anything less would have been seen as lacking credibility. The policy took the form of the 1991 Convertibility Law, which made the national currency freely convertible into dollars at a fixed and unchanging value. The law ended contract indexation and prohibited the central bank from printing money to cover deficits unless new currency emissions were backed by gold or foreign reserves. The law had to be shocking to make it clear that hyperinflation would not recur, but this alone would not have made Cavallo so different from some of his predecessors.

The genius of Cavallo's strategy was to use democratic constraints to implement this policy. He chose to act through congressional action, rather than by decree, and in the future to require prior congressional authorization for any change in the exchange rate or the printing of more money. Through congressional approval, Cavallo was signaling the commitment of the executive and legislature to alter permanently the course of Argentina's macroeconomic policies. Cavallo induced the congress to assume responsibility for macroeconomic stability and tied his hands via the democratic process. Self-binding behavior is a long-recognized strategy to demonstrate credibility and to address the problem of rational expectations.[36] Henceforth, the president or the central bank would find it much more difficult to change monetary policy; henceforth, the basis for macroeconomic policy would be supported even by Peronists, those who had hitherto been most suspected of recklessness.

Cavallo believed that Argentina's past economic problems had not been

technical. The technical problems were understood; good technical prescriptions existed as well. Cavallo accurately diagnosed the problem as
political; this political problem could only be addressed via democratic
procedures. For this technopol, democracy was not an option; it was a
necessity. Only by binding himself, his president, his government, and his
party allies to the consent of congress could Cavallo persuade rational
actors to believe that, this time, Argentines, indeed, the Peronists, meant to
get their house in order.

The remainder of Cavallo's unprecedented economic program was consistent with his opening salvo. The national government deficit was sharply
curtailed, state enterprises were privatized, provincial governments were
cajoled into fiscal restraint. Cavallo urged voters to unseat governors who
failed to reform. In October 1991, the government adopted a far-reaching
program of deregulation. Cavallo also sharply reduced tariffs and other
forms of trade protection in order to open up Argentina's economy to the
forces of the world market. His search for freer trade agreements was also
an effort to use self-binding constraints to institutionalize the rules of an
open economy.

And yet, as with the other technopols, Cavallo was particularly interested not in weakening the state but in making it competent. His comprehensive tax reforms sought the inconceivable. As Cavallo has stated, the
only miraculous thing his ministry achieved was to get Argentines to pay
taxes. In addition to various tax policy changes, Cavallo strengthened the
state's capacity to collect taxes. He also greatly fortified the state's capacity
to regulate the markets created through the privatization of state enterprises.

Cavallo's accomplishments, therefore, featured the use of democratic procedures to address the problem of rational expectations and to transform
the state so that it could govern at last. That he was also technically highly
skilled was, of course, necessary to the task but not so remarkable. Cavallo
is more unusual for his political skill than for his economics, and so he is an
example of a democratic technopol.

The Mexican miracle—restoring growth while reducing inflation—is
more a collective than a personal accomplishment, because Pedro Aspe's
role was less singular than those of Foxley and Cavallo. (President Carlos
Salinas de Gortari played a far more salient role in fashioning economic policies than did Presidents Aylwin and Menem.) Nonetheless, Aspe played a
key role in recrafting the Mexican state, making it fit to govern.

As in Argentina and Chile, a far-reaching program of privatization of
state enterprises was also undertaken in Mexico under Aspe's general pur-
view. Aspe's ministry also worked in sustained and effective fashion to im-

prove tax collection and to increase the state's revenues. The proceeds from privatization in Mexico were directed to pay off parts of the public debt, thus freeing budget funds to be spent on health, education, housing, and basic infrastructure. Regular tax revenues were also directed to these purposes. The reduction of poverty became an objective of the Salinas presidency; in turn, this goal was made possible by Aspe's successful financial policies. The channeling of public funds to address the social deficit was an integral part of Aspe's intellectual concerns before his rise through the bureaucracy; as a scholar, Aspe had worked thoughtfully on problems of inequality and poverty.

There was, perhaps, a second Mexican miracle, namely, the ability to make significant progress without a Cavallo-like policy shock but also under a politics of elite inclusion in a nondemocratic system. In October 1987, the Mexican stock market crashed more severely than world stock markets did; an unexpected run on the peso sent inflation out of control. At that very moment, Carlos Salinas had been nominated as the ruling party's presidential candidate, and Pedro Aspe had become budget and planning secretary. The ingenious and impressively effective solution to this crisis was a social pact of the sort that scholars seem to think never works.

The Economic Solidarity Pact was based on the recognition that the government could not address all problems by decree. The state could not impose a solution; labor and business had to agree to bear some of the burden. And by making policy through negotiations, leading to mutually binding commitments, Aspe and the government increased the likelihood that the pact would be credible at home and abroad. Within a half-year of its enactment, the pact had brought Mexican inflation down to just over 1 percent per month; the pact would subsequently be renegotiated various times, but Mexican inflation would remain low through the first half of the 1990s.

Little about this pact was truly new. Aspe had learned from the failures of previous inflation control efforts in Argentina and Brazil and from successes in Israel and Spain; he understood that only fiscal discipline would provide a stable underpinning to price and wage controls. Aspe may have learned a more important lesson from his MIT mentor, Dornbusch, who believes that economic stabilization is, above all, not a technical issue but a political one. Aspe applied this concept to Mexico through negotiation of concerted action among key economic and political actors to avoid shock policies and to succeed in slaying the inflation dragon. Political inclusion was needed, though it fell well short of the democratic politics of Cavallo and Foxley.

By intention and, in the cases of the ministers, by accomplishment, these technopols sought to recraft the state. The state has shed (or is in the process of shedding) its fat in order to become more competent (fit) to tackle a narrower array of tasks that only it can perform. Technopols not only privatize state enterprises in the belief that the state is generally not capable enough of conducting such business, but they also raise taxes so that the state's public finances are sound. Especially in Chile, Mexico, and Brazil, these technopols took seriously the state's obligations to address the social deficit and increased government spending on education, health, and basic infrastructure. The support for the competent state is a value shared among these technopols, no matter how much they may differ in other aspects of their politics.

These technopols have also understood that rational investors expect policy continuity. To achieve this fundamental objective, the technopols followed two strategies. The first harkened back to their founding cosmopolitan vision. They pursued international trade agreements to lock in their country's new, freer, market-oriented policies well into the future and thus set the market rules that will meet the rational expectations of investors. The second strategy was to foster a political opening to ensure that all key actors participate in the shaping of the new policies and, as a result, remain committed to them. In Brazil, where such consent was most elusive, less had been accomplished by the mid-1990s to reorient the economy and secure the bases of democratic politics, though President Cardoso accelerated the pace of change. Where such consent remained imperfect because transparent democratic procedures had not characterized the polity—as in Mexico— greater uncertainties remained. Nonetheless, the commitment to market-oriented reforms seemed strong by the mid-1990s. Even after Mexico's financial crisis and economic recession of 1994–95 (and a less severe but still noteworthy simultaneous economic crisis in Argentina), all four governments remained committed to market-oriented policies.

Foxley and Cavallo, therefore, were the most successful of these technopols, for their behavior and their policies fostered freer trade as well as the consent of the governed with regard to market-oriented policies under democratic politics. The democratic center-left parties in Chile and the Peronists in Argentina could demonstrate better than any military government that the countries' new commitments would endure, and in this way democratic politics responded effectively to the rational expectations problem.

The Deepening of Democracy

The political actions of these technopols have advanced the practice of democracy in each of these countries, though to varying degrees. For the most part, they have acted to deepen democracy, because they believe in its values; at a minimum, they have sought to deepen democracy because obtaining the consent of the governed, especially that of the actual or potential partisan or sectoral opposition, is the most effective way in the long run to consolidate their preferred economic policies.

Foxley and Matthei worked jointly to bridge the gap between parties that had been adversaries in the preceding presidential elections and for the duration of the Pinochet regime. For Matthei, the political risks were higher. She was the daughter of an air force general who had served on the military junta during the Pinochet regime. Her party had just begun life in the opposition. She had barely entered national politics and lacked a strong partisan base. She had to change the right's expectation that it would lack the ability to influence policies under the new government. Even for Foxley, there were risks: would the Christian Democrats in power betray their campaign promises to bring greater fairness to Chile? The Pinochet dictatorship had been accustomed to giving orders as its method of rule. The constitution that President Aylwin and Minister Foxley had inherited vested great powers in the executive branch; instead, they turned to congress to govern democratically. Led by Aylwin and Foxley, the government reached out to the congressional opposition, led among others by Matthei, to reach an agreement on tax increases and new government expenditures. Foxley repeated as minister the technique that he had first developed within the opposition coalition: the forging of agreements on a sound technical basis to advance policy goals. For her part, Matthei innovated a strategy for her party as the loyal opposition, credible and capable of government. As teacher to the nation, she communicated a new, caring, democratic image for the parties of the right that should serve them and Chilean democracy well.

Within the government, Foxley spent much time defending his policies before his party and its coalition partners and before the congress. He fostered the growth of various means for regular political consultation. Foxley also reached out to a dynamic business class, which had long distrusted him, his party, and his party's allies, at a time when business was being asked to accept tax increases and labor law changes that they opposed. Foxley also worked to develop fluid conversations with labor and among business, labor, and the government. Democracy required, above all, that both the political and the economic right remain allegiant; Foxley bargained with the right in Congress and dealt professionally with business.

Foxley also became a teacher to the nation, using television and other mass media successfully. His public persona emphasized sober competence and effectiveness. Matthei, too, had made exemplary use of television and other media to portray a caring, as well as a competent, image. In Chile, democrats understood that democracy required that the Weberian scholar hidden within a technopol should surface to consolidate public beliefs in the utility and efficacy of democracy.

Cardoso's central contributions to Brazilian democratic politics have been discussed in an earlier section: the creation of a team, an intellectual institution, a political party, and the sustained effort to insert programmatic ideas into party programs and political discourse. As finance minister and later as president, Cardoso worked with congress to enact economic reform measures, even though congress was often an obstacle to the adoption of such measures. The 1993 dispute over wage adjustments illustrates Cardoso's approach. In June, the congress had enacted a law to guarantee monthly wage adjustments to ensure that workers' pay would remain abreast of inflation. Cardoso's Finance Ministry prepared a technical analysis that showed the highly inflationary effects of such a measure, while Cardoso's team lobbied members of congress. In August, congress changed the wage law to dampen the inflationary flames. Democracy had to be made to work in Brazil; that had been and remained Cardoso's commitment.

Cardoso has also made three other important contributions to Brazilian democracy. First, he is the peerless teacher to his nation, combining a lively sense of humor and a gift for phrase making with an accessible public demeanor that is unmatched by the other technopols under study except for Matthei. His ability to transform important abstract thoughts into more readily understood concepts has helped to deepen mass democracy. Second, Cardoso has been accused by critics of having shifted his views according to prevailing political winds. In fact, Cardoso has been consistent in the central features of his thought, though he has also made numerous changes of emphasis and substance. That is, of course, what ought to happen in democratic politics. Politicians should shed dogmas in response to new facts; Cardoso has exemplified how this is to be done: in public. Finally, in a political system marked by infidelity to parties, Cardoso has been respectful of his party's discipline, even turning down an early offer to become foreign minister because his party had chosen not to join the president's political alliance. Democratic governance requires party discipline; Cardoso has practiced what he has preached.

As finance minister in a nondemocratic political system, Aspe's role in furthering Mexico's political opening was modest. Nonetheless, as noted earlier, the design of the 1987 Economic Solidarity Pact featured political inclusion within the elite. More important, during the 1980s the Mexican congress assumed a more active role in questioning government ministers; this role increased once the opposition made major gains in the 1988 national elections. Aspe appeared before congress regularly and often. Although he occasionally lost his temper, Aspe, too, became a teacher to the nation through his congressional testimony.

Cavallo's contribution to deepening Argentina's democratic practice is the most surprising because he had worked for the military government in 1981–82 and because President Menem had demonstrated a penchant for ruling by decree. And yet, as minister, Cavallo, too, made a net contribution to democracy in his country. This process began but did not end with the 1991 Convertibility Law. At times, Cavallo was criticized for having compromised too much in his dealings with congress, but that is of the essence of democratic politics. To secure support from Peronist backbenchers and from the main opposition, the Radical Party, Cavallo permitted the congress to scrutinize and approve every major step in the reform of the state. Privatizations had been carried out by presidential decree, but Cavallo preferred that those decisions, too, require congressional approval. He understood clearly that congressional and opposition participation increased the likelihood that such privatizations would be seen as broadly legitimate. Cavallo knew that his democratic predecessors had failed in congress; it was therefore not only desirable but also efficient to engage the congress.

In the Economy Ministry, Cavallo built not just a technical team versed in economics but also a political team versed in dealing with congress, the parties, and the provinces; this team was institutionalized through a new undersecretary's office in the Economy Ministry. Cavallo understood that the making of economic policy was too important to be left to economists alone. Cavallo insisted that the economy had to be governed by laws, not by decrees, as a means to ensure endurance of the new rules. Cavallo became a teacher to his nation by appearing in congress and on television talk shows, by speaking wherever he had an opportunity to educate his president, his party, the congress, and the nation at large that the time had come at last to break with Argentina's unstable and undemocratic past and to link democracy and markets in the building of a more secure future. As a scholar, he spoke about things as they were, not about the promises of an imaginary utopia. Cavallo became, as well, a teacher to the international community, to change the expectation that Argentina would forever be an economic or political pariah. In this fashion, Cavallo redeemed his nationalist credentials in defense of the country's interests.

The time that Cavallo, Cardoso, Foxley, and Aspe spent in political work also had an economic payoff. By working to improve the government's relations with both labor and business, technopols, through more open politics (and in Argentina and Chile, specifically democratic politics), built a consensus behind efficient and realistic policies while reducing transaction costs—fewer strikes, fewer budget allocations for repression, the end of the international isolation of more authoritarian regimes, and less likelihood of business support for coups. Brazil lagged in the development of this market-oriented policy consensus, but the effort to achieve these objectives began in earnest in 1994. (Mexico's delayed democratization was associated with increased protests demanding greater political opening.) The reduction in transaction costs in Argentina, Brazil, and Chile also probably increased business support for democracy.

More generally, in each of these cases (except Mexico) democratic technopols sought to deepen democracy as an integral part of their task and as a component of their own self-definition in politics. Political openings, and democracy more specifically, moved forward in these countries thanks to the political acts of these technopols.

The Contradictions: Techno versus Pol

The role of technopol features inherent contradictions, some of which are noted earlier. This chapter reports not only the successes of technopols but also less fortuitous outcomes. One was Matthei's alienation from her party. In 1992, she was suspended for ten years from all political activity in her party for covering up her indirect participation in the wiretapping of a political rival's private telephone conversation. Beyond the specifics of her case is the larger problem evident in all the cases, namely, that the skills and predispositions that make for the technical side of the technopol are in some tension with those that make for the political side. To this extent, the themes that have long concerned scholars who have focused on technocrats remain pertinent, namely, whether the technical virtues may undermine the democratic possibilities. I disagree with the extant scholarship in that I believe that it has exaggerated the problem, not that it has lacked a fundamental insight.[37]

Three distinct though related factors may account for Matthei's political difficulties. She lacked a team, a think tank, an institutional base of her own that would enrich her ideas and values and temper her political actions. Her technical training had not prepared her for the formation of alliances and the building of institutional bases that are essential for successful political action and that are present to a greater degree in the other four cases. Nor did Matthei have a good sense of timing. To some degree, her meteoric rise in national politics was part of her near undoing; her business background and technical training had not prepared her adequately for the circumspection at times required in political action. Nor did she have enough time to hone the skills for making political judgments in the earlier period of her political career.

The tensions within the role of technopol had different effects on Aspe.

His actions fostered some political inclusion at the elite level, but Mexican politics did not become democratic; and Aspe, unlike the others, did not act in a democratic context. As with Cavallo and Foxley, Aspe, too, could display the arrogance of the technically trained, express impatience and disdain for members of congress, and become too preachy in his approach to the public, the press, and the parliament. Constrained in part by the division of labor between economic and political affairs within President Salinas' cabinet, Aspe resolved the tensions within the role of technopol by eschewing the building of democracy; in so doing, he differed in important ways from the other four technopols.

The insider style of Mexico's technopols made it more difficult for them to develop the skills of conciliation and negotiation associated with more openly competitive politics, an observation that echoes the analysis of some of Matthei's political difficulties. What made Mexico's technopols successful in their country also made it less likely that they would press to open up the political system. Aspe was never a member of an opposition political party, unlike the four others. The unpreparedness of Mexican technopols for democracy may have made them less sensitive as well to the greater readiness of Mexican citizens for democratic politics (for elaboration, see chapter 5). Salinas's team of technopols listened too little and too late to the demands for a more open political system; in 1994, those demands were among the factors that would contribute to the unraveling of the economic policies so carefully fashioned by Salinas and Aspe. Salinas, Aspe, and their associates thought that they were more skillful in reforming the Mexican economy than Mikhail Gorbachev was in reforming the Soviet Union's economy. Gorbachev's project may have been undone by the general breakdown of the Soviet system; the Salinas-Aspe project was gravely injured, in part, by its democratic "deficit." A key question for Mexico's future is whether a more democratic political regime can fashion better and more sustainable economic policies.

In economic terms, Aspe is also the least successful of the finance ministers. Mexico's financial panic of December 1994, and the fiscal and monetary policy errors committed by the Mexican government during that year, contributed to a severe economic recession in Mexico during 1995. The lack of democratic procedures in Mexico to compel the executive to listen to criticism and take it into account insulated top decision makers to an extent unprecedented elsewhere, and at a political and economic cost not found anywhere else in the continent.[38] A short-term political rationale (to win the August 1994 election for the governing party) along with the democratic deficit contributed to the unmaking of elite economic policies and threatened the decades-old rule of the Institutional Revolutionary Party.

Related problems are evident also in the other cases. Cavallo had little patience for congressional questioning or for delays attributable to mere political factors. This impatience stemmed from the intensity and clarity of his convictions; that is, the more persuaded he became of the technical soundness of his view, the less effective he could be at getting such views accepted politically. This is the Cavallo who lost his temper and shouted at members of congress; the thoughtful teacher turned into a shrill preacher. The same candid and sincere Cavallo could make condescending statements in public. There was both an authoritarian streak in the Olympian technical skills and an ill preparedness for the normal rough and tumble of democratic politics that stemmed as well from his technical training, orientation, and demeanor.

Institutionally, more worrisome was Cavallo's continued reliance on government by decree to sidestep the congress because it might overrepresent those most resistant to change. This was the reason to deregulate by decree rather than by congressional law. Democratic procedures, then, might be seen as optional tools to be used, then discarded, in the building of the altar of market-oriented reforms. To this extent, there remained an incompatibility between Cavallo's technical and democratic-political dimensions. And yet, in reorienting the economy within a democratic polity, Cavallo bested Chile's record under Pinochet and Mexico's under Salinas.

The tensions between techno and pol were evident as well in Foxley's case. Perhaps Foxley's most important political action was his veto of the economic program that the technical committees of the opposition parties negotiated in 1989. In the end, the parties were well served electorally by succumbing to Foxley, but Foxley seemed to expect compliance to defer to expertise. Foxley's occasional flashes of arrogance and extensive use of the mass media could suggest a discomfort with some of the normal conduct of democratic politics.

More seriously, Foxley sought to prevent the congress, and especially the parties in his coalition, from constraining his technically "correct" policies, because he preferred to retain maximum flexibility. He also continued to see value in the institutional obstacles to party and congressional exercise of power that were inherited from the authoritarian regime because they forced wide agreements prior to the implementation of major policies. Moreover, Foxley also played on labor unions' fear of the authoritarian regime to moderate labor demands. And yet, Foxley was the first finance minister in Chilean history to succeed at maintaining and developing market-oriented economic policies in a fundamentally democratic context. Foxley experienced the tensions within the role of technopol more vividly when he became Christian Democrat party president in 1994. In that new job, he found it difficult to cope with the murky and often personalized nuances of party politics. His commitment to emphasize ideas as the guiding star of politics was at times overwhelmed by the need to attend to egos, jealousies, and interests that palpitate at the heart of politics.

The tensions in the role of technopol also had different consequences for Cardoso, who can be located at the opposite end of the spectrum from Aspe. Cardoso never had the love for the state evident among so many Brazilians on the political left or in the armed forces, but Cardoso has always been suspicious of the "magic" of the market. With the passing of time and with his growing frustration with the corruption and abuse of the bloated Brazilian state, Cardoso's interest in and respect for markets rose, though Cardoso continued to find it difficult to celebrate a market-oriented economic policy in the same manner that comes so easily to the lips of the others. Cardoso, in short, resolved the tensions within the role of technopol by emphasizing the primacy of political goals and methods.

Technopols discover ongoing difficulties in reconciling the various dimensions included within this role. In part for that reason, Matthei's political career nearly aborted after a very promising start. Also in part for that reason, Aspe—and for a long time, Cardoso—addressed these internal role contradictions by focusing on one dimension at the expense of the other. Cavallo and Foxley, and eventually Cardoso as finance minister and president, wrestled with these contradictions with far greater effectiveness. By this I do not exempt Cavallo, Foxley, and the latter-day Cardoso from criticism, but I believe that they should be held to realistic standards in the context of their countries and the region as a whole. No finance minister in Chile and no economy minister in Argentina had pursued market-oriented economic policies in a democratic context as successfully as these two, and no Brazilian president had attempted ambitious and joint democratic and economic reforms.[39] These were historic accomplishments.

Conclusion

"Look at a success story," U.S. Undersecretary of the Treasury designate (and former World Bank vice president) Lawrence Summers exhorted his audience at the 1993 annual meeting of the Inter-American Development Bank. After praising the general trend toward "popular, democratic elections and institutions," Summers continued: "Chile is an excellent example of a country that has implemented far-reaching macroeconomic reforms [and] encouraged the development of the private sector and markets. . . . Now the government can concentrate its resources on the social sector. . . . Chile has demonstrated the political will to make social programs a priority. This is a good example for other countries."[40] After a decade-long economic decline in most Latin American countries in the 1980s, growth resumed in most countries in the early 1990s. After a legacy of political instability, Argentine and Brazilian civilian governments in the late 1980s and early 1990s survived the sort of hyperinflation that brought European and Latin American governments tumbling down earlier in the twentieth century.

In this chapter, I argue that there was a structural political and economic origin of the changes evident in several major Latin American countries in the early 1990s but that there has been a voluntarist resolution through the effective use of each nation's institutions. The structural crisis posed the problems; its severity forced elites to consider a wider range of policy options. The fact of an economic crisis does not by itself explain the course of policy adopted in the early 1990s. For example, in the 1980s and early 1990s Brazil suffered a similar crisis but only belatedly did it begin to adopt policies comparable to those of Argentina, Chile, or Mexico. Similarly, Argentina suffered a severe economic crisis earlier in the 1980s; while it shifted toward democratic politics, it did not at that time adopt the market-oriented policies that it adopted in the early 1990s. The explanation for the joint adoption of policies that would foster freer markets and freer politics lies in the strategic actions of technopols working with their allies through democratic institutions to formulate new policy designs. They learned from the failures in democratic or economic policy of their authoritarian and democratic predecessors.

The more successful outcomes have been those shaped by political leaders whose ideas were forged in both national and cosmopolitan contexts. They drew on the available international pool of ideas about the utility of markets to legitimize their views and, at a critical juncture, acted to turn ideas into policy. There was a second international pool of available ideas: respect for democracy. Fortunately for the fate of political openings, authoritarian regimes everywhere but in Chile had failed to deliver sound economic policies, depriving them of political support and opening the gates for new political regimes.

In Argentina, Brazil, and Chile the leaders under study drew upon both sets of international ideas to fashion new market-oriented economic policies and to advance toward and consolidate more open politics rooted in each country's national experience. (In Mexico, the reforms focused mainly on economic issues.) This comprehensive shift was in place only by the early 1990s, ten years after the birth of the economic crisis in most Latin American countries—one reason that the crisis is only a background factor, not the explanation for the direction and content of the new policies.

These political leaders are not Reagan, Thatcher, or International Monetary Fund clones. In fact, Cardoso since the 1960s and Aspe and Foxley since the 1970s have spent much time and intellectual energy, in speeches and publications, calling attention to the need for state action to address not only the problems of growth but also those of poverty. These technopols not only drew from but also helped to change the international consensus directing greater attention and channeling greater resources to social policies in the midst of economic adjustment and market liberalization. Cavallo's dissertation was a critique of the monetarist policies of Argentina's military government in the late 1970s, a critique (in which he was joined by the others studied in this chapter) of policies once favored by the international community.

From Matthei on the center-right to Cardoso on the center-left, all five leaders studied in this chapter have advocated or implemented improvements in the state's capacity to tax. "Read my lips, pay your taxes" seemed to be their shared motto. These technopols helped to change the international consensus: the state has to be recrafted, not merely reduced, nations need competent governments, not puny ones. They are neoliberals neither in their views and policies on the social deficit nor in their views and policies on the state. They forced the state to shed its fat not to kill it by starvation but to render it fit to serve the nation's interests.

These political leaders learned early on the importance of ideas and high professional standards. They internalized the norms of their respective technical professions. They returned home to build teams that would seek to conquer the state. They were classic idea carriers, who went on to implement those ideas. They had a passion for open politics and open markets and were responsible for the consequences of those beliefs and guided generally by a sense of proportion: in these ways, they were classic Weberian politicians. As scholars in Weber's sense, they became teachers to the nation. And though they came to function in bureaucracies, theirs was a more varied career pattern than that of Weberian bureaucrats and, as a result, more open to democratic politics.

As finance ministers, Aspe, Cavallo, Cardoso, and Foxley suffered to some degree from Turgot's difficult relations with constitutional government, and Aspe, Cavallo, and Matthei had worked for governments in undemocratic regimes. The trend for them over time, however, was away from the temptations of Pharaoh's Joseph and toward political openings. The tensions inherent in the role of a democratic technopol can never be entirely solved, but these leaders addressed them far better than their predecessors, or than scholars on technocrats have led us to believe.

Their superior performance stemmed less from their technical skill, high as it was, and more from their understanding of the importance of politics to their goals. These findings are consistent with Conaghan and Malloy's comparative study of Bolivia, Ecuador, and Peru—three cases in which elected civilian presidents sought to reorient economic policies in the 1980s. Political craftsmanship was the reason that Bolivia's shift toward a more market-oriented economy was much more successful than similar attempts in Ecuador and Peru. "In the final analysis [Bolivia's president Víctor] Paz Estenssoro's vision—his understanding of the intimate connection between political change and economic change—was what differentiated his administration from those of [Ecuador's president León] Febres Cordero and [Peru's president Fernando] Belaúnde. Paz's accomplishments as an economic policy maker lay in his recognition that neoliberalism required reinventing Bolivia politically as well as economically."[41] In fact, this chapter's technopols politically outperformed Paz Estenssoro's government. The Bolivian politico-economic team "did not devote much energy . . . [to] how to organize support for their policies once in power." In Argentina, Brazil, Chile, and Mexico, politico-economic leaders spent considerable time explaining their programs and building and consolidating governing coalitions.[42]

In late 1992, Richard Feinberg asked Foxley whether he accepted the label *technopol*. Foxley said he did and went on to define the term: "First is the realization that to do a good technical job in managing the economy you have to be a politician. If you do not have the capacity to articulate your vision, to persuade antagonists, to bring people around on some unpopular measure, then you are going to be a total failure. . . . Economists must not only know their economic models, but also understand politics, interests, conflicts, passions—the essence of collective life. For a brief period of time you could make most changes by decree; but to let them persist, you have to build coalitions and bring people around. You have to be a politician."[43]

Speaking for himself and his peers, Foxley sketched the procedural utility of democracy for the implementation and consolidation of market-oriented policies. And so, the economists in this study learned much about democratic politics, just as Cardoso, the only sociologist learned about markets, jointly narrowing their past differences. Democracy is useful to bring about market-oriented reforms and, above all, to make them last. Foxley's understanding of democracy does not purge it of its conflicts and passions but, instead, seeks to harness the forces of democracy to set the rules and institutions that will shape and respond to the rational expectations of economic actors. Democracy also lowers transactions costs that stem from instability or authoritarian repression.

For these reasons, Chilean democracy accomplished what Pinochet's Chicago Boys never could in an authoritarian context: it bound the nation's future to the market by means of the nation's consent. The Chicago Boys willfully ignored the search for consent and could not institutionalize their policies. Democratic technopols understand the necessity and worth of politics. Cavallo's strategic use of congressional laws to bind himself, the government, and the nation to a new program of market-oriented policies was perhaps the most dramatic example of the efficacy of democratic mechanisms in fostering a healthy market. As Foxley also told Feinberg, the Argentine and Chilean cases show that "democracy can be effective and efficient in producing change."[44] Moreover, for Cardoso and Foxley always, eventually for Matthei and Cavallo, least so for Aspe, democratic politics may also be valued for itself. Cardoso and Foxley, in particular, have devoted much of their adult lives to making democratic politics work.

To anchor political openings in markets, all five supported an opening toward international trade, though Cardoso did so with reservations. Those who served as finance ministers liberalized trade and sought to institutionalize freer trade by means of free trade agreements that would lock in the market reforms abroad just as consensual democratic agreement locked in such reforms at home. In this sense, the foundational cosmopolitanism of their ideas came to be implemented through their market internationalism.

Much remains to be done, however. Mexican politics have much room for a further opening; Brazil has barely begun to implement significant changes in economic policies. The near-term future of Argentine and Mexican policies remain somewhat uncertain, even if the overall direction of policy seems settled.

In all four countries, there is already evidence that the privatization of state enterprises has led to the consolidation of certain private and barely regulated monopolies and oligopolies; if this trend continues, privatization may turn out to be market illiberal. And yet, all five leaders seem conscious of the public loss from such concentrated private power, holding the hope that democratic governance and institutional transparency committed to markets may induce even alleged capitalists to welcome capitalism. As Aspe has often said, in the long run market policies will only work if the private sector itself is privatized and becomes less dependent on state protection, subsidies, and contracts. Democracy will prosper best if private economic power is not so concentrated. The search for market liberalism, not simply for the private ownership of the means of production, will serve the rational expectations of democrats who expect such policies from democratic technopols.

Moreover, the Mexican case reminds us that there is no easy and instant correspondence between market-oriented economic reforms and political democratization. Mexican leaders attempted the first while, at the same time, limiting the second. It remains possible, however, that Mexico, too, will feature a market-oriented economy and more democratic politics as the new millennium begins.

"The philosophers have only *interpreted* the world, in various ways," wrote Karl Marx in his eleventh thesis on Feuerbach. "The point, however, is to *change* it."[45] These technopols would agree. For them, too, the point has been to change the world in their respective countries and, they hope, to succeed more than Marx did.

5   Norms of Mexican Citizenship

Are Mexicans "Democrats"?

with James A. McCann

Are Mexicans "democrats"? A long tradition of scholarship has sought to address this question—a question that remains unanswerable to some extent and that can only be addressed in part through survey research. To understand the nature of the Mexican political system and the circumstances that foster or hinder democratic politics, one must look at political, economic, and social structures and institutions in addition to studying opinions. One should not take an exclusively national perspective but should also study local communities and their traditions.[1] Nonetheless, the beliefs of citizens do, in the aggregate, matter to an understanding of the history of a political system and the prospects for change. If political institutions were to open up more than they have, are Mexican citizens ready for democracy?

A possible explanation for Mexico's long-standing experience with authoritarian rule is that its citizens may demand it. In England in the seventeenth century, Thomas Hobbes argued in *The Leviathan* that citizens in the midst of prolonged and brutal war, and severe uncertainty about the prospects for political stability, should choose order, even authoritarian order, above all else. Heirs to one of the world's most violent revolutions, Mexicans too might prefer authoritarian order. We cannot assess, of course, whether a *Leviathan*-like social contract might have appealed to war-ravaged Mexico in the late 1920s, but as recently as the late 1950s there was some evidence of mass public support for aspects of authoritarianism in Mexican politics. From the late 1950s to the late 1980s, however, democratic politics became possible.

In this chapter we focus on certain minimal standards for democratic politics. First, we ponder the level of interest, attention, and involvement that Mexicans display with regard to politics. An apathetic public would permit routine authoritarian rule. An interested, attentive, and involved public might suffer from, but not contribute to, authoritarian rule. This first concern should help us to determine whether the extant authoritarian practices in Mexico are better explained by the structures of the political regime or by the beliefs of Mexicans. We also assess the dimensions of national pride and its complex relationship to democratic politics. National pride can serve as a ruler's weapon to stifle the opposition, but it can also enhance a nation's coherence by means of support for those aspects of politics and society that might foster democratization. Finally, we discuss the attitudes toward specific political objects that, in various settings, have been associated with the prospects for democracy. Do Mexicans prefer strong leaders as their governors, do they call for clerical participation in politics or military participation in the general tasks of government, and do they approve of the authoritarian practices of the long-governing party, the Institutional Revolutionary Party (PRI)?

We argue that democratic politics is indeed possible in Mexico. The remaining authoritarian features in Mexican politics are best explained with reference to factors other than the beliefs of Mexican citizens. Despite some ambiguous responses and some residual problems, Mexicans are ready for a more democratic polity. By the late 1980s and early 1990s, moreover, the attitudes of Mexican citizens toward politics had become much more nationalized than in the past; that is, on important questions the differences that have existed among Mexicans by education, gender, region, or social class had attenuated.

This finding bears on the scholarship on democratization. Although the values of Mexican citizens became more consistent with the practice of democratic politics, the structures of the Mexican political system changed much less. A change in public norms does not democratize a political regime in the absence of other strategic actions by political elites.[2] On the other hand, the public's demand for democratization increased markedly during the 1980s and 1990s and put pressure on elites to speed up the pace of democratization. The demand for greater democracy was a central concern of the opposition parties in the 1988, 1991, and 1994 elections. The democratization of public values makes it more likely that the political regime would some day become more democratic.

The Mexican Context

Mexico's political regime has long been undemocratic and highly centralized.[3] At its apex the president has combined the godlike majesty of the office and the impressive technical resources of the national government. Mexico's political leaders have often governed wisely and well, but to maintain their political control they have also resorted regularly to electoral fraud and abuse of power.

The strongly presidentialist character of Mexican politics has been one of its most distinctive and enduring features; it explains the regime's most authoritarian features as well as the high stakes of presidential elections.[4] In practice, presidents have chosen their own successors as well as most state governors, members of Congress, judges, heads of state enterprises, and government officials down to midlevel bureaucrats; presidents can arbitrarily remove state governors, PRI legislators, and labor union leaders who oppose them or perform poorly on the job.[5] The constitutional prohibition of the reelection of members of Congress prevents the development of a cadre of experienced and powerful legislators who might challenge the executive branch, or at least monitor it effectively.[6] This pronounced presidentialism—reproduced as executive dominance at the state and local levels—enforces discipline and loyalty.

A key political means to extend to reach of the presidency has been the ruling party, the PRI. The party dates its history to 1929, when the military chieftains and regional bosses who survived the Mexican revolution created the National Revolutionary Party (PNR) to put an end to two decades of often-brutal civil war.[7] Through 1988, the PRI and its partisan predecessors had never acknowledged the loss of a presidential election and had always controlled both houses of congress by huge majorities. Going into the 1988 national elections, the PRI held 72 percent of the seats in the Chamber of Deputies. Until 1988, the PRI had controlled all the seats in the Senate. Until 1989, no opposition party member had ever been acknowledged as having won a gubernatorial election. This combination of factors made democracy problematic at best in Mexico.[8]

The PRI's distinctiveness from the state has at times been difficult to discern. The party has long nurtured this blurring of the boundaries between itself and state; the colors and configuration of the national flag and those of the party logo are identical. Not until the 1994 presidential election did Mexico begin to acquire legislation and means of enforcement to curb government financing of PRI election activities (and even then such constraints were modest). Government officials have routinely used the power of their offices to support the PRI. The close connections between the government and the privately owned mass media have also given a marked advantage in media, especially television, coverage to the PRI and its candidates, even in the 1994 presidential election.[9]

Since the 1930s, the PRI's internal structure has been sectoral; that is, the party has been constituted through the affiliation of organizations grouped in its labor, peasant, and popular sectors. In this fashion, the PRI has co-opted and controlled the organizations that otherwise might have represented the autonomous interests of society and economy. Moreover, because of the state's central role in the economy, even business federations have rarely challenged the government or the PRI; they have preferred to work informally to advance their goals. Over the years, the government and the PRI have also combined to commit electoral fraud with impunity. As Craig and Cornelius have noted, agents of the PRI-government have stuffed ballot boxes, intimidated opposition candidates, disqualified opposition poll watchers, relocated voting places at the last minute, manipulated voter registration lists, issued multiple voting credentials to PRI supporters, manipulated voting tallies, and even nullified adverse electoral outcomes.[10]

The July 1988 national elections were a political earthquake, given that history. Carlos Salinas de Gortari was the PRI's candidate; he claimed barely more than half the votes cast. The combined opposition parties commanded 48 percent of the seats in the Chamber of Deputies, the highest proportion ever in Mexican history.

Competitive nationwide congressional elections were also held in 1991. Contrary to the expectations of many that the PRI would continue to weaken, the ruling party rebounded in these elections, winning 64 percent of the seats in the Chamber of Deputies; Carlos Salinas had become an immensely popular president who seemed to have single-handedly turned Mexico's economic fortunes around. The era of one-party government had seemed to end in 1988 only to be reborn, phoenixlike, in 1991.

The 1994 national elections were also quite competitive—and fairer than previous elections. There were, however, many remaining inequities in the electoral process. Heading the PRI ticket, Ernesto Zedillo was elected president of Mexico with just under 49 percent of the officially tabulated votes. The combined opposition captured 40 percent of the seats in the Chamber of Deputies and 25 percent in the Senate. Mexico had taken important strides along the path of democratization, but a full transition to democracy was not yet complete.

Another important aspect of Mexico's experience during the 1980s was the economic crisis. In August 1982 the world's international "debt crisis" was born in Mexico. Within a short span of time the Mexican government ran out of cash to meet its international financial obligations. It could not continue to service its international debt and so sought a major rescheduling of its international financial obligations. The international financial community, in turn, expected Mexico to adjust economically to its new circumstances and to adopt an appropriate economic stabilization program in order to become solvent once again. Mexico did so, but with severe costs to its standard of living.

Mexico's gross domestic product per capita in 1988 constant dollars fell each and every year between 1982 and 1988, from $2,192 in 1982 to $1,920 in 1988, that is, a cumulative drop of 12.4 percent.[11] This economic decline hit workers hard, and workers had long been one of the key constituencies of the official party—and one of the pillars of state authority.[12] Setting an index of average annual real wages (that is, adjusted for inflation) in manufacturing to equal 100 in 1980, such wages plummeted from 104.4 in 1982 to 71.7 in 1988. That is, real average manufacturing wages dropped by about a third in this six-year period. All citizens were hurt by the acceleration of inflation. In the late 1970s and early 1980s, Mexico's annual consumer price index (CPI) rose just below 30 percent. In 1982, inflation jumped by nearly 100 percent. The CPI decelerated to an annual rate just below 60 percent in 1984, whereupon it accelerated again to reach a peak of nearly 160 percent in 1987.[13]

A modest recovery began in the late 1980s. Gross domestic product per capita (in constant 1980 prices) grew 1.0 percent in 1989, 2.2 percent in 1990, and 1.4 percent in 1991. Given the marked decline in the preceding years, these growth rates were too modest to restore the standard of living of most Mexicans; on the eve of the August 1991 elections, Mexico's gross domestic product per capita was still below the level that it had achieved ten years earlier. The deceleration of inflation was a more impressive accomplishment. The CPI dropped each year from its high of 159.2 in 1987 to 18.8 in 1991. Real average wages in manufacturing recovered. As noted above, this index (with 1980 = 100) had reached 71.7 in 1988, but it rose steadily to 83.0 in 1991.[14]

The Scholarly Literature
General Considerations

"The development and maintenance of democracy," Larry Diamond and Juan Linz have argued, "is greatly facilitated by values and behavioral dispositions (particularly at the elite level) of compromise, flexibility, tolerance, conciliation, moderation, and restraint."[15] Seymour Martin Lipset has emphasized a similar point, though he anchors it in the recognition of specific citizen rights. "Democracy requires," in his view, "the acceptance by the citizenry and political elites of principles underlying freedom of speech, media, assembly, religion, of the rights of opposition parties, of the rule of law, of human rights, and the like."[16]

There is a lively scholarly debate on whether there are prerequisites for the establishment and consolidation of democracy. For example, Terry Karl has argued that the search for preconditions for democracy is "futile"; instead, she suggests, the study of democratic transitions ought to focus on elite "strategic interactions," which "help to determine whether political democracy will emerge and survive."[17] One often- mentioned prerequisite is political culture or, more specifically, democratic norms. In a related vein, Edward Muller and Mitchell Seligson have shown that interpersonal trust is unrelated to changes in a country's level of democracy; thus such attitudes could not be a major cause of democracy.[18]

We agree with the position sketched by Diamond and Linz: "Historically, the choice of democracy by political elites clearly preceded . . . the presence of democratic values among the general public or other elites." On the other hand, they also argue, "democratic culture helps to maintain" democracy. Thus the relationship between political attitudes and structures is "reciprocal."[19] This view was articulated much earlier by Gabriel Almond and Sidney Verba in their work on the civic culture in five countries (including Mexico): "It is quite clear that political culture is treated as both an independent and a dependent variable, as causing structure and as being caused by it."[20] Where the values typically found in democracies are strong and widespread, democracy's eventual emergence and, especially, consolidation are more likely.

In this chapter, we argue that the emergence and consolidation of democracy in Mexico are facilitated by the shift in the public's values but that such values by themselves have not caused democracy to emerge in the Mexican political system. We are conscious that this research does not exhaust the discussion of democratization in Mexico—the role of the state, the parties, and the behavior of elites matter greatly as well—but we believe equally firmly that no discussion of democracy can ignore the beliefs and behavior of the nation's citizens.

Scholarship on Public Opinion in Mexico

In a lecture delivered in 1960, the late Daniel Cosío Villegas, distinguished Mexican historian, focused on "the situation of the government in Mexican society." He argued that the government's "political power is almost unlimited" and vested in specific leaders: "the President in all the Republic . . . the governors in their respective States as regards local matters; and . . . the municipal authorities in their respective jurisdictions as regards the minor matters that they manage." He wondered about the "basis" for this concentration of power in a few very strong leaders and argued that it stemmed in part from "the laws themselves, since the federal Constitution gives the executive very broad powers, and the local constitutions also give very broad powers to the governors of the States" but also in part from "the fact that when legal power does not suffice . . . the law is simply ignored." Cosío Villegas observed that in "a real democracy" one corrective for this use and abuse of power was the role of the courts and another was a "public opinion" that "denounces the abuse and compels the authority to correct it." In Mexico, he noted with sadness, "these two checks function sporadically and ineffectively."[21]

The year before Cosío Villegas's lecture, Almond and Verba surveyed the opinions of Mexicans who lived in communities with populations larger than ten thousand. In their pathbreaking book, *The Civic Culture*, they characterized Mexican politics as follows: "What have been most striking in the Mexican pattern of political culture are the imbalances and inconsistencies. Mexico is lowest of all five countries [the United States, the United Kingdom, West Germany, Italy, and Mexico] in the frequency with which impact and significance are attributed to government and in its citizens' expectation of equal and considerate treatment at the hands of the bureaucracy and police. At the same time, the frequency with which Mexicans express pride in their political system is considerably higher than that of the Germans or Italians." And they record that "the objects of this pride tend predominantly to be the Mexican Revolution and the presidency." They go on to note that "what sense of participation there is appears to be relatively independent of a sense of satisfaction with governmental output."[22]

In this chapter, we compare responses to questions first asked in 1959 to the responses to identical questions repeated nationwide by the Gallup poll in Mexico in 1986, 1988, and 1991. We also make use of the fine survey conducted by Miguel Basáñez in 1983.[23] Our purpose is to assess the trends in the responses to questions that shed light on the citizenry's normative orientations toward politics as well as to consider the attitudinal outcome in the early 1990s. In particular, is there greater support for democratic practices since 1959 and are there variations beyond those noted by Almond and Verba?

Education and Gender

In addition to the explicit cross-national aspects of their research design, Almond and Verba focused on some intracountry sources of variation. They found that educational attainment had the most important demographic effect on political attitudes. Among other findings, the better educated person felt freer to discuss politics with a wider range of people, was more likely to follow politics and to pay attention to election campaigns, was more likely to feel capable of influencing the government, and was more likely to believe that other people are trustworthy and helpful. Almond and Verba also found that gender made a difference in political attitudes, though this varied by country and by level of education. In Mexico, women were much less likely to discuss politics, to follow political campaigns, to be aware of and participate in politics, or to feel that they could influence government and politics. In contrast, Almond and Verba found that social class did not matter much once education was considered on its own terms, in part because educational differences captured the effects of class differences. They also found that church attendance did not matter much. Their analysis did not focus at all on subnational regional variations.[24]

The Demographic Underpinnings of Political Participation

In their extensive sociological investigation in 1982 of the values held by Mexicans on various topics, Alberto Hernández Medina, Luis Narro Rodríguez, and their associates focused part of their attention on certain political values. Although they found that only about 4 percent of Mexicans reported being politically active, an additional 43 percent considered themselves interested though not active. Consistent with Almond and Verba's findings, women were much less likely to be interested or to participate in politics; university graduates as well as those of higher socioeconomic status were much more likely to be interested and to participate in politics than those who had not completed primary schooling or whose socioeconomic status was lower. Age did not make a difference in the likelihood of interest or participation.[25] More general sociological research by Mexican scholars suggests as well that education and gender help to shape important values held by Mexicans on a wide array of topics.[26]

Democracy's Meanings and Social Class Variation

In their study of politics in the city of Jalapa (Veracruz state) in 1966, Richard Fagen and William Tuohy found that Jalapeños across social classes were nearly unanimous in their support for democracy as the best form of government, for the election of public officials by majority vote, and for according an equal chance to every citizen to influence government policy. But when they asked beyond what they called these "platitudinous formulations" about the rights of minorities, opposition groups, women, and illiterates to free expression and the franchise, they found a much lower acceptance of democratic practices, revealing greater complexity in public opinion. Unlike Almond and Verba, but like Hernández Medina and Narro Rodríguez, Fagen and Tuohy found that social class made a difference. The lower classes were more supportive of reform-oriented economic programs but less supportive of democratic political practices as identified by Fagen and Tuohy.[27] This last observation is generally consistent with the broader cross-national argument made years earlier by Seymour Martin Lipset about what he called "working-class authoritarianism."[28]

Democracy's Likelihood and the Leader-Law Relationship

Another aspect of this complex picture was explored in 1969 by Rafael Segovia in his fine study of the political socialization of Mexican schoolchildren. Segovia found ample evidence of authoritarian attitudes among these children, though he also noted that the likelihood of democratic orientations increased markedly as levels of education increased, an observation consistent with that of Almond and Verba and Hernández Medina and Narro Rodríguez. Segovia found that the image of the president of the republic was more associated with his maintenance of public order than with his representativeness of public opinion; the president is most admired for his capacity to command, for his strength far more than for his benevolence. Moreover, as Cosío Villegas might also have expected, in the view of the schoolchildren, the law "c'est le fait du prince" (is the prince's business)."[29]

Authoritarianism and Problem Solving?

In his comprehensive study of the migrant poor in Mexico city in 1970, Wayne Cornelius found that there was "a positive relationship between authoritarianism (defined here as a preference for strong, autocratic leadership and a low level of tolerance for minority opinions) and political participation." Those migrants who were participants in a broad array of endeavors were especially likely to exhibit such tendencies. Cornelius hypothesized that this could derive from the action of local bosses, or caciques, who spent a good deal of time in political mobilization. Cornelius also suggested, however, that support for these local bosses could be a rational way for urban migrant poor people to solve some of their community's problems: "Demonstrated performance in securing benefits for the community is particularly important," he noted, as a way to explain how bosses retained support.[30]

Economic Stakes

Henry Landsberger and Bobby Gierisch studied various aspects of peasant participation in one of Mexico's most important agricultural regions, La Laguna, in the northern states of Durango and Coahuila. Levels of participation were found to have been quite high, but they were not explained by value systems: "Neither modern values, nor modernizing experience, nor even parental socialization in any direct sense, seem to predict the individual's propensity to participate. What does so is above all the size of the individual's economic stake. . . . The less the stake, the less the propensity to participate." The second best explanation was the by now familiar level of education, including mass media involvement.[31]

A Democratic Political Culture, Gender, Education, and Social Class

In 1978–79, John Booth and Mitchell Seligson studied the political attitudes of middle-class and working-class Mexicans in seven cities, focusing on support for widespread political participation and for the right to dissent. They found rather strong and consistent democratic, libertarian support for all but one of the eleven items measured. They also found that in all but one case workers were on the liberal democratic side of the spectrum, though they were less supportive of those practices than were middle-class Mexicans. In this sense, though social class made a difference, there was no basis to speak of working-class authoritarianism. Women were less supportive of democratic liberties than men; the difference was statistically significant but not large. Education played its familiar, key role, dwarfing the effect of social class (which by itself was not statistically significant).[32]

In brief, pertinent scholarly work has focused generally on an assessment of authoritarian or democratic values. Our review of such related scholarship suggests that support for authoritarianism may have weakened between the 1960s and the early 1980s, perhaps to the point at which majority support would exist for democratic values. Education remained an important source of explanation for variance in support for or opposition to authoritarian values; gender seemed to matter as well. Some studies suggest that economic stakes and instrumental motivations may explain the range of variation in support for authoritarian values. Religiosity did not seem to explain authoritarian propensities. There was no consensus on whether social class was a helpful explanation for such variance.[33]

Unlike these studies of political culture, Miguel Basáñez's studies of electoral behavior in the 1980s suggest that both regionalism and social class are important explanations of voter attitudes. The differences by region, albeit noteworthy, are more modest than the differences among occupational categories.[34]

Describing the Pattern of Beliefs
Political Interest, Attentiveness, and Talkativeness

Significant portions of the Mexican electorate express an interest in politics and in political campaigns. As evident in table 5-1, about two-fifths of the electorate expresses some to great interest in politics during a presidential election year (1988); this proportion is nearly identical to that found by Hernández Medina and Narro Rodríguez for the 1982 presidential elections. During the 1988 presidential campaign, nearly half of the electorate gave "some" to "great" attention to the campaign.

More surprising is the relative constancy of political interest and attentiveness. When there was no national election (1986), 35 percent of the electorate expressed "some" or "great" political interest. When there was a national election for Congress but not for the presidency (1991), 33 percent expressed a comparable level of political interest. And when there was a national election for both presidency and Congress (1988), the level of interest rose but only to 39 percent. In short, not fewer than one-third of Mexi-

Table 5-1. Political Interest, Campaign Attentiveness,
and Sources of Political Information (percent)

	1986	1988	1991
Political interest			
Great	11	16	12
Some	24	23	21
Little	35	32	34
None	30	29	33
Attention given to the current political campaign			
Great	—	30	25
Some	—	19	19
Little	—	35	39
None		15	17
Media used to obtain political information			
Television	—	92	—
Radio	—	75	—
Newspapers/magazines	—	54	—
International newspapers	—	3	—
Cable	—	1	—

Source: *New York Times* Mexico survey, 1986; IMOP S.A. (Gallup) polls, May 1988 and July 1991.
Note: N = 1,899 (weighted, 1986), 2,960 (1988), and 3,053 (1991).

cans express political interest at any time, with that proportion rising only during a presidential campaign and then just slightly. So too with attention to a current political campaign. During the 1988 presidential campaign, 49 percent paid "some" to "great" attention to it; during the 1991 congressional election, the comparable statistic was 44 percent. Clearly, short-term electoral stimuli have little impact on level of political interest and campaign attentiveness, which appear to be both relatively high and constant.

In the late 1980s, the level of political interest expressed by Mexicans was similar to that expressed by citizens of several advanced industrial democracies. Figure 5-1 presents data for Mexico's 1988 presidential election (the percentage of those expressing "great" interest in politics) along with data for West European democracies for 1989 and for the United States during the 1988 presidential election.[35] As the evidence reported in figure 5-1 shows, the level of political interest expressed in Mexico in 1988 was comparable to levels of political interest in Germany and Greece; it was exceeded but only slightly by levels of political interest in Denmark and the United States. The level of political interest was higher in Mexico than in the Netherlands, the United Kingdom, France, Canada, Ireland, Belgium, Spain, Italy, and Portugal.

Nearly all Mexicans obtain political information from television, which underscores the influence of the country's only important television network, TELEVISA (table 5-1). Only 8 percent of Mexicans claimed not to use television to obtain political information. To be sure, the fact that Mexicans obtain much of their political information from television makes them similar to citizens in advanced industrial democracies (for example, in the 1988 General Social Survey only 3 percent of U.S. respondents claimed never to watch television). What is strikingly different in the case of Mexico, however, is the disproportionate reliance on television as the medium of choice to obtain information. Whereas only 5 percent of U.S. respondents to the

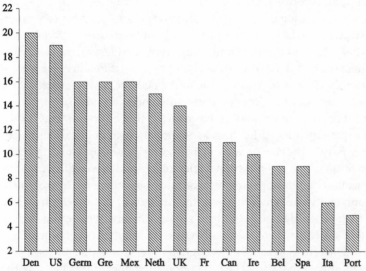

Figure 5-1. Mexican Political Interest in Comparative Perspective (percentage expressing great interest)

Source: Euro-Barometer Study, no. 31, March-April 1989 (data made available through the Inter-University Consortium for Political and Social Research, ICPSR study no. 9322); United States General Social Survey, 1972–91 (National Opinion Research Center of the University of Chicago, data made available through ICPSR study no. 9710); Canadian National Election Study, 1988 (originally collected by the Institute for Social Research, under the direction of Richard Johnston et al., data made available through ICPSR study no. 9386); IMOP S.A. (Gallup) poll in Mexico, May 1988.

Note: Euro-Barometer smallest country N = 991. In the U.S. General Social Survey, the item on political interest appears in 1987; N = 353. Canadian National Election Study N = 3,609. IMOP S.A. N = 2,960.

General Social Survey claimed never to read newspapers, 46 percent of Mexican respondents claimed never to do so.[36]

What has happened to the level of attentiveness to political campaigns over time? Unfortunately, we cannot answer with precision because the 1959 Civic Culture survey was conducted at a time when there was no nationwide campaign under way in Mexico. Nonetheless, the evidence in table 5-2 suggests a significant jump in the level of attentiveness between 1959 and the two more recent surveys. Given the discussion, above, about what appeared to be relatively high and constant levels of political interest from the mid-1980s to the early 1990s—a level of interest that held up even in 1986, when there was no national election—the difference between 1959, on the one hand, and 1988 and 1991, on the other, can be plausibly attributed to change over time rather than to the accidents of campaign timing.

The most important finding is the trend toward the nationalization of Mexican politics between the late 1950s and the early 1990s. In 1959 there was very wide regional variance in attentiveness to political campaigns (high in the Federal District and low in northern Mexico). By 1988 and 1991 those differences had narrowed: the north remained less attentive to campaigns than the rest of the country, but other regional differences were modest. Curiously, central Mexico outside of the Federal District scored at the top in both 1988 and 1991, though these differences are small.

As mentioned, Almond and Verba reported that education was an important explanation for differences in attentiveness to political campaigns and other issues. We concur with their findings for 1959. The differences between those with a secondary education or less and those with a preparatory education had disappeared by 1988 and 1991, however. In 1988 those with a university education followed the campaign with much greater intensity than other Mexicans, but by 1991 the university educated had reverted to their earlier level of attentiveness. In 1991, education helped to explain attentiveness to campaigns but to a lesser extent than in 1959.

Almond and Verba also called attention to gender differences, as did Hernández Medina and Narro Rodríguez and Booth and Seligson. The evidence in table 5-2 suggests the gradual disappearance of the gender gap. Once again we concur with Almond and Verba's findings for 1959. Booth and Seligson's research in the late 1970s indicated that gender made some—but not a major—difference in explaining political attitudes; pertinent to the finding in table 5-2 for 1988, the Booth and Seligson observation serves as an intermediate link in this long behavioral chain. By the 1991 congressional election, gender differences did not seem to explain variance in attentiveness to the campaign at all.

In 1959 there was a large social class difference in attentiveness to politi-

Table 5-2. Changes in Attentiveness to Political Campaigns
(percentage expressing great interest)

	1959	1988	1991
Whole sample	15	30	25
Region			
North	9	28	21
Central	12	33	29
South	19	29	23
Federal District	24	30	25
Education			
Secondary or less	13	27	23
Preparatory	25	27	24
University	24	40	29
Age			
18–25	10	24	21
26–35	16	31	26
36–50	19	33	26
51+	14	36	26
Gender			
Female	11	27	24
Male	22	33	25
Class			
Upper	23	32	23
Lower/middle	14	29	25
Church attendance			
Weekly	13	28	27
Less than weekly	20	32	23

Source: Mexican component of the *Civic Culture* study; IMOP S.A.
(Gallup) polls, May 1988 and July 1991.

  Note: N = 1,295 (weighted, 1959), 2,960 (1988), and 3,053 (1991).

cal campaigns. That finding is consistent with Fagen and Tuohy's 1966 study
in Jalapa. Hernández Medina and Narro Rodríguez also found that social
class helped to explain variance in political interest in 1982, though the differences were modest. Basáñez reported that social class mattered in shaping electoral preferences in elections during the 1980s. The evidence in table
5-2 indicates, however, that social class differences in campaign attentiveness were quite minor in 1988 and 1991.

  Religiosity, measured by church attendance, was also an important factor in 1959, but its significance seemed to have weakened by 1988 and 1991.
In 1991, moreover, weekly church attenders were more attentive to the cam-

paign, reversing the findings for previous years. And except for the lower campaign attentiveness of voters between the ages of eighteen and twenty-five—typical of first-time voters in most countries—age has never made much difference in explaining campaign attentiveness.

The relationship among these variables when they are included in the same multivariate summary regression equation is shown in table 5-3. In each case we seek to "predict" interest in political campaigns by means of the demographic factors reported in table 5-2. With some exceptions the results of this more comprehensive analysis are consistent with the discussion above.

Regionalism, education, and gender are statistically significant explanations for interest in political campaigns in all three surveys, but their importance lessened between the late 1950s and the early 1990s. In 1959, regional differences clearly demarcated different geographic political environments, but by the late 1980s and early 1990s residence in the Federal District no longer separated its citizens from the rest of the country on this dimension (e.g., the regression coefficient for the Federal District was no longer statistically significant). Education was a consistently important factor, but it had become less important by the late 1980s and early 1990s (the coefficient for education was cut in half between 1959 and the later surveys). The pattern for gender is the same as for education, namely, important throughout but markedly less so by the late 1980s and early 1990s. (This finding contradicts the inference drawn from table 5-2 simply because the multiple statistical controls present in table 5-3 allow us to see the enduring though declining importance of gender as an explanatory variable.)

Consistent with the previous discussion, the importance of social class as an explanatory factor for interest in campaigns weakened steadily over time until it became insignificant in 1991. Age mattered only in the 1988 election but was otherwise insignificant. The finding for religiosity in table 5-3 is somewhat different from the inference drawn from table 5-2. The importance of religiosity did weaken between the late 1950s and the late 1980s, but in the early 1990s it appears to have become significant again, though this time because churchgoers had become more interested in campaigns.

In conclusion, by the early 1990s the Mexican political system had become more homogeneous in terms of the political interests of its citizens. Whereas in 1959 there were marked regional, educational, gender, social class, and religious differences, by 1988 and 1991 nearly all of these differences had weakened. In 1991 there was still a regional gap, albeit a modest one, between the north and the center. The differences in education and gender still mattered but had narrowed greatly; social class had become statistically insignificant. Only religiosity had become more important as churchgoer

Table 5-3. Predicting Interest in Campaigns: A Multivariate Model

	1959	1988	1991
North	−.11 (.05) *	−.07 (.03) *	−.09 (.03) **
South	.05 (.06)	−.06 (.04)	.05 (.03)
Federal District	.21 (.05) **	−.06 (.04)	.05 (.03)
Education	.16 (.05) **	.09 (.02) **	.08 (.02) **
Age	−.17 (.10)	.27 (.07) **	.03 (.06)
Female	−.29 (.04) **	−.08 (.02) **	−.06 (.02) **
Class	.11 (.03) **	.06 (.02) **	−.02 (.02)
Religiosity	−.08 (.04) *	−.03 (.02)	.09 (.02) **
Constant term	1.76 (.15) **	1.96 (.07) **	1.82 (.06) **
Adjusted R^2	.11	.03	.02

Source: Mexican component of the Civic Culture study; IMOP S.A. (Gallup) polls, May 1988 and July 1991.

Note: The coefficients above are unstandardized linear regression estimates. Standard errors appear in parentheses. N = 1,206 (weighted, 1959), 2,926 (1988), and 2,956 (1991). The scaling of each variable is consistent across samples.

* = $p < .05$.   ** = $p < .01$.

interest in campaigns rose. Mexico had, indeed, changed politically during this third of the century. Its people had become more interested in political campaigns, and the demographic differences in their level of interest had generally narrowed (the proportion of the total variance in political interest explained by these combined demographic factors dropped from 11 percent in 1959 to 2 percent in 1991, as measured by the adjusted R^2). Mexicans had become one people—and a more politically attentive one.

If Mexicans had become more attentive to political campaigns, and more uniformly so, had they also begun to talk more openly about their political views? The data in table 5-4 suggest that the answer is yes. In 1959, 19 percent of Mexicans talked freely about politics with anyone; in 1991, that statistic had risen to 27 percent. The likelihood of speaking freely about politics with everyone rose for women and for men, for each of the country's regions, for each of the educational, religious, and social class categories, and for each age group. Such a consistent pattern of increase is remarkable.

There is, however, greater complexity to this pattern of change. In 1959 the Federal District's citizens were the most reluctant to discuss politics with anyone. The proportion of Federal District citizens willing to engage in that kind of behavior had more than doubled by 1991, when the district led the country. Similarly, in 1959 the most highly educated were the most reticent to discuss politics with anyone. By 1991 the willingness of the most highly

Table 5-4. Willingness to Discuss Politics (percent)

	Talk Freely about Politics with Anyone		Never Talk about Politics	
	1959	1991	1959	1991
Whole sample	19	27	21	20
Region				
North	20	25	23	18
Central	20	23	20	24
South	20	30	23	18
Federal District	14	32	19	21
Education				
Secondary or less	20	24	22	24
Preparatory	15	33	11	18
University	14	32	11	12
Age				
18–25	22	29	17	19
26–35	14	28	19	19
36–50	20	25	18	21
51+	20	28	29	24
Gender				
Female	18	25	25	23
Male	20	29	13	28
Class				
Upper	14	25	13	16
Lower/middle	20	28	22	21
Church attendance				
Weekly	19	27	22	21
Less than weekly	17	27	18	20

Source: Mexican component of the *Civic Culture* study; IMOP S.A. (Gallup) poll, July 1991.

Note: N = 1,295 (weighted, 1959) and 3,053 (1991).

educated to talk politics with anyone had more than doubled. It is as if the best-informed Mexicans in 1959 might have known that it could be imprudent to talk about politics with anyone; such reluctance had declined markedly by the early 1990s.

Unlike our findings with regard to political interest and attentiveness to political campaigns, the differences among categories of citizens in their willingness to discuss politics with anyone had not narrowed between 1959 and 1991, but they were not wide in either year. For example, the gap be-

tween the Federal District and other parts of central Mexico in the willingness to discuss politics with anyone was about the same in 1959 as in 1991
(though the gap had widened a bit, and the rank order had been reversed).
Similarly, the gap between educational categories remained fairly similar
(though widening and with the rank order also being reversed). Differences
by gender and church attendance were quite narrow in both years, but
the gender gap widened slightly while the religious gap disappeared altogether. Differences among age groups also disappeared, but they had also
been modest. The only category where the gap narrowed appreciably was
social class.

Finally, there also developed a wider political stratification between 1959
and 1991, namely, the proportion of Mexicans who never talk about politics remained unchanged, while the proportion who talk quite freely about
politics increased. Among these politically uncommunicative Mexicans,
there was a trend toward somewhat greater uniformity from 1959 to 1991.
Differences narrowed among age groups, among educational, social class,
and religious categories, and between men and women; they widened only
slightly among regions. This greater homogeneity among the politically
uncommunicative and the unchanged demographic variance among the
politically talkative indicate that the differences that widened between the
late 1950s and early 1990s were political, not sociological. For reasons that
we observe but cannot explain, Mexicans differed more in 1991 than in 1959
in their willingness to talk about politics; these differences are not seemingly related to demographic factors.

In short, Mexicans have become more willing to discuss politics. Mexicans from all walks of life have become more politically talkative. The
best-informed Mexicans—those who reside in the Federal District or have
a university education—have become much less politically suspicious. The
likelihood of discussing politics is not explained by sociological categories;
that is, poorer or less well educated Mexicans are not markedly less likely
to discuss politics than those with greater resources. Thus the greater gap
among Mexicans in 1991 in terms of their willingness to discuss politics is
itself an eminently political phenomenon, one that we deem favorable for
the future of democratic politics.

National Pride

What, then, of national pride in Mexico? Despite the country's severe economic difficulties in the 1980s, Mexicans expressed great pride in Mexico in
both 1988 and 1991. (In each case Mexicans were asked whether they agreed
with the statement, "I am very proud of my country." Table 5-5 reports those
who agreed or strongly agreed with that statement.) The increase in pride

Table 5-5. Pride in Mexico (percentage expressing pride)

	1988	1991
Whole sample	89	96
Region		
North	88	97
Central	92	96
South	92	96
Federal District	84	94
Education		
Secondary or less	91	96
Preparatory	87	96
University	83	94
Age		
18–25	86	95
26–35	89	96
36–50	91	96
51+	91	96
Gender		
Female	89	96
Male	88	96
Class		
Upper	91	95
Lower/middle	88	96
Church attendance		
Weekly	91	97
Less than weekly	87	95

Source: IMOP S.A. (Gallup) polls, May 1988 and July 1991.

Note: N = 2,960 (1988) and 3,053 (1991).

between those two dates was also marked, perhaps reflecting the Mexican economy's modest recovery during those years. This increase in pride between 1988 and 1991 is evident for all regions, for all educational, social class, and religious categories, for all age groups, and for both men and women. This uniform increase in national pride is extraordinary.

In 1988 there were some demographic differences in the likelihood of expressing pride in Mexico. Residents of the Federal District and the university educated were less likely to express pride in Mexico. Younger Mexicans were also somewhat less likely to express such pride. The differences by gender, social, class, and religiosity did not matter. By 1991, however, all such differences had disappeared. There was, alas, "national unity" concerning national pride.

In the 1989 Euro-Barometer study, few countries in the European Community had a measure of citizen pride as high as Mexico's in 1988, and none of the largest European countries did. For example, only 65 percent of West Germans said that they were "extremely" or "moderately" proud to be German; the comparable statistics were 78 percent for France and 81 percent for the United Kingdom.[37]

We turn, then, to a related question, namely, an examination of pride in *political* attributes. Table 5-6 shows the extent to which the source of pride was specifically political (the state, the Constitution, democracy, or equality in Mexico). These views surfaced in response to similar open-ended questions that were asked in both 1959 and 1991. Whereas in 1959, 28 percent of Mexicans expressed pride in such political attributes, that statistic had risen to 35 percent in 1991.

This increase in pride in the Mexican political system was especially noteworthy in northern Mexico and among women and upper-class respondents, but increased political pride was manifest for all age groups and all social class and religious categories. There was a slight drop among preparatory-school-educated Mexicans and among residents of the Federal District, basically no change among men, but an increase in all other regions and in the other two educational categories.

No doubt the legitimacy of Mexico's political system was sharply contested in 1988 and, to a lesser degree, in 1991, but there is also no doubt that a significant proportion of Mexicans volunteered that they were proud of Mexico's political institutions, practices, and outcomes. Such feelings of political pride or the more expansive national pride were not themselves hostile to democratic politics, for Mexicans chose to name constitutional government and democracy among the reasons for their pride. Nonetheless, the specific content of the views of Mexicans about democratic institutions and practices needs to be assessed; to that we now turn.

Political Leaders, Institutions, and Practices

In 1959, Almond and Verba asked Mexicans whether they agreed with the statement, "A few strong leaders would do more for Mexico than all the laws and talk." That question was repeated in the 1988 and 1991 surveys; the results are presented in table 5-7. A majority of Mexicans agreed with such a statement even in 1991, but there was a substantial decline in agreement with that statement since 1959 and even some decline since 1988. Over time, Mexicans have become more attached to the rule of law, though there remains considerable room for improvement.

Table 5-6. Pride in the Mexican Political System
(percentage expressing pride)

	1959	1991
Whole sample	28	35
Region		
North	23	38
Central	31	39
South	26	34
Federal District	32	28
Education		
Secondary or less	27	33
Preparatory	39	36
University	38	41
Age		
18–25	26	32
26–35	26	34
36–50	33	37
51+	28	37
Gender		
Female	23	33
Male	38	37
Class		
Upper	34	48
Lower/middle	28	33
Church attendance		
Weekly	29	37
Less than weekly	27	33

Source: Mexican component of the Civic Culture study;
IMOP S.A. (Gallup) poll, July 1991.
   Note: N = 1,295 (weighted, 1959) and 3,053 (1991).

From 1959 to 1988, with one important exception, and again from 1988 to
1991, the preference for strong leaders declined for each of the categories in
table 5-7; that is, with the passing of years such preference for strong leaders fell for both men and women, all age groups and regions, all religious
and social class categories, and all educational categories except for the university educated. There was a stunning increase in the likelihood that university-educated Mexicans would prefer strong leaders in 1988 and even in
1991, as compared to 1959.

In 1959 by far the single best explanation for variance in the preference
for strong leaders was education; the university educated were much less

Table 5-7. "A Few Strong Leaders Would Do More for Mexico than All the Laws and Talk" (percentage agreeing)

	1959	1988	1991
Whole sample	67	59	54
Region			
North	62	53	49
Central	68	61	60
South	68	61	51
Federal District	72	64	56
Education			
Secondary or less	69	61	55
Preparatory	65	58	54
University	38	57	51
Age			
18–25	63	59	55
26–35	66	62	53
36–50	70	60	55
51+	69	55	53
Gender			
Female	67	62	55
Male	67	57	54
Class			
Upper	66	59	54
Lower/middle	67	60	54
Church attendance			
Weekly	69	62	55
Less than weekly	66	57	53

Source: Mexican component of the Civic Culture study; IMOP S.A. (Gallup) polls, May 1988 and July 1991.

Note: N = 1,295 (weighted, 1959), 2,960 (1988), and 3,053 (1991).

likely to express such preferences. The other important factor was region, with citizens from northern Mexico being less likely to prefer such strong leaders than residents of the Federal District. Younger Mexicans were also less likely to prefer strong leaders. Gender, social class, and religiosity hardly mattered.

By 1988, region had become the single most important explanation, with the north still remaining the region least likely to prefer strong leaders. Education still mattered, but much less than in 1959, as an explanation for variance in the preference for strong leaders. Some modest differences had appeared in terms of gender and religiosity, but social class continued to be unimportant. Age had an interesting role. The group over age fifty-one in 1988 and in 1991 is the same, of course, as those below age twenty-five in 1959. In all three surveys these citizens consistently showed the lowest preference for strong leaders. Their formative political socialization experiences endured over three decades.

By 1991, age, gender, social class, and religious differences explained none of the variance in the preference for strong leaders. Education's explanatory importance continued to decline. Region had become the only important explanation, but it was important in a new way. Whereas the preference for strong leaders had declined markedly over time in the north, the south, and the Federal District, it had declined much less in other parts of central Mexico, which had become for the first time the region with the strongest support for such strong leaders.

The roots of Mexican authoritarianism is assessed by means of a multivariate model in table 5-8. Its results are consistent with the preceding analysis.

Education was the most important factor in the variance in authoritarian attitudes in 1959, but its importance had declined markedly by 1988 (the regression coefficient is much smaller), and by 1991 it had become statistically insignificant. Age was statistically significant only in 1959 and gender and religiosity only in 1988; they did not contribute to the explanation over time. Regionalism rose in importance from 1959 to 1988, and by 1991 it was the only factor that helped to explain variance in authoritarian attitudes. Because education was so important as an explanation for authoritarian attitudes in the late 1950s, we focus on it more directly in table 5-9, for which we computed the hypothetical expected probabilities of preferring "a few strong leaders" over "all the laws and talk." In table 5-9 the expected probabilities calculation controls for all the other variables included in table 5-8 so that only education varies; thus its effect can be seen most plainly.

Consistent with the previous discussion, education made a marked difference in 1959, less difference in 1988, and hardly any difference in 1991. But this more refined analysis permits us to reflect upon an important analytical point. The probability that a Mexican with limited education would prefer strong leaders fell from 78 percent in 1959 to 59 percent in 1991 once all other statistical controls apply. In the same vein and following the same calculation, the probability that Mexicans with intermediate levels of education would prefer strong leaders fell from 66 percent in 1959 to 57 percent in 1991. Consistent with our inference from table 5-7, the probability that university-educated Mexicans would prefer strong leaders did rise from 1959 to 1988, while it fell back in 1991. But once the full panoply of statistical controls is applied, the increase over time in the likelihood of such pref-

Table 5-8. The Roots of Mexican Authoritarianism:
A Multivariate Model

	1959	1988	1991
North	−.39 (.18) *	−.63 (.12) **	−.47 (.11) **
South	−.02 (.23)	−.33 (.12) **	−.36 (.13) **
Federal District	.32 (.20)	−.11 (.12)	−.28 (.11) *
Education	−.62 (.16) **	−.17 (.06) **	−.09 (.05)
Age	.08 (.04) *	−.02 (.02)	.01 (.02)
Female	.19 (.15)	.26 (.08) **	.11 (.08)
Class	.16 (.12)	−.01 (.06)	−.09 (.06)
Religiosity	.04 (.15)	.13 (.06) *	.02 (.07)
Constant term	1.13 (.52) **	.81 (.23) **	.73 (.22) **

Source: Mexican component of the *Civic Culture* study; IMOP S.A.
(Gallup) polls, May 1988 and July 1991.

Note: The coefficients above are maximum likelihood logit estimates.
For each year, the dependent variable was coded 1 if respondents preferred "strong leaders" over "all the laws and talk" and 0 otherwise.
Standard errors appear in parentheses. Initially the *LLF* equaled −768.7
(1959), −1,875.7 (1988), and −1,924.9 (1991); at convergence the *LLF* equaled
−597.2 (1959), −1,723.4 (1988), and −1,874.3 (1991). The model correctly
predicted 76.2 percent (1959), 65.3 percent (1988), and 57.1 percent (1991)
of the cases. $N = 1,109$ (weighted, 1959), 2,706 (1988), and 2,777 (1991). The
scaling of each variable is consistent across samples.
    * $= p < .05$.   ** $= p < .01$.

erences by university-educated Mexicans turns out to be quite modest and
therefore much less alarming.

Returning to the arguments in an earlier section, we can also affirm with
confidence that these data provide no support for a "working-class authoritarianism" argument. Social class was never a useful predictor of attitudes
toward strong leaders, and education—a close proxy for social class—came
to matter less and less as an explanatory factor.

On the other hand, we cannot quite gauge what the preference for strong
leaders means in the late 1980s and early 1990s. In 1959, education was the
overriding explanation for variance in leadership preferences. An argument
about political culture might have sufficed. In more recent years, arguments
about education, or even about regional subcultures, are much less persuasive. Those who might claim, for example, that the north is the cradle of a
democratic Mexico would be unable to explain why the differences in 1991
between northern and southern respondents are so modest, given that the
south does not have the reputation for democratic political practices. It is
possible, but we cannot prove it, that the preference for strong leaders in the
late 1980s and early 1990s might respond to the perceived need for such

Table 5-9. Educational Levels and Expected Probabilities of
Preferring "A Few Strong Leaders" over "All the Laws and Talk"

	1959	1988	1991
University	.51	.59	.55
Secondary	.66	.64	.57
Less than secondary	.78	.67	.59

Note: These probabilities were derived from the equations in table 5-8, where all independent variables except education have been set to their mean values.

leaders to rescue Mexico from its economic and political crises of those times. If so, then the reason for the remaining high preference for strong leaders could be instrumental: the tough-minded, problem-solving leader of whom Wayne Cornelius has written. We leave this hypothesis as speculation for further research.

Beyond the preference for a strong leader, we were interested in the views of Mexicans about the proper political role of institutions that are themselves not internally democratic. Table 5-10 records the responses to two questions asked in 1983, namely, should the Roman Catholic Church participate in politics, and should the military participate in government? These questions address in part the need for a democratic political system to retain its autonomy from institutions that are not internally democratic. Thus we move here from abstract democratic norms to consider the more practical question of the state's autonomy.

In the Mexican context, these questions may evoke memories of a highly conflictive national history. Armies fought each other during Mexico's revolution earlier in the twentieth century. Warlords shaped Mexican politics at least into the 1930s. One aspect of Mexico's civil wars was a religious conflict, which in the late 1920s was the central factor in the so-called Cristero war. This specific Mexican context may help to explain the different responses to the questions about clerical and military involvement in politics. Just as important, the questions address quite different themes. The church is part of civil society, not of the government; we seek to understand what Mexicans believe about the appropriateness of church engagement in politics. The military is a part of the state; we seek to understand what Mexicans believe about the appropriateness of a generalized military involvement in the government.

In 1983 two-thirds of Mexicans opposed participation in politics by the Roman Catholic Church. Fewer than one-tenth of Mexicans favored church participation in politics. Church-state relations have remained quite controversial in contemporary Mexico, even though the church does not threaten Mexico's established political institutions.[38] Even though the military is an arm of the state, fewer than half of all Mexicans support its participation in the general tasks of the government. Only about one-fifth of all Mexicans favored military participation in the government. As Alain Rouquié has put it, "Few Armies in the [American] continent appear to be less politically involved."[39] The overall proportions in Mexican attitudes toward church and military participation in politics and government changed little during the remainder of the 1980s.[40]

Opposition to church participation in politics was strongest among the university educated, the wealthy, men, and government workers. Indeed,

Table 5-10. Attitudes toward the State's Autonomy (percent)

	Believe the Church Should Not Participate in Politics	Believe the Military Should Not Participate in Government
Whole sample	66	44
Education		
Secondary or less	60	38
Preparatory	69	50
University	74	53
Age		
18–25	68	45
26–35	68	46
36–50	62	45
51+	65	40
Gender		
Female	59	39
Male	69	47
Monthly income (pesos)		
Less than 10,000	61	40
10,000–40,000	69	46
40,000–80,000	72	51
More than 80,000	72	59
Employment		
Government worker	73	47
Nongovernment worker	66	45
Unemployed	59	42

Source: Miguel Basáñez poll, March 1983.
Note: N = 7,051.

Table 5-11. How Should the PRI Choose Its Presidental
Nominee? (percent)

	Primary Elections	Party Conventions	Presidential Prerogative
Whole sample	60	24	4
Region			
North	63	18	4
Central	65	20	3
South	57	32	2
Federal District	56	26	6
Education			
Secondary or less	62	21	5
Preparatory	60	26	3
University	57	30	3
Age			
18–25	62	24	4
26–35	61	25	3
36–50	59	24	4
51+	59	21	4
Gender			
Female	59	23	4
Male	62	25	3
Class			
Upper	53	33	4
Lower/middle	62	22	3
Church attendance			
Weekly	60	23	3
Less than weekly	60	24	4

Source: IMOP S.A. (Gallup) poll, May 1988.
Note: N = 2,960.

only age did not seem to matter much as an explanation. Opposition to military participation in government was also substantial; it was strongest among the university educated, the wealthy, and men, but age and occupation did not make a difference.

In short, education, social class, and gender were not helpful in understanding variation in the preferences for strong leaders in the 1980s, but they help to explain the varying levels of opposition to clerical and military involvement in politics and government, respectively. The dimensions of democratization in Mexico differ, therefore, depending on whether one considers norms or practices, leadership styles or institutional roles.

Finally, we look at the extent of authoritarian or democratic preferences within the context of the PRI. Table 5-11 reports the results of a practical question: How should the PRI's presidential nominee be chosen? The selection of the PRI's candidate formally rests with PRI institutions, but in effect the party's candidate has been chosen by the outgoing president, who consults informally but retains the decisive power.[41] This informal but effective presidential prerogative in choosing the next president has been the operative norm of Mexican politics for decades. In 1988 only 4 percent of Mexicans supported it.

In 1988, Mexicans strongly supported changing the way in which PRI presidential candidates were nominated; most Mexicans preferred primary elections to party conventions. This lopsided preference is evident throughout all the categories listed in table 5-11, but there are some differences in the intensity of such preferences. The preference for party conventions is strongest among upper-class Mexicans and among the university educated, who may believe that they might have greater influence on a party convention than on the results of a primary election. (Support for a party convention is also strong in southern Mexico.) In contrast, gender, religion, and age seem to explain little about the variance with regard to such preferences.

Conclusion

The attitudes of Mexican citizens have changed in important and consistent ways since the late 1950s. By the early 1990s, Mexicans had become much more likely to be interested in politics, to be attentive to political campaigns, and to discuss politics freely. The rising level of politicization of the electorate is still high when Mexico is compared with advanced industrial democracies. It remained high both in years when Mexico held national elections and when it did not. As time has passed, Mexicans have also become less likely to prefer to rely on strong leaders rather than on the rule of law; they do not favor the participation of nondemocratic institutions in political life; and they strongly favor the internal democratization of the ruling party's presidential nomination practices.

Not everything had changed, however. As in the late 1950s, Mexicans in the early 1990s were extraordinarily proud of their homeland. The level of national pride Mexicans exhibited in an economic recession year (1988) continued to exceed that found in Western European countries when their economies were growing (1989). The pride of Mexicans was focused on the nation's political institutions to a considerable degree. This pride was not hostile to democratic institutions, however. In the 1950s as in the 1990s, pride was connected to certain democratic political practices.

Our findings agree with those of other scholars, whose work is reviewed in this chapter and who suggest that the trend over time in the attitudes of Mexican citizens has been favorable to the possibilities of democratic politics. The residues of authoritarian practices in Mexican politics are best explained in terms of existing institutions and policies, not the preferences of Mexican citizens.[42] Especially noteworthy is the fact that the most highly educated Mexicans have become less suspicious of and less alienated from politics. By the late 1980s, Mexicans were ready to give Thomas Hobbes's *Leviathan* a decent burial.

We have confirmed a number of the demographic differences noted by other scholars and summarized earlier in this chapter. Nonetheless, our findings suggest that Mexican politics has become more nationalized. The differences among demographic categories, such as education or gender, that concerned Almond and Verba and other scholars have, in general, narrowed over time. The point is not that Almond and Verba or the others were incorrect in their analysis; they were not. The point is that Mexico has changed and that its citizens are ready for a more democratic polity.

Explaining Attitude Changes

Why did the political attitudes of Mexicans change between the 1950s and the 1980s, even though the institutions of the political regime did not? Our answer to this important question is less certain and more speculative. Four explanations emerge from our data.

One explanation is the spread of elementary education. In 1960, just after the Almond and Verba survey, over 40 percent of Mexican adults did not know how to read and write; on the eve of the 1988 presidential election, that proportion had dropped below 10 percent. As recently as 1970 the median schooling level of the population age twelve and older was 3.5 years; by 1990 the median schooling level for that population had risen to 6.4 years.[43] The narrowing of the education gap in the attitudes of Mexicans can be attributed to a significant degree to the virtual elimination of illiteracy and to the upgrading of the population's educational levels. Educationally, Mexicans became more alike with the passing of time.

A second factor, evident also in the surveys, is the relative insignificance of church attendance as an explanation for democratic attitudes. Roman Catholics and secular citizens have comparable commitments to democracy. As Samuel Huntington has argued most explicitly, the "third wave" of democratization has been especially noteworthy among Catholic countries, and it is attributable to some extent to the important worldwide changes that have occurred since the 1960s within the Roman Catholic Church.[44]

Third, Roman Catholic aggiornamento has permitted the wider incorporation of women in social life outside the home, thereby reducing the role of gender as an explanation for differences in political attitudes. A contributing factor to the narrowing of the attitudinal differences between men and women is exposure to cosmopolitan international influences, particularly television programs and films from the United States, which are quite pervasive in Mexico.[45]

Finally, there is a potential for reciprocity between attitudes and political processes. Even though the nation's governing institutions have, for the most part, remained closed to the opposition, Mexican politics in the 1990s had become much more competitive than in the 1950s. The very fact of such increased competition may help to explain why Mexicans have become more interested in politics, more willing to participate, and less dependent on a few strong leaders for solving problems. As E. E. Schattschneider first argued about the United States in the 1950s, party competition can be "contagious." As parties take sides on issues and battle each other, citizens are drawn into the electoral arena; their predispositions to engage in democratic politics change as a consequence.[46] And as Mexicans have become more democratic in their values, they have placed further pressures on governing elites to reform political processes even more.[47]

Mexico in Comparative Perspective

In the early 1990s Mexico was much less democratic than the attitudes of its citizens might lead us to expect. This observation supports the argument of those who stress that the construction of a democratic political regime requires, above all, a change in elite strategies and behavior.[48] From the 1950s to the 1980s a change in the mass public in the direction of democratic values did not bring about a democratic regime.

Scott Mainwaring has noted one consequence of the scholarly focus on elite behavior, however: the "dismissal of the importance of a normative commitment to democracy" as a subject for research and reflection. This has had two regrettable consequences. First, it ignores the ample evidence that the construction of democratic political regimes in contemporary Latin America has certainly involved "people who have devoted much of their lives to the democratic cause." Second, "a society in which there is limited support for democracy does not bode very well for this form of government."[49] The likelihood of the consolidation of democracy increases if there is mass support for it.

Mexico's slow process of democratization in the 1980s cannot be understood without reference to the change in public attitudes. Mexicans began to demand democracy. These demands were localized at first, as in the state of Chihuahua in widespread protest against fraud in the 1986 gubernatorial elections,[50] but they soon spread. These mass-based national demands for democracy are evident in what Soledad Loaeza has labeled "the call to the voting booth"[51]—the belief, growing in the late 1980s and in the 1990s, that elections ought to be fair and decisive. In this chapter, we document the increasing support for democratic practices during the 1980s; such growing support accounts well for the content and significance of the campaigns of opposition parties in the 1988 presidential election.[52] The perception of substantial fraud committed during and just after that election brought forth what some have called a "civic insurrection."[53]

These demands for greater democracy through fair elections resurfaced loudly during the 1994 presidential elections and are one part of the explanation for the important reforms in electoral procedures that were adopted during the months prior to the 1994 election.[54] These societal demands explain as well the belated but nonetheless effective blossoming in the early 1990s of organizations in civil society concerned with the defense of human rights—and in particular, organizations (such as the Civic Alliance) concerned with the defense of the fairness of the electoral process.

Consequently, prior to a transition to a fully democratic political regime, the demand for democracy has been more long-lasting in Mexico—in part because the transition has been slow and prolonged—than in other cases of democratization.[55] The Mexican transition toward democracy resembles the slow-moving mass-based experience of democratization in Poland more than it does other Latin American cases.[56] Mexican citizens pressured elites to democratize the political regime and in so doing have become actors on the nation's public stage. The changed attitudes and behavior of Mexicans have induced elites to change their own strategies and behavior.

Most optimistically, the shift in the matrix of political attitudes makes it more likely that a democratic political regime could be consolidated in Mexico in the future. Economic growth may well help to consolidate the Mexican political system in the future, after Mexico recovers from the recession begun in 1995, but comparative studies show, as Ronald Inglehart has put it, "that economic development per se does not necessarily lead to democracy."[57] Whether economic growth consolidates an authoritarian or a democratic regime is strongly affected by political attitudes. Where democratic norms have come to prevail, as is increasingly the case in Mexico, the likelihood of democratic consolidation rises.[58]

The Transition to Somewhere

Foreign firms are investing, tourists bask in the sunshine, and illegal markets boom. Is this still Fidel Castro's Cuba? In the early 1990s, Cuba began its "transition to somewhere." I do not know what specific form the future of Cuba will take but there is no doubt that a significant transition is under way and that its eventual outcome will be very different from that of the past three decades. Some of the outlines of Cuba's future can be sketched already. Above all, Cuba's foreseeable short- to medium-term future will be grim no matter who is the nation's president or what is the form of its political regime.

The sharp decline of Cuba's economy, the erosion of its political system, its international isolation, and the fraying of its institutions did not begin with the collapse of European communist regimes but were greatly exacerbated by it. By its government's own reckoning, gross domestic product (GDP; in constant 1981 prices) fell 40.1 percent between 1989 and 1993. By the end of 1995, the economy had stabilized, but GDP was still only 67 percent of its level in 1989.[1] (Between 1986 and 1990, according to Cuban government statistics, global social product per capita in constant 1981 prices fell about 3.7%.)[2] Faced with such a catastrophe, the Cuban government began to change several policies and has been forced to tolerate behaviors that it would otherwise have sought to stop.

Cuba's international trade shrunk badly, helping to accelerate the country's international isolation and deepening the domestic economic crisis. The value of exports of goods dropped 80 percent from 1989 to 1993, while the value of imports of goods dropped 75 percent during those same years. By the end of 1995, trade had recovered a bit, but still exports were only 27 percent and imports 28 percent of their respective levels in 1989.[3] The loss of Soviet political and military support (including the loss of weapons transfers free of charge) also rendered Cuba much more internationally vulnerable than at any time since the political regime's founding in 1959.

Nonetheless, Cuba's economic performance in 1996 suggests that the worst decline may have passed. The economy performed well during the first half of the year, led by sugar cane, mining, and tourism. International financial obligations were met. The economy may have been adversely affected by the enactment of the U.S. Helms-Burton Act (formally called the Cuban Liberty and Democratic Solidarity Act) in March 1996, though principally through the decisions of would-be investors not to invest and the consequent increase of the cost to Cuba of attracting replacement investors. Although during the second half of 1996 the economy grew at only about half the rate as during the first half, the government reported that GDP for the year grew 7.8 percent. Nonetheless, even under the most optimistic economic scenarios, Cuba is not likely to return to its 1985 economic level until well into the twenty-first century.[4]

In the next section, I present a baseline scenario to organize thinking about Cuba's future by characterizing the current responses of Cuba's government and people: a tight, repressive government control of politics, an important opening to foreign investment, booming illegal markets, and persistent overall economic difficulties. Four principal scenarios about Cuba's future follow: these are labeled "*China," and "Cuba–," "Cuba=," and "Cuba+." The *China scenario describes the Cuban leadership's preferred future, namely, continued political monopoly with economic growth through more rapid market openings.

The Cuba– scenario assumes that the *China scenario would fail economically and, as a result, violent protests would arise and be met with increased repression. Within the Cuba– scenario, two variants are considered to ponder the possibilities of violence. In one variant, the regime remains strong enough either to prevail over its opponents or to remain in the field during a civil war. In another variant with a much weaker regime in the more distant future, the violence succeeds in defeating the government swiftly; but that is because Cuba's economic collapse will have become all the more dire.

The Cuba= scenario explores the political regime's efforts to obtain renewed political support with much less economic growth than envisaged in the *China scenario. Within the Cuba= scenario, two power-sharing variants are considered (in one, Fidel Castro turns over power to other Communist Party elites; in the other, the Communist Party shares power with the opposition). The Cuba+ scenario speculates about Cuba after a major political regime transition, paying special attention to the weight of cultural, historical, and legal traditions. It expects the establishment of a new, strong, centralized government, with personalistic politics and high demand for state provision of services. Taking into account the baseline scenario, the four principal scenarios, and the two variants within the Cuba–

and Cuba= scenarios, there are nine Cuba scenarios. In a later section, these are further developed and compared to four transition scenarios observed in other countries.

Beginning with the Cuba= scenario but turning toward the Cuba+ scenario, the analysis goes past what I call the "poof moment," that historical moment when the old political regime changes enough or has been replaced so that market economy policies can be applied successfully. This whimsical label is adopted to underscore, in humility, the point that no one has a good account of how or when this decisive, conceptual moment might be reached. Writing about the period past the poof moment has become a growth industry in some circles in the United States; the U.S. Helms-Burton Act devotes an entire (long) chapter to its prescriptions for Cuba past the poof moment. My analysis portrays various alternatives for Cuba's stylized future while also admitting that I cannot shed sufficient light on the critical turning point.

In the discussion of the scenarios but, especially, later in the chapter, I consider three issues that any political transition in Cuba would face: the utility of crime with impunity, before, during, and after a major transition, to facilitate both a market transition and political peace; the problem of how to govern a long-submerged but emerging, possibly vibrant, civil society unaccustomed to rule-governed markets and noncoercive, peaceful politics; and the likely strength of some authoritarian institutions along with the observable weakness of potentially democratic institutions—also before, during, and after a major transition.[5]

The Baseline Scenario

A political transition has already begun in Cuba. This is not necessarily the kind of transition that readers of this book, or I, would prefer, but it is real, nevertheless. Structures and practices have been changing, and will continue to change, to make Cuba's political regime rather different from what it has been. For example, in the early 1990s, Cuba's political regime is far more personalized than was the case from the early 1970s to the mid-1980s. The reassertion of President Fidel Castro's personal centrality for regime survival harkens back to the founding days of the 1960s.

Along with personalization, there has been deideologization. There is less reliance on Marxism-Leninism as the regime's guiding body of thought. Although the significance of formal doctrine—in contrast to the undoubted importance of Fidel Castro's ideas—for Cuban politics during the past several decades has always been debatable, in recent years doctrinal purity has come to matter much less. In official political discourse and in the 1992 Constitution, references to the sacred texts of European communism have become infrequent or have been expunged altogether. The 1992 Constitution proclaims, in Article 8, that the state is secular but no longer atheist. It purges the language of class struggle from old Articles 1, 4, and 5. In Article 5, the new Constitution locates the Communist Party's claim to legitimacy under the shade of Cuba's palm trees and the legacy of the official national hero, José Martí. Cuba's political leaders now claim to incarnate the Cuban nation, not alien doctrines.[6] Nationalism has overtaken universalism—in form as well as in practice—as the doctrinal foundation of Cuba's political regime.

There has developed a considerable diversity among "tendencies" within the government and the party. These tendencies are best understood as amorphous and changing currents of opinion rather than as factions, especially if by the latter one means groupings with a defined identity over some political cleavage, in which there has been a consistent "taking of sides" on issue after issue. The existence of shifting and varied currents of opinion suggests an element of elite pluralism along with persistently weak intra-elite contestation, a combination that strengthened the political regime in the short run. There is enough openness to retain enough unity within an increasingly heterogeneous coalition under conditions of economic hardship, but there is not enough contestation to threaten a split.

As a means of collective and individual adjustment to the crises, there has been a turn to the street and neighborhood levels. Ordinary Cubans have rediscovered each other and the need to rely on themselves and each other more than on the power of the (weakened) state. Regime-sponsored mass organizations have lost social support, but the government, too, has turned to the street and the neighborhood through such developments as People's Councils (Consejos Populares), rapid response brigades, and the decentralization of the administration of justice.

The People's Councils were created in 1988 and have spread throughout the country. They tackle the local tasks of daily life that municipal governments cannot. Ordinary citizens and members of the People's Councils and of municipal government account for over 40 percent of National Assembly deputies elected in February 1993. Rapid response brigades are bands of thugs who allegedly rise spontaneously at the local level to defend the government's honor and to beat up regime opponents. In fact officially sponsored, these bands first surfaced in advance of the summer 1991 Pan American Games and have remained in sporadic operation ever since. Similarly, provincial courts have established branches in municipal capitals, while the powers of municipal courts have increased and efforts have been made to enhance the prestige and capabilities of local police forces. For the first time since 1959, there has been a simultaneous increase in repression and decentralization.

In terms of the relationship between the state and the economy, there are several important changes: the official opening to foreign direct investment, the boom in illegal markets, the growth of lawful quasi-private firms, the rise in lawful individual entrepreneurship, and the legalization of the holding and use of U.S. dollars for retail trade transactions.[7]

The Cuban government's welcome to private foreign investment is a major turning point for Cuban politics. Cuba's revolutionary socialism was founded in part on the expropriation of foreign firms. Symbolically and politically, the reliance on direct foreign investment as a strategy for development signals a fundamental change. Much of this foreign investment has gone to the tourism sector; some of it has gone to labor-intensive manufacturing, often known as *maquiladoras*. These new economic policies make Cuba look, alas, like a Caribbean country.

The growing presence of foreign firms has already begun to affect labor-management relations and political discussions with regard to them. Foreign firms have been persuaded to accept labor unions in the tourism sector, for example, on the grounds that such unions would contribute to higher productivity. As Haroldo Dilla has written, it may be possible that "Cuban workers would sing the firm's anthem every morning with sincere enthusiasm, but that would certainly not lead to the construction of a participatory democracy in which each person—not just the technocratic or entrepreneurial elites—would become an effective participant in the making of significant decisions."[8] The politics of more contentious labor-management tensions lie over the horizon.

Much economic activity is illegal, however. There has been an erosion of respect for law. In its boldest form, reported common crime has increased, but perhaps its most important manifestation is the routine mass reliance on illegal markets—even by government and party officials—to satisfy basic needs. By 1993, the majority of Cuba's retail commercial transactions probably occurred, legally or illegally, within the context of a market economy. Over the following three years, the proportion of legal market transactions increased gradually while that of illegal transactions probably fell, but the overall pattern change was confirmed. To put it boldly, Cuba is already engaged in a transition to a market economy, albeit one that remains illegal to a substantial extent.[9]

At issue in Cuba's future, therefore, is a transition to a rule-governed market economy—given that a transition to illegal markets is under way—as well as a fuller transition toward a market economy for the lawful operation of the nation's productive enterprises. This more important transition is already authorized (though in an odd way) by the 1992 Constitution's Article 14, which emphasizes that Cuba's sugar mills, basic manufacturing plants, and other means of transportation, production, and finance that were once expropriated "cannot" be privatized. But Article 14 also provides that privatization can go forward if it would serve the nation's development and would be so approved by the handful of members of the executive committee of the Council of Ministers.

There is also what might be called "anticipatory Sandinization" of certain state enterprises. After the defeat of Nicaragua's Sandinista Front for National Liberation in the February 1990 elections, the Sandinista government transferred property over certain housing units and enterprises to its own cadres in reward for their "historical services." There were no competitive bids for the property or recognition of alternative property claims. No criteria of economic efficiency or developmental objectives were applied. The transfer of property from the state to private persons was justified in political terms, but it was lawful; for that reason, it differs from the unlawful do-it-yourself privatization evident in various parts of the former Soviet Union.

Cuba's evolving national private sector could come to look like Nicaragua's, except that the changes in Cuba precede a formal transfer of power from the ruling party to the opposition. The change in Cuba is certainly lawful under the 1992 Constitution. Its Article 23 recognizes the right of private enterprise in Cuba's economy to foreigners as well as nationals. *Sociedades anónimas* can be established by any person. Many of the existing *sociedades anónimas* are quasi-private firms: they are closely linked to the state and use what had been public patrimony in their business. The state formally remains the sole shareholder but its rights as shareholder are exercised by individuals who serve as its trustees (*fideicomiso*).[10] In their form of operation and their control over the use of profits, these firms have become something other than mere state enterprises.

Between the growth of illegal markets and the growth of quasi-private firms, there is another zone of market activity: lawful individual entrepreneurship. The number of private salaried workers and self-employed persons grew substantially during the first half of the 1990s. While this trend is best explained as the sum of individual responses to economic crises, the government and the Communist Party have recognized and legalized much of this behavior. The Fourth Party Congress authorized the lawful development of self-employment in the service sector, even envisaging the legalization of other private individual economic activities "within the constraints and possibilities that the circumstances of the special period [of severe economic austerity] have imposed" on Cuba.[11]

Aspects of this rise in lawful individual entrepreneurship are also evident in the countryside. The number of peasants in state-sponsored cooperatives fell by nearly 23 percent between 1983 and 1989. In the nonsugar sectors of the agricultural economy, in which government control is weaker, defections from cooperatives were even higher. From 1983 to 1989, nearly 35 percent of the members of tobacco cooperatives and more than 36 percent of the members of coffee cooperatives abandoned the cooperatives.[12] It comes as no surprise that the 1991 Agricultural Household Survey of the University of Havana found that peasants who worked their land individually had significantly higher net incomes per capita than those who pooled their land in agricultural cooperatives and, especially, than agricultural workers on state farms. These results held true for quite different regions in three Cuban provinces.[13]

In August 1993, the Cuban government began to permit the lawful holding and use of U.S. dollars for various transactions; the government had been widening the scope for their lawful use during the previous two years. The political consequences of formal dollarization are complex; its immediate beneficiaries were those who acquired dollars illegally and those who had retained close contact with Cubans overseas; those least likely to benefit were those who abided by the law and those so loyal to the regime they had broken ties with relatives who had emigrated. In the longer term, legalizing the use of the dollar will help the Cuban government politically only if additional measures are undertaken to stimulate production in Cuba, decisions that the Cuban leadership has been slow to make.

Overall, there is an important contradiction in the government's evolving policies. The state's repression of small human rights and opposition groups has become harsher. In politics, even would-be reformers fear that the path to reform may also be the path to their perdition, a perception that may also strengthen the regime in the short run. If officeholders fear that "reform communism" is an oxymoron and if the attempt to introduce some changes is seen as inevitably leading to regime breakdown, then officeholders are more likely to close ranks in support of a regime that they would otherwise wish to change for fear that they would lose power, status, and resources after a transition. On the other hand, even the toughest of hard-liners believe that some significant market openings are necessary if the political regime is to survive. Among the strongest supporters for bolder economic reforms are the ultimate guardians of order, the armed forces.

Cuba's official leaders are torn, therefore, between their long-standing belief that the market will ruin the nation (and especially ruin them) and their more recent reasoning that some market mechanisms can save the nation. The attempt to reconcile these contradictory opinions is embodied in their pursuit of what I call the *China scenario.

The *China Scenario

How do Cuban leaders think about the future? Extrapolating both from
current trends and leadership preferences, the *China scenario rests on the
premise that a "transition to somewhere" has begun; I call this first approx-
imation of "somewhere" the *China scenario to distinguish it both from
Cuba and from the real China (for elaboration, see later section). The *China
scenario sketches the current preferences of the Cuban leadership for the
maintenance of political control via a market opening more limited than
China's.

> The *China scenario and Cuba are much more personalized than is
> China. Fidel Castro's role exceeds that of China's late Deng Hsiaoping.
> There is no evidence of change toward a reduced role for Fidel Castro
> (despite occasional statements about his possible retirement).

> Justification in terms of nationalism, and a concomitant decline in re-
> liance on European Marxism-Leninism, are evident in China and Cuba
> and are part of the *China scenario.

> The *China scenario and Cuba are more successfully repressive than is
> China. Cuba has yet to have an episode such as that of Tiananmen
> Square: the Cuban armed forces have not shot at a large public gather-
> ing of Cubans. In the first half of the 1990s, the Cuban government
> repressed its enemies while employing only moderate levels of overt
> physical force. Thus, political control seems more effective in Cuba
> than in China. Cuba, however, differs from the *China scenario. Cuba
> suffers from a breakdown in respect for law; citizen allegiance to the
> laws that govern the economy has been lost rapidly. Sustained control
> and respect for law well beyond Cuba's current practice are essential to
> the *China scenario, in which rulers would also not compromise with
> alternative political forces.

> Substantial political decentralization is feasible both in *China and in
> China. Authority roles are transferred in varying degrees from the cen-
> ter to the intermediate and local levels. Decentralization need not
> require depoliticization or the Communist Party's loss of control. Cuba
> has made some moves toward decentralization, but it remains much
> more centralized than China or *China. (Remember that Cuba is
> smaller than most Chinese provinces.)

> Cuba's transition to a lawful market economy remains distant from
> the Chinese experience. The *China scenario rests on a policy of wel-
> coming substantial foreign investment as well as on the growth of

quasi-private (but not fully private) firms. In this way, the *China scenario differs from both China and Cuba: Cuba has yet to have truly substantial foreign investment and has few, if any, genuinely private "purely Cuban" firms, while China features much foreign investment and many lawful private firms in many economic sectors. More important, the *China scenario suggests that the government would avoid a transition to a fully private market economy. Instead, some market mechanisms would be adopted, and Cuban quasi-private firms would operate alongside foreign and state firms. Freer markets have reappeared in agriculture, but these have not, and need not, require a further change in the property regime. Cuba's leaders have claimed credit for the modest economic improvements that have occurred as a result of these limited market openings.

The leadership of the *China scenario is marked by variety within unity. There is not yet that much variety in Cuba; there is more variety in China. Whether Cuba could reach a greater level of effective variety within the *China scenario under Fidel Castro's leadership is debatable, perhaps doubtful.

Cuba is not yet near the *China scenario; nonetheless, its transition toward the *China scenario has begun and has some prospects of political and economic success; the 1996 economic growth rate reassures its supporters within the Cuban leadership. In so arguing, I am not forecasting that the *China scenario will become a reality; I do argue that, to varying degrees, most currents of opinion within the Cuban leadership wish to move toward it. Nor am I suggesting that the *China scenario's economic reforms will suffice to launch Cuba's economic recovery. Even the least dogmatic of Cuba's current leaders have political difficulty envisaging a fully private and market-oriented economy, an ideological constraint that will limit Cuba's gains from this scenario.

The main obstacles to the realization of the *China scenario are Fidel Castro's allergy to the market and political pluralism; the leadership's loss of political support; the growth of illegal markets; and the persistence of international isolation, which will continue as long as Cuba does not move beyond the *China scenario and even beyond a "real China" scenario.

Fearing the Cuba– Scenario

In some respects, the scenario I call Cuba– almost occurred in the early 1990s when the economy collapsed. The Cuban economy's prospects for renewed and sustained growth under current structures and policies remain problematic, and the public discourse of Cuban government officials is not much more encouraging. In effect, the Cuba– scenario is the early 1990s projected onto the future.

The Cuba– scenario is based on the assumption that Cuban leaders will fail in their pursuit of the *China scenario. There are several reasons. First, there will not be sufficient foreign investment and profitable enough tourism, perhaps because the U.S. Helms-Burton Act will dissuade international investors. Second, Cuban leaders will constrain the "excessive" spread of market forces, denying Cuba the economic benefits of the *China scenario. Third, political rigidities will prevent political decentralization and other means to gather support and enhance institutional flexibility. The grimness of the country's prospects can be gleaned from a consideration of Cuba's comparative advantages as enumerated by Julio Carranza, one of Cuba's most thoughtful analysts:[14]

> *Cuba has a large industrial infrastructure for a country of its size.* Yes, but much of it is highly inefficient and internationally uncompetitive. Its development since the 1960s at virtually "any cost" made sense only in the context of Cuba's quasi-war economy.

> *Cuba has an extensive physical infrastructure of roads, bridges, airports, electrification, and communications.* Yes, but there has been woefully inadequate maintenance. Much of the nation's infrastructure is near collapse and requires very large investments to reach minimally acceptable levels. Telephone and other forms of electronic communications are at a primitive level of development. Electric power outages lasting for hours occur regularly.

> *Cuba has a well-educated workforce, especially in technical and scientific areas.* Yes, but work habits have slackened because incentives to work hard have been so weak. Even with a restoration of effective economic incentives, there may be a lag in the recovery of efficient work habits. More seriously, Cuba lacks a well-educated workforce for the delivery of efficient services, quality control over production and services, management and marketing, and related work skills essential for a modern economy inserted into world markets.

> *Cuba has political stability derived from the consensus "that has been achieved up to now" in support of the "revolutionary people's project."* Yes, but it is debatable how that consensus can be ascertained in the absence of free politics, and it is equally debatable whether that consensus, even if it can be ascertained, would still lend support to the political regime in the 1990s. Telling enough may be Carranza's own formulation: "up to

now." If economic actors are motivated by rational expectations, the uncertainty about Cuba's political future provides a disincentive to foreigners to invest.

The Cuba– scenario is not just about economics, however. The record of the recent past suggests a government willingness to crack down on even mild forms of overt opposition. The rapid response brigades of the early 1990s was a novel means of repression. The modest opening that permitted the formation of human rights and overt political opposition groupings in the late 1980s was followed by a narrowing of officially tolerated political space in the mid-1990s.

In early 1996, the government harshly repressed the Concilio Cubano. Founded on October 10, 1995 (the anniversary of the beginning of Cuba's first war of independence), the Concilio was an attempt by some 140 small unofficial opposition groups to coalesce around a minimum program. The Concilio's aims were a general amnesty for all political prisoners, full respect for the present Constitution and fundamental laws, a call on the Cuban government to fulfill its obligations to respect human rights under the United Nations Charter, a demand for freedom of economic organization, and a call for free and direct elections on the basis of the pluralist nature of society. In November, the Concilio reaffirmed its commitment to use only peaceful means to achieve its aims. In short, the Concilio respected the country's Constitution and legal framework while demanding changes within them. In December, the Concilio formally asked the government for permission to hold a large gathering on February 24, 1996 (the anniversary of the beginning of Cuba's last war of independence). On February 15, however, the government launched a wave of repression against Concilio leaders and members; the next day, it banned the gathering.[15] The political regime's means to elicit political support have weakened, and as result, there is a greater reliance on coercion.

One of the clearest arguments on behalf of heightened repression was made by Carlos Aldana before the National Assembly in December 1992.[16] Because Aldana had seemed among the more open of the top leaders, only he could convey their resolute commitment to narrow the political space available for dissent. Aldana's public warnings covered even the mildest forms of criticism of government and party policies. This repressive political orientation was evident as well in the Political Bureau's report to the Fifth Plenum of the Communist Party's Central Committee, held in March 1996 and read by General Raúl Castro. The report attacked even the Communist Party's own think tanks for alleged ideological deviance in their research on Cuba and, in particular, for their contacts with international scholars.[17] The report narrowed the prospects (never wide) for normal academic research by Cuban scholars on their country.

Another dimension of the Cuba– scenario is the limits of Fidel Castro's flexibility. Fidel Castro has shown extraordinary flexibility throughout his public career. Even in the 1990s, he has demonstrated a willingness to reverse past policies on foreign direct investment, on the holding and use of U.S. dollars, and on various market mechanisms, some of which he denounced in years past. He has drawn closer to the People's Republic of China, whose government's market-oriented policies he once criticized. He has demoted from public office many of those who had served him loyally for decades; Cuba's top elite had changed little from the mid-1960s to the mid-1980s, but it has been almost entirely renovated since then.[18] Fidel Castro can be and has been very flexible.

There are limits to his flexibility, nevertheless. He does not share power. He does not delegate effectively for sustained periods of time (that is, either he delegates too much and provides inadequate supervision or he insists on sustained micromanagement). His level of economic literacy is modest, but he refuses to recognize it as such. The political regime has been redefined once again in the 1990s to associate his continued personal rule with the fate of the revolution, socialism, and the nation. In the final analysis, he is the principal obstacle to the *China scenario (reluctance to allow extensive private ownership and far-reaching moves toward a market economy) as well as to the Cuba+ and Cuba= scenario and its variants (see later sections) just as he is the main explanation for Cuba's difficulty in truly escaping the Cuba– scenario.

Thus, Cuba remains at risk of further economic decline and, possibly, of political violence. The prospects for rapid and substantial political and economic improvement under current and foreseeable circumstances are modest. The level of economic hardship for ordinary people is likely to persist. The level of political repression may increase. In August 1994, for the first time since the early 1960s, a major riot involving thousands of people broke out in downtown Havana over state security attempts to punish those who were trying to emigrate without an official permit. Such instances of political protest could recur. More generally, social pressures might lead to violent eruptions, some of which the government may find difficult to control.

Such antiregime violence is unlikely to succeed in the near to medium term, however. In the face of violence, which could lead to civil war, the top elite would close ranks, notwithstanding other policy differences among them. And the government's insistence on involving much of the population in the maintenance of public order at the street level has "contaminated" many people with responsibility for some acts of repression; such persons have less incentive to side with those whom they have repressed, for fear of eventual retribution. Thus, if substantial violence were to break out in the near term, the government remains strong enough to resist. If some in the military were to attempt a coup, it is likely that many other officers would remain loyal, so the regime either would prevail outright or would be engaged in a civil war between factions of the military and other security forces. Under circumstances of sustained political violence, some Cuban Americans would participate directly and would ask the U.S. government and international institutions to intervene.[19] The greater the level of direct participation by Cuban Americans in a Cuban civil war, the greater the chances that U.S. armed forces would be drawn into such a war.

If substantial violence were to break out only in the longer term, years after further economic decline and further loss of political support for the government, the government and the party might be too weak to resist and the transition might be quick—along the lines of what occurred in 1989 in Eastern Europe. In those economically dire circumstances in the next century, the chiefs of the armed forces might jointly remove the top leaders of government and the party. Cuba would be even more bankrupt, however, and its prospects for economic recovery even more remote. The consequences of the Cuba– scenario, therefore, are (a) higher levels of violence soon (over the next three years), with possible U.S. military intervention, to end the political regime before there is further economic collapse, or (b) low levels of violence in the next century, which would bring about regime change swiftly and without U.S. military intervention but at the cost of even worse economic deterioration. Neither of these outcomes is normatively desirable for any potential participant: not for Fidel Castro, not for the U.S. government, not for Cubans or Cuban Americans, not for the international community. And yet the pattern of domestic and international circumstances could make this outcome likely.[20]

Assessing the Cuba= Scenario

Instead of the grimness of the Cuba– scenario, Cuba's political regime can survive. The Cuba= scenario includes a revivified political regime under severe economic constraints. The Cuba= scenario (as does the Cuba– scenario) presumes that the economic gains of the *China scenario remain elusive, for the most part; there is no sustained economic growth for Cuba under the Cuba= scenario (though, as in 1996, there may be spurts of growth). In contrast to the Cuba– scenario, in the Cuba= scenario the Cuban government and Communist Party adapt their institutions and obtain new political support. This is a relatively optimistic scenario from the political regime's perspective, because the Cuba= scenario rests on the proposition that it can become stronger even if the economy might not.

The strategy to political recovery rests on the implementation of the process of *perfeccionamiento* launched by the Fourth Party Congress in October 1991. As the Spanish word indicates, the goal is to improve the efficacy of the existing regime. One key to this strategy is institutional redesign. Greater authority would be devolved to provincial and municipal governments. The pre-1992 executive committees of the municipal and provincial assemblies would be terminated to empower the assemblies politically. The already mentioned People's Councils would help ordinary people shape politics and act on behalf of the government as well as gain access to leaders who would pay attention to their concerns. This change of the regime's institutions closest to the street and the neighborhood would make it more feasible, at least in theory, for citizens to affect the politics of greatest pertinence to their lives. Mass organizations would also evolve; the old organizations would not have a monopoly on state support. New social organizations might arise to meet new needs and receive government support toward those ends.

There is a parallel electoral strategy. For the first time since 1959, under the 1992 Constitution members of the national and provincial assemblies are elected directly by the people. In this fashion, leaders at the middle and upper levels of politics would reestablish grassroots connections.

Another pillar of *perfeccionamiento* is symbolic and ideological; namely, the heightened sense of nationalism of a nation in danger from its international enemies. This is an attempt to recover the "spirit of 1959" nearly four decades after the fact. The government and party have even reached out to certain religious believers, especially though not exclusively those associated with Afro-Cuban religiosity, seeking to incorporate them in the "Cuban nation." (The Pope has been invited to visit Cuba in 1998.)

At the elite political level, there is room for diversity based on age, institutional location, and personal temperament. These tendencies operate within the existing political rules, however.

At the level of implementation, the government and the party seek to engage citizens in acts of regime defense through, among other ways, the development of the Unified Vigilance and Protection System (SUVP), which also includes specialized organizations for peasants and state farm and factory workers. At times, these acts of regime defense would include organized mob violence against regime opponents. By exercising repression through these more decentralized means that do not involve the military, the internal security forces, or the police, the government protects these institutions from the onus of repression, and in that way it may contain the loss of legitimacy that accrues from repressive acts.

Within the common core of this Cuba= scenario, there are two longer-term variants.

Power Sharing within the Elite

One variant of the Cuba= scenario would move to a gradual but substantial and peaceful liberalization and democratization, relying less on repressive acts, and leading to somewhat competitive elections, which the Communist Party would win. This outcome resembles the experience of Mexico's long-ruling official party, the Institutional Revolutionary Party (PRI), until the 1980s.

Following Guillermo O'Donnell and Philippe Schmitter, "by *liberalization* we mean the process of making effective certain rights that protect both individual and social groups from arbitrary or illegal acts committed by the state or third parties."[21] These are the basic freedoms of the liberal tradition: expression, association, and so forth. By *democratization* I mean the turn to free, fair, and competitive elections, held at regular intervals, in the context of guaranteed civil and political rights, responsible government (i.e., the accountability of the executive, administrative, and coercive arms of the state to elected representatives), and political inclusion (i.e., universal suffrage and nonproscription of parties). The guarantees of rights and institutions would be embodied in a convention of constitutionalism, that is, the presumption that political change should only occur in accordance with rules and precedents.[22]

How might this scenario for power sharing within the elite unfold? If the elections were free enough and under international monitoring, the Communist Party might be relegitimized. But the PRI analogy suggests the possibility of some electoral fraud and, at a minimum, the biased use of state resources (including the mass media) to support the official party. Consistent with the main features of the Cuba= scenario, the still-ruling Cuban Communist Party would rely more on co-optation than on coercion to woo support from the population and even from the opposition. It is highly unlikely, however, that such an outcome would lead to U.S. economic assistance to Cuba or to much investment by Cuban Americans.

I believe that power sharing within the Cuban elite—a PRI-like strategy—is feasible, albeit difficult, in Cuba, and that it is not beyond belief that Fidel Castro could adopt it, even if it is not likely. A shift toward a scenario of power sharing within the elite has several advantages.

It would be evidence of an opening of the Cuban political system and would hold the promise of other openings. There would be a gain in domestic political support and in international support, though perhaps not from the United States.

It would render U.S.-Cuban relations more complex. Even if they remain cool, the most hostile aspects of the long-standing adversarial relationship might be eroded enough for the Cuban government to begin to demobilize its armed forces and save substantial resources. Cuba's public finance might be stabilized if Cuba's military expenditures were to fall to the level of Mexico's. Such a shift would allow further economic structural adjustments to unfold.

It might make it easier for foreign firms to invest in Cuba, thereby bringing Cuba closer to the *China scenario. And it would provide means for non-U.S. foreign investors to influence Cuban policies and thus to gain some greater "ownership" over the government that regulates their activities.

Consistent with long-standing PRI practices, there would be growth in quasi-private firms. Private wealth grew in Mexico when the winners of its revolution appropriated public resources or made use of opportunities that depended on their government roles (they anticipated the events of the late 1980s in Nicaragua and communist Europe).[23] This process, already under way in Cuba, would just expand.

The Cuban Communist Party and its ancillary organizations would get closer to the grass roots and begin to engage in the politics of listening and bargaining, not just commanding, thereby making it likelier that the party and the regime might endure.

Finally, at various times high-ranking government leaders have spoken as if openings that would not challenge the Communist Party's grip on power might be thinkable. If Fidel Castro can contemplate stepping down from power at least for the purpose of impressing his questioner, why should it be inconceivable that he might shift to a political system that would give him, and then his brother, and then his colleagues many more years as they rotate the wielding of power?

Power Sharing with Other Parties

A second variant of the Cuba= scenario would move to a gradual but substantial and peaceful regime transition that would rely less on repressive acts and lead to competitive elections that the Communist Party would lose. Nonetheless, the Communist Party would retain significant influence in the new political context through its legislative representation and the allegiance of many in the military, the police, and the bureaucracy. This outcome resembles that of Nicaragua in 1990. As with Nicaragua in the early 1990s, Cuba's economic recovery prospects would remain poor; the likelihood of substantial U.S. economic assistance or investment by Cuban Americans would be low.[24] The practical likelihood of this variant remains remote.

Difficulties

Cuba's leaders—above all, Fidel Castro—have not been willing to implement the nonrepressive aspects of their own political strategy. Fidel Castro has been hoarding power, not sharing it. The devolution of authority and, especially, of resources to the local level has been meager. The People's Councils have developed their own bureaucracies, their own hardening of the arteries. The December 1992 municipal elections revealed a surprisingly high level of discontent. The government and the Communist Party rallied all their forces, therefore, to obtain the highest possible expression of political support in the February 1993 elections for the National Assembly. This effort succeeded in demonstrating the party's enduring capacity to mobilize, but it simultaneously deprived the regime of a valid measure of political support. Nor did the February 1993 elections nourish voluntary forms of political allegiance. Official controls remained equally tight during the 1995 municipal elections. The Communist Party has yet to learn the art of bargaining and listening effectively.

Even within the elite, the removal and official disgrace of Political Bureau member Carlos Aldana in the fall of 1992—at the time the top leader most open to political and economic experimentation—provided strong disincentives for would-be liberals to move past the narrow boundaries of the official elite consensus; such officials have been remarkably circumspect in the mid-1990s. In brief, the elements for a Cuba= scenario exist, but Fidel Castro and other leaders have not yet been willing to liberalize this much.

Imagining the Cuba+ Scenario

What might a Cuba different from the present look like, a Cuba past the poof moment? What would Cuba look like if the current political regime were to be replaced? I call this scenario Cuba+. One way to explore it is to look into Cuba's past, particularly the years from the 1930s to the 1950s. Looking to history is analytically useful to understand the possible future of former communist regimes.

Cubans have long demonstrated a preference for strong, centralized government. Such a government might crack down on crime, seek to reimpose respect for law, and curtail the autonomy of neighborhood and street-level behavior. Moreover, Cubans have a preference for strong leaders and are comfortable with caudillo rule.

Cubans have also believed that the state should provide basic services and wrote a democratic constitution in 1940 that is highly interventionist into society and the economy. (The Cuban state did not succeed in doing this, but Cubans wished it to be so.)

Mediating groups of various kinds, including racial and ethnic associations, have been politically ineffective. Nonetheless, the future might differ somewhat from the past. Afro-Cuban religiosity, vibrant before the revolution, will outlive the regime heir to that revolution and has been growing stronger. In 1994–95, for example, female participants in Afro-Cuban religious practices in the city of Havana were younger and better educated than in previous years; the proportion of white participants in these religious activities had also risen.[25] New social movements might emerge in the context of a better educated and, in this future, more autonomous population.

Cubans have been nationalists. One target of such nationalism has been the United States, especially its government and U.S. firms but, at times, even its tourists.[26] The complex attitude toward tourism helps to explain why the Castro government's tourist development policy has been so controversial in Cuba and why any Cuban government's future tourist development policy would be likewise.

The prospects for the unfolding of the politics of revenge and resentment are worrisome, given their historical and intellectual roots. The politics of resentment may complicate relations among Cubans and between them and Cuban Americans, the U.S. government, and U.S. firms.

Let us explore some of these issues in greater detail. Cuba's 1940 Constitution is surprisingly illiberal.[27] Article 33 authorized discretionary limits on freedom of expression if its exercise "threatened the honor of persons, the social order, or public peace." Article 37 permitted the regulation of freedom of association "to guarantee public order," and it prohibited the formation of "political organizations contrary to the [constitutionally mandated] regime." These constitutional texts are remarkably similar to Article 62 of the 1992 Constitution.

The 1940 Constitution is statist in its economics. Several articles are detrimental to the establishment of a market economy. Articles 66, 67, and 77 introduce rigidities in employment and job termination practices; the likely effect of these articles is to raise labor costs and discourage job creation. Article 70 requires and protects professional associations; its effects restrict the supply of highly skilled labor and raise costs. Article 256 authorizes the creation of compulsory membership producers' cartels in every sector of the economy. Article 275 mandates extensive state intervention in the sugar industry to set output levels for cane and milled sugar and to set prices. In addition, Article 52 mandated that the Ministry of Education's budget had to be larger than that of any other ministry and that "the monthly salary of an elementary schoolteacher could, in no instance, be lower than one-millionth of the total national budget," introducing thereby extraordinary rigidity in budget management as well as strong incentives to corrupt the budget process in order to avoid implementing such provisions.

Alternatively, the 1992 Constitution might be suitable for a transition period provided it is amended. For this scenario, the discretionary powers accorded to the state to regulate the exercise of rights would be repealed (just as they would have to be under the 1940 Constitution, were it to be reinstalled). The 1992 Constitution has an adequate and comprehensive listing of rights. For a Cuba+ scenario, Articles 5 and 62 would be repealed; Article 5 establishes the supremacy of the Communist Party, while Article 62 empowers the state to restrict any and all of the constitutional rights. The bill of rights would be purged of ideological references to socialism. (Changes would also be required in Articles 6, 7, 14, and 121, among others.) Similarly, the 1992 electoral law would be changed to permit competitive elections, but the constitutional framework on elections could endure during a transition period. The 1992 Constitution and associated legislation create an effective normative base for the transition to a market economy and the protection of property rights held by nationals and foreigners.

The 1992 Constitution creates a strong executive, which would be useful to implement major changes. Strong presidential powers have been essential to economic policy reforms in Chile, Mexico, Peru, El Salvador, Bolivia,

Brazil, and Argentina, for example. Retaining the 1992 Constitution might also make it easier to retain the allegiance of old regime elites, especially in the military, while making it less necessary for millions of Cubans to learn a new legal framework overnight.

While major constitutional and legal reforms would be necessary, this analysis suggests, paradoxically, that the 1940 Constitution might make a political and market transition more difficult, while the 1992 Constitution might facilitate it. The preference for strong, centralized executive powers might be the best means to constrain the nation's historic dependency on a paternalistic state.

With regard to nationalism, in the Cuba+ scenario one important question would be, Who is a Cuban and what are the rights of Cubans? Article 32 of both the 1976 and 1992 Constitutions mandates the loss of Cuban citizenship when another citizenship is acquired; so, too, did Article 15 of the 1940 Constitution. As a practical matter, Cuban governments have not enforced this requirement; notwithstanding the 1976 Constitution, for example, for internal security reasons the government continued to require Cuban-born U.S. citizens to travel to Cuba with a Cuban passport even if they explicitly stated that they wished to travel with a U.S. passport. The most politically pertinent constraint is to be found not in the Constitution but in the 1992 electoral law, which deprives Cuban citizens of voting rights unless they have been Cuban residents for the two years prior to the elections. Moreover, Cuban citizens cannot be elected to office unless they have been Cuban residents for the five years prior to the elections. Under a Cuba+ scenario, these prior residency requirements would most likely be cut to, say, six months. Voters would retain the right, of course, not to vote for someone who had lived abroad for long periods of time.

Under a Cuba+ scenario, the government would also have to design a law of return. Article 33 of the 1992 Constitution makes it possible for those who had become citizens of other countries to reclaim their Cuban citizenship and, presumably, even to demand social services from a probably bankrupt government and compete for scarce jobs with long-resident Cubans.

The Cuba+ scenario presents several paradoxes, therefore. In search of political liberty as a consequence of a full regime transition, Cubans might turn to a strong leader for the sake of order and efficacy, and that leader might limit some of the newly acquired liberties. But if so, will social organizations become tools of the new ruler, as they were tools of rulers previously? Or will these organizations resist on behalf of a fuller realization of a democratic ideal? Will the search for order clash with the hopes for the full expression of a new associational life and with the manifestations of individualism?

Although hopeful that the market might rescue the economy, Cubans may wish to retain the strongly interventionist state to which they and their great-grandparents have long been committed. This statist predisposition might seek to protect the so-called gains of the revolution, namely, the high public investments in schools, health, and the social safety net.[28] Nationwide public opinion surveys suggest that Cubans in the early 1990s valued their schools and health facilities highly but also wanted improvements in transportation, the food supply, and so forth.[29] And yet, the current level of public social expenditure could not be sustained. All the transitions from communist regimes have been accompanied by severe economic downturns, which last, in the best of cases, not less than four years. Will Cubans have the patience not to abort a market transition and turn instead to the state, or a caudillo, as savior? This statist predisposition might also seek to prevent the economy's denationalization, that is, its falling into the hands of foreigners. This raises again the question whether Cuban Americans are "Cuban enough." Were such efforts to be undertaken, however, policies of economic adjustment and a return to market-based economic growth will become unfeasible or, at a minimum, much less effective. Will Cubans' "fatal attraction" for the state cripple a transition to a market economy?

The legacy of Cuban culture lives on in the present and in the institutions and symbols that Cubans carry in their minds. That legacy makes the construction of a stable, cosmopolitan, market-oriented, liberal democracy difficult. The Cuba+ scenario may be much more desirable than its alternatives, but it is also unstable. Surprisingly, the more useful legal framework to advance the goals of the transition and to constrain the ghosts of Cuba's economic past may be the 1992 Constitution, provided that it is purged of its ideological biases and its excessively authoritarian features and that its complementary legislation is amended to conform to liberal democratic practices.

Lessons from International Scenarios

In the short to medium term, the experience of other transitions away from communism suggest that there may be an incompatibility between the prior successful reform of the economic system—by which I mean a transition toward greater reliance on market means—and the subsequent successful reform of the political system, by which I mean political liberalization and democratization, as defined earlier.[30] Were the current regime to become economically stronger, in the short to medium term its incentive to open up politics may well decline. Only in the longer term (perhaps in the new century) might the market opening lead also to a full political opening. To assess this observation, and to further develop and compare the earlier scenarios, I turn to some international comparisons.

China-Related Scenarios

The *China scenario and, even more so, the China analogy imply a substantial transition toward reliance on market means. The *China scenario
focuses on elite efforts to consolidate an authoritarian regime, while the
China analogy suggests an even greater market opening whose spectacular
results would strengthen the authoritarian regime.

Cuba's political system has some comparative advantage in moving toward either a *China scenario or a China scenario. Fidel Castro legitimized
the welcome to private direct investment and the readoption of certain market mechanisms in the early 1990s, thereby making a modified economic
transition feasible. These China-related scenarios appeal to Cuban leaders
because they hold the promise of economic reactivation with much less
need to accept criticism, ideological adjustment, or negotiations with political foes; they would also not require extensive involvement by Cuban
Americans. These China-related scenarios would allow current elites to
hold on to power by implementing important but not radical changes.

Cuba's economy is much smaller than China's, however, and also much
more dependent on the international economy and on a single export crop.
The smaller market makes it more difficult to attract foreign investment,
while the international vulnerability narrows the government's freedom of
maneuver. Moreover, the different history of U.S. relations with these two
countries suggests that a *China or China scenario in Cuba would not
produce significant enough improvement in U.S.-Cuban relations. In addition, China did not suffer from the macroeconomic imbalances that plague
Cuba's economy because much of China's success came from an early and
thorough marketization of agriculture. In contrast, Fidel Castro has resisted
freeing peasant markets; Cuba's agricultural reforms are timid and limited.
There is also the risk for Cuban leaders that, once embarked on the path to
some reforms, Cuba would be able to secure further necessary international
support only if it were to extend the reforms.

Curiously, what makes the China-like strategy feasible in the first place
is also what makes it much less effective at achieving China-like economic
outcomes, namely, Fidel Castro's allergy to markets. The economic reforms
that Castro would grudgingly support are likely to be too limited. Castro's
presence, in short, makes an economic opening simultaneously possible
and insufficient. Of course, the final chapter to China's story has yet to be
written. China's liberalization and democratization may have been only interrupted at Tiananmen Square, not necessarily stopped for all time.

Cuba's current government may be able to move with some success down
the path of the *China scenario, at least. Although this scenario would not

lead to the impressive economic gains that China has registered, it would stop the economy's decline and extend the life of the political regime; this was certainly the hope of many Cuban leaders in early 1996 just before the U.S. government enacted the Helms-Burton bill into law. This path along the *China scenario remains difficult, however.

A Mexican Scenario

Another international scenario is exemplified by Mexico. One key to the success of a Mexico-like scenario, and one reason that it is unlikely to be applicable in Cuba, is the close economic relations between the United States and Mexico. Were the Cuban Communist Party to win a freely competitive election, U.S.-Cuban relations might not be so hostile but it is improbable that they would become cordial. Were the Cuban Communist Party to win elections as the Mexican PRI once did, namely, through extensive use of government resources in support of the official party and the recurrent practice of electoral fraud, the U.S. government may not accept the election results at all. Whereas Mexican Americans for the most part have not sought to foster U.S. government intervention on behalf of democratizing Mexico, Cuban Americans are unlikely to find a Mexico-like political outcome satisfactory in Cuba.[31]

In addition, Fidel Castro and other Cuban leaders may find it difficult to emulate the Mexican PRI. Opposition parties in Mexico compete for public office and, in the 1990s, win elections from time to time. Opposition parties are represented in the Mexican congress and in various state and local legislative bodies; in the 1990s some governors have been elected from the opposition. There has been considerable liberalization in Mexico; the government and its leaders are regularly criticized in the mass media. Individuals, groups, and parties regularly call for the official party's defeat. Nothing in what Fidel Castro has said and done suggests that he is prepared for any of this, and he might dislike the no-presidential-reelection rule that is at the heart of the Mexican regime.

The Communist Party of Cuba may also lack the political skills that made the PRI successful. The PRI negotiates and co-opts; the Cuban Communist Party commands and controls. The PRI is accustomed to clientelism and pork barrel politics; though these practices are not alien to the Cuban Communist Party, in Cuba they are seen as corrupt. The Communist Party's public values of probity and self-sacrifice would need to be jettisoned for it to be born again, phoenixlike, as the PRI.

Earlier, I explained why I think that a Mexico-like scenario is feasible. Nonetheless, the discussion of the Cuba= scenario and this more extended comparison should indicate that the prospects for this outcome remain poor because Fidel Castro and other Cuban leaders have failed to enact, or have undermined, the policies that might lead them to it.

Power Sharing with Other Parties

Yet a third international scenario is power sharing, as suggested by the cases of Poland, Hungary, Nicaragua, Romania, Lithuania, Slovakia, and Bulgaria. In all of them, former communists (in Nicaragua, the Sandinistas) have either won national elections again or done extremely well even if they lost; in the latter case, their clout is sufficient to protect their interests and to have considerable impact on government policies. The political discourse of Cuba's would-be former communists is easy to imagine: "We are the heirs of over one hundred years of struggle to defend the Cuban nation. In the face of promarket zealotry, we defend industry and labor against the ravages of neoliberal policies that shut down factories and create unemployment. We defend consumers who are victims of the lifting of price controls. We oppose the proposed destruction of the revolution's social and economic gains, the curtailment of social expenditures, the promises of economic decline followed by more decline, and the efforts to dismantle the national patrimony and turn it over to vulture capitalists." Or words to that effect. So a power-sharing scenario would be feasible only after Fidel Castro's departure from power. And yet, many current Cuban government and party officials could survive politically under such a scenario. As the earlier discussion of the creation of quasi-private firms indicates, many elites are already positioning themselves economically for such a negotiated transition.

In short, this international scenario is much more distant and less likely than those suggested by the experiences of China and Mexico mainly because Fidel Castro is still in command. In his absence, its likelihood would rise markedly. It could become the most likely scenario if the "right time" were some years after further economic decline fostered a consensus in Cuba on the need to arrange a transition that would be accepted by the U.S. government and a large proportion of Cuban Americans.

Regime Collapse

The most decisive international scenario is that of regime collapse. It is suggested by the happy cases of the Czech Republic, Poland, and Hungary, and also by the less happy cases of the Soviet Union and Yugoslavia.[32] The former were peaceful, the latter have been more violent. All have in common a colossal leadership blunder: that is, leaders thought mistakenly that they could control the transition. In the Czech Republic, Poland, and Hungary, in the first free national election, Communist Parties turned out to have the support of only about 10 percent of the electorates (in Poland and Hungary, however, reborn Communist Parties had returned to power by the mid-1990s). This is the strategy that Cuban leaders most seek to avoid as well as the political outcome that Cuban Americans and the U.S. government most seek to foster. There is little evidence, however, that Cuban leaders are likely to commit the political blunders that made the regime transition so relatively simple in Hungary and Czechoslovakia. They have learned what to avoid from the Eastern European experiences. And the ethnic violence that marked the breakup of Yugoslavia (and that is evident in several former Soviet Republics) is unlikely in Cuba.

The domestic counterpart of this international scenario is, of course, the Cuba— scenario in either of its variants. In the violent but quicker scenario, the economic costs of reconstructing Cuba would be increased by whatever destruction were brought about by the violence. In the less violent but delayed scenario, the initial readiness of Cuba's economy for a market transition would be quite poor, but it would be politically easier to implement market-oriented economic reforms because the Cuban Communist Party would be too weak to resist. Subsequent to a regime collapse, the circumstances of the Cuba+ scenario would apply.

Issues during the Transition to Somewhere
The Utility of Crime with Impunity

There has been a stunning decline in respect for law in contemporary Cuba. Cuba's economic transition has featured the illegalization of the majority of retail commercial transactions. The political regime's survival rests in part on the very kind of illegal market activity that it wishes to suppress: were it not for illegal markets, citizens would find it much more difficult to satisfy their basic necessities. Thanks to the illegal economic transition already under way, the political regime has survived. Its leaders know this, and thus they tolerate such activity. This do-it-yourself economic transition bears remarkable similarity to aspects of China's experience.[33] The point here is that Cuban capitalism is being reborn, in part, as common crime.

Under the current political regime, quasi-private firms may evolve lawfully into fully private firms. If so, some may believe that these firms result from unethical devolutions of state resources. Alternatively, quasi-private firms might become fully private but not lawfully so, either under the current or a successor regime. Thus, this more formal aspect of a transition toward markets may be either unethical or illegal.

When the poof moment arrives, Cuban government decision makers will have two options. They can denationalize the economy, selling it to foreign investors (including Cuban Americans). Or they can legalize past crimes in order to retain the economy in the hands of nationals. Will patriotic criminals or expatriate traitors prevail? In either case, it will be problematic, if not impossible, to punish those who broke the law to survive economically or even to enrich themselves prior to the poof moment. It is difficult to imagine that any Cuban government would seek to dispossess thousands of entrepreneurs at the time when the country needs entrepreneurs or that any Cuban military or police force (which would have engaged in similar behavior) would enforce the law. If there were a U.S. military occupation, some such law enforcement might be more likely; but even so, the most probable result would be a blanket amnesty. The incentives to Cubans to break the law are strong.

Prior to the poof moment, common crime has played a significant role in the reemergence of Cuba's civil society. Crime is a form of everyday resistance, one means for quotidian survival.[34] As groups of friends and neighbors cooperate to help each other, Cuba's civil society reemerges through networks of mutual assistance; citizens would meet at last without their government's supervision—and all the while they break the law. Cuba's grassroots democracy and autonomous associational life are also being reborn in crime.

Crime may also protect the post-poof-moment state from having to pay as much compensation for property once expropriated by the Cuban government. Property restitution and property compensation claims in Cuba's future will be complex because factories, farms, machinery and equipment, housing units, and so forth have been expanded, torn down, modified, moved, or otherwise rendered different from the original. To the extent that crime further alters the landscape of Cuba's properties, then restitution may become unfeasible, making compensation the only viable avenue. Moreover, the disappearance or dismantling of property through crime will simplify the question of compensation: at the poof moment, much property would also have gone poof.

Democratic Distemper

Cuba's civil society is slouching toward Bethlehem to be born. This civil society's growth raises questions about the relationship between state and society. Cuban civil society has long been submerged or controlled by the state, even well before the 1959 revolution. In the mid to late 1980s, Cuba's civil society began to emerge. Perhaps the largest group of religious believers in Cuba is identified with Afro-Cuban religiosity.[35] And yet, the institutions of Afro-Cuban religiosity have been typically decentralized and have survived at the sufferance of, or in opposition to, the state. Can a new Cuban government, or some version of the current one, design a relationship with Afro-Cuban religious believers that respects their dignity and that brings them into the mainstream of the nation's social life? That did not happen in Cuba before the 1959 revolution; it began to happen to some modest degree in the late 1980s, but there is much distance yet to go.

Domestic opposition political parties and human rights groups have been small, fragmented, competitive, and not well organized, despite the short-lived attempt in late 1995 and early 1996 to create a confederation of such groups through Concilio Cubano. Many of these groups, though ideologically liberal in their opposition to the government, identify still with some notion of "the revolution" and have views about markets that would make the economic transition more difficult.

On what basis could Cuba's democracy be born if the strongest entities in civil society are organized so weakly, articulated so poorly, and accustomed more to the role of witness than to that of politician? How well will Cuba be served if, or when, Cuban American politicians seek to be elected to public office in Cuba? Can an "alien" Miami civil society merge easily or well with the legacies of postcommunist Cuba? Will post-poof-moment Cuba cope with race relations problems as Cuban society typically has, namely, by denying that there is a problem? Or will there be an emergence of greater racial consciousness and racial tension in Cuba? Will returning Cuban Americans reproduce in Cuba the contentious pattern of race relations that they have helped construct in Miami? Independent of such outcomes, the structure of race relations in Cuba has been changing subtly. For example, by the late 1980s and continuing into the 1990s, there was a tendency for university students to be drawn from white professional families, a pattern reminiscent of prerevolutionary years.[36]

Old Bottles for New Wine

A key issue in Cuba's political transition to somewhere is the situation of public institutions. The formal institutions for crime control are among those most likely to persist for the duration of the existing political regime. They may also transit to a modified or successor regime, because the costs of dismantling them may be too high even in a replacement regime; such a regime will be concerned above all with changing political, military, and economic institutions. Common crime will be defined as an enemy by any government of Cuba. Oddly, this would suggest that aspects of the internal security apparatus, albeit not those focused on political crimes, may survive well into the future.

Similarly, even if much of the personnel that staffs the police and the courts is changed, the formal frameworks for these institutions are likely to linger, just as they did from the prerevolutionary to the revolutionary period. This has been a common experience throughout regime transitions in

Latin America. One question is whether the old regime's forces of order can be trusted to serve new liberal democratic masters. Can these institutional old bottles contain the new wine of more open politics?

One way to oversee such institutional legacies of an authoritarian regime would be to depend on the informational legacy of Cuba's human rights movement. But these groups have not yet been able to perform the tasks that comparable groups, more successful than Cuba's, were able to perform in other authoritarian settings in Latin America. Cuba's human rights groups have not been able to conduct much research, nor to develop means to diagnose emerging problems, nor have they had means to disseminate information effectively, nor means to check facts as rumors spread. These groups lack the analytical basis to nurture the oversight institutions of the future.

Thus, Cuba's transition to somewhere might be burdened by the continued strength of some of the institutions of the old regime and by the continued weakness of the institutions created by the democratic opposition, as the nation seeks to construct a new relationship between state and society.

Finally, the reliability of the political regime's own electoral institutions has declined. Perhaps one-third of the citizens of the city of Havana cast null or blank ballots in the December 1992 elections; the proportion of such ballots nationwide may have been one-fifth.[37] And yet, two months after those elections the government announced that the proportion of blank and null ballots nationwide was only 10 percent. Had these official figures been correct, it would have made no sense for the government and party to mobilize such impressive resources, as they did, to prevent the casting of blank or null ballots in the February 1993 elections (according to the official figures, 7 percent of the population did so nationwide).[38]

Perhaps for the first time since it began to hold municipal elections, the government may have committed fraud in the reporting of the results for the December 1992 (and, less clearly, in the February 1993) elections. Although the political environment for Cuban elections had always been highly adverse to the opposition, the results had been counted fairly on election day. This may have changed. This change may facilitate a regime transition along the lines of Mexico's PRI, but electoral fraud would make it more difficult for the opposition to trust the electoral results once a wider political opening were to become possible.

In short, the institutional foundations of regime transition in Cuba are weak and may have become even weaker. The capacity to substitute for the police and the courts or to monitor their work is poor, and the democratic reliability of once-reliable regime institutions may have declined.

Conclusion

Cubans have suffered many hardships in the 1990s. Their standard of living has declined. The possibilities for the full expression of their personality have narrowed. Their ability to shape the nation's politics is severely constrained. Even for Cuba's political leaders, the 1990s have been turbulent and tragic. Cuba's political and economic transitions, both already under way (though at different rates), have not yet produced successful outcomes.

I have generated a variety of scenarios to organize the available evidence. The possibilities for Cuba's future cut across a wide spectrum of outcomes. Neither full regime replacement nor the current leadership's preferred options would spare the Cuban people from even worse suffering for several more years. An appreciably more liberal, more democratic, and more prosperous Cuba is unlikely before the new millennium.

Cuba's stylized future may have a millenarian dimension in the more metaphorical meaning of that word. The most likely scenario for Cuba's future might be understood in terms of an analogy from evolutionary research. S. J. Gould and N. Eldredge have argued that evolutionary change is characterized by what they term punctuated equilibrium.[39] They contrast their position with Charles Darwin's. Under punctuated equilibrium, long periods of stasis are broken by short (in geologic time) episodes of rapid speciation. Sharp breaks occur in fossil records because one variant of a species quickly replaces its ancestor as a result of shifts in environmental conditions. Change occurs in response to constraints imposed by previous choices: earlier adaptations, or earlier elimination of certain species, channel subsequent developments. Change thus responds to structural legacies, not just to individual adjustment. In Darwin's synthesis, in contrast, change is slow, steady, gradual, and individualistic.

Thinking in these terms about Cuba's future, there may a period of stasis (the baseline scenario) along with Darwinian efforts at adaptation by individual will (the *China scenario or the less ambitious Cuba= scenario). Not much would change for some years (long, in political time). Nor would a quick and easy overthrow soon bring about a wholly different political and economic regime because change is difficult, constrained as it is by previous choices, structures, the wider environment, and human action. As also happens with earthquakes and volcanic explosions, however, tensions would build as successive efforts at adaptation fail to solve fundamental problems. I cannot foresee when this poof moment might arrive, but it is likely to be somewhat unexpected, swift, perhaps violent, and most likely comprehensive in its consequences.

The alternative to such a scenario—adverse for everyone who cares about

Cuba—would require sustained initiatives in Cuba and in the international community to open up Cuba's politics peacefully and to reorient its economy. This pious wish seems unlikely to be realized soon, however, so the forecast remains one of equilibrium waiting for punctuation, slow decline waiting for a catastrophe.

Conclusion

"And thus let Hope be the ever-lasting vision among us," wrote the Nicaraguan Rubén Darío (1867–1916) in the penultimate line to his poem, "The Optimist's Salutation."[1] And yet, optimism about politics seemed so un–Latin American for so long, certainly difficult for a Nicaraguan, and unlikely in a region heir to the pessimism recorded in *Martín Fierro* (see introduction). Scholars and politicians had long rightly emphasized the significance of values, structures, habits, traditions, international vulnerability, and plain bad luck that helped to account for the feebleness of democracy in this part of the world. As the millennium ends, however, many people in Latin America and the Caribbean are optimistic that a past of dictatorship and abuse is over and that a vision of democratic politics lies ahead.

This book shares an optimistic expectation about the prospects for democratic politics in these countries. I remain mindful, of course, of continuing evidence of profound dissatisfaction with the workings of democracy and the lot of ordinary citizens. Even as I write, the daily news reports violent clashes between police and demonstrators in Ecuador, Venezuela, and Haiti—and that is just one day's events. Nonetheless, Latin America, especially, is much better off as the century closes than it was not all that long ago under the boot of military dictators or the sway of torturers justifying their application of electric shock to their victims in the name of anticommunism, Roman Catholicism, and the defense of Western civilization. The quotidian failings of democratic politics should not obscure the stunning historical achievements of democratic governments, politicians, and ordinary citizens in constructing a new civic life and reopening the chances for prosperity.

These final reflections draw from the preceding chapters four general themes about this region's recent experience and likely future, situating these cases in a wider context of democratic politics through comparisons with Central and Eastern European cases. I emphasize the differences in my findings from those of some of the best scholars of democratization and democracy in order to call attention to the need for further analysis and re-search to ascertain the validity of these generalizations. In my judgment, scholarship about Latin America and the Caribbean has underemphasized the positive effect of international factors and the actions of ordinary citi-zens as voters on the process of the consolidation of democracy. Scholars should also attend more closely to the historic shift in the relationship be-tween the armed forces and the process of the consolidation of democracy. Finally, the scholarly literature has surely emphasized the role of strategy, choice, and craftsmanship in the making of the democratic transition, but it has underappreciated the skill of politicians in overcoming or working around many hurdles to foster the consolidation of democracy.

The International Effects on Democratization and Democracy

There has been no common or similar impact of the international system on specific transitions to democracy in Latin America and the Caribbean from the late 1970s to the 1990s.[2] There has been no uniform regional effect on the likelihood of democratization—that is, the transition from authoritarian re-gimes to constitutional governments through free, fair, and competitive elections. There has been, however, a strong and positive effect of the inter-national system on the prospects for the consolidation of democracy after such a political transition throughout the Latin American and the Carib-bean region. To understand the variation, I distinguish according to sub-region, time period, and issue areas.

In the Anglophone Caribbean, the United Kingdom long shielded these island countries from the winds of the Cold War and contributed its gov-ernmental, partisan, and civic institutional examples to help fashion endur-ing democratic polities. In the Spanish Caribbean, the results are mixed. In 1978 and in 1996, the United States fostered the transfer of power from one civilian president to another through fair and free elections in the Domini-can Republic; in 1978, U.S. pressure was decisive in bringing about this out-come. With regard to Cuba, however, in the 1990s U.S. policy unwittingly helped the government and the Communist Party to rally nationalist elite and popular support in the face of increasingly interventionist U.S. law and policy. The Communist Parties of China, Russia, Vietnam, and Serbia, among others, have demonstrated a capacity to assume the mantle of nation-alism; the Cuban Communist Party has done so as well. The United States probably retarded Cuba's democratization in the 1990s.

Several Central American countries, in contrast, are closer to the experi-ence of the former communist countries of Central and Eastern Europe. Democratization could advance in Nicaragua, El Salvador, and Guatemala, as in former communist Europe, only upon the ending of the Cold War and thanks to a marked change in the foreign policy of the most proximate super-power. Until the late 1980s, the United States and the Soviet Union opposed most negotiations between the government and the antiregime opposition in the respective regions—the very negotiations that would, eventually, prove to be the key to a political opening and, in Central America, to paci-fication as well.

U.S. military intervention has also had the long-term effect of opening the gates to democratization in the circum-Caribbean in recent decades; in due course, democratization followed U.S. military interventions in the Do-minican Republic in 1965, Grenada in 1983, Panama in 1989, and Haiti in 1994. This is a strikingly consistent finding. Troubled as these countries re-main—Haiti, most so—their politics became clearly more open and demo-cratic after U.S. military intervention than they had been. In the latter three cases, U.S. forces smashed the domestic military establishment that had underpinned each dictatorship, thereby making more democratic politics possible.

The South American experience has been more varied. In no South Amer-ican case except Argentina are international variables as important in ex-plaining the likelihood of democratization, as in Central America, or democ-racy's endurance, as in the Anglophone Caribbean. Moreover, the variation in the relative weight of international variables in the South American cases is noteworthy. Argentina's defeat in the 1982 war with the United Kingdom over sovereignty in the South Atlantic islands broke the power of the mili-tary junta, opening the way for a democratic transition.[3] The effects of U.S. policy, however, have been quite variable over time. In the late 1970s, U.S. policy probably contributed to the transition to democracy in Ecuador and Peru. In the early 1980s, in contrast, U.S. policy probably retarded democ-ratization in the Southern Cone countries. Finally, U.S. policy assisted the likelihood of democratization in Chile and Paraguay at the end of that dec-ade. International factors were least important in the eventual transitions in Brazil and Uruguay. The utility of international variables in explaining the likelihood and timing of democratization, therefore, is best focused on Cen-tral America and the Caribbean as well as on former communist Europe.

The international system has had a more consistent regional effect on the process of consolidation of democracy. All the Latin American countries suffered dramatically from the debt crisis that broke out in 1982–83; its con-sequences depressed Latin America's economic growth rates for the bal-ance of the decade. From 1981 to 1990, all but four Latin American countries had negative rates of change in gross domestic product per capita; the best performer, Colombia, grew barely a cumulative 18 percent for the entire decade. The wreckage of the debt crisis and its wider economic effects was far more severe in Latin America than elsewhere in the world (most African countries had not been creditworthy enough to get into such high levels of debt). East Asia, Europe, and North America recovered much more quickly than Latin America from the economic recession of the early 1980s.[4]

Latin America's great depression of the 1980s posed extraordinary challenges for economic management by democratic governments.[5] Perhaps most important, this economic crisis broke the back of the old economic models and opened the windows to new ideas about economic policy and about the connections between markets and democracy. The ideological tsunami that swept through the international system in the late 1980s and early 1990s helped reshape the cognitive map of decision makers about democracy and markets.[6] The turn toward democratic capitalism in Latin America and the Caribbean was nearly uniform by the late 1990s; the international diffusion of ideas made a powerful contribution to this common outcome.

In terms of the process of democratic consolidation, the Latin American cases share some features with the former communist countries of Europe. In both of these regions, there has been an attempted double transition toward democracy and markets from prior conditions of dictatorship and statist economics during approximately the same period of time.[7] In Central and Eastern Europe as in Latin America, the two transitions have been complex. In both regions, international organizations, led by the major powers (which sometimes have acted alone), have sought to defend democratic institutions; the Council of Europe, the European Union, and the Organization of American States have played these roles in various ways.[8] The United States has generally played a constructive role. In Latin America in the 1990s, international actions with strong U.S. participation helped to protect constitutional government in Guatemala, Haiti, Venezuela, and Paraguay by helping to deter or overturn military coup attempts; in the 1980s, the United States pressured domestic actors to prevent coup attempts in El Salvador, Honduras, Bolivia, and Ecuador. The record of success in Latin America in gradually strengthening democratic institutions and practices is so far generally positive, though much remains to be done. The record of success in Europe is much more variable; the greater success in strengthening democratic institutions and practices is evident in Poland, the Czech Republic, Hungary, and Slovenia, which are also, not surprisingly, among the countries most likely to be accepted into the European Union or the North Atlantic Treaty Organization (NATO), or both.

In brief, the connection between the international system and the likelihood of democratization is quite variable in Latin America and at times weak, but the connection between the international system and processes of democratic consolidation in Latin America, the Caribbean, and former communist Europe is much stronger and unidirectional. The reason for this difference is the strong ideological change in the international system that began in the 1980s and continues in the 1990s. The major powers came to believe that democracy matters for international order, and they have been much more willing to act accordingly, alone and through international organizations. The effects have been large and important in Latin America and the Caribbean (except in Cuba), where democratic forces have long been at work. The effects are noteworthy but less uniformly decisive in former communist Europe, where the strength of domestic democratic forces is more varied and, in some countries, much weaker. In short, the international system can and has tilted domestic politics quite effectively, especially in countries where prior domestic political forces are already favoring democratic consolidation.

"There are two ways of constructing an international order," Henry Kissinger wrote in explaining the formalization of the concert of European powers at the Congress of Vienna, "by will or by renunciation; by conquest or by legitimacy."[9] In the 1990s, there is a notable effort to build the international order, at least in part, on the shoulders of democratic polities. This international explanation, therefore, may be the clue as to why the past pendular swings between democracy and dictatorship in Latin America (noted in the introduction) may remain simply part of the past.

Citizen Effects on Democratization and Democracy

The role of ordinary citizens in explaining democratic transitions in Latin America has characteristically been seen as secondary. Guillermo O'Donnell and Philippe Schmitter set the tone in their agenda-setting book. For their explanation, they emphasized "elite dispositions, calculations, and pacts . . . because they largely determine whether or not an opening will occur at all." Then and only then, "a generalized mobilization is likely to occur, which we choose to describe as the 'resurrection of civil society.'"[10] Indeed, the record of Latin American cases supports their finding, but the experience in former communist Europe suggests a wider range of possibilities.

The effect of rapid political mobilization was much more decisive in the transitions in East Germany and Czechoslovakia than in any Latin American case, and a revolution backed by the military toppled the Rumanian communist regime.[11] Civil society also played a long-term role in the slow-moving transition in Poland. Arguably, there are important similarities between the processes of transition in Poland and Mexico. In each country, the authoritarian regime was less harsh than elsewhere in their respective regions. In each, the transition was protracted. And in each, the transition began when ordinary folks shocked the elites into action: the widespread worker strikes in Poland in the summer of 1980[12] and the unexpected large vote for the opposition in Mexico in July 1988. On balance, civil society played a protagonist's role in the process of democratization in several of the European cases, more so than in Latin America, and for this reason the assessment of the role of ordinary citizens in democratization remains indeterminate on a wider comparative basis.

The role of citizens, however, is much more uniformly important in explaining the likelihood of democratic consolidation. Voters have played a key role in shaping the rhythm and content of democratic politics after the transition, though they have done so with some delay. At first, as Susan Stokes has argued, "majority preferences in economic policy, as expressed in elections, failed to translate into government policy" in several countries in Latin America and the Caribbean.[13] The gap between campaign election discourse and eventual government policy was most marked in the 1982 election of Salvador Jorge Blanco in the Dominican Republic, the 1989 election of Carlos Menem in Argentina, and the 1990 election of Alberto Fujimori in Peru. The gap was also considerable in the 1985 election of Víctor Paz Estenssoro in Bolivia, the 1989 election of Carlos Andrés Pérez in Venezuela, and the 1989 election of Michael Manley in Jamaica. Many voters, understandably, thought that politicians had lied. The connection between the preferences of voters and the actions of elected government officials had been severed at democracy's peril.

But voters had subsequent chances to pass judgment on the liars and the relative merits of the programs eventually adopted. In the Dominican Republic and Venezuela, voters punished the Dominican Revolutionary Party (PRD) and Acción Democrática (AD) in the next presidential elections. In Argentina and Peru, voters approved a change in the constitution to permit the incumbent president's immediate reelection—and then reelected Menem and Fujimori. And in Jamaica the People's National Party was also rewarded with the electoral ratification of its incumbency and its economic program. In these second elections after the politicians sinned, voters discerned differently in various countries according to the efficacy of results. Democracy malfunctions when politicians lie; it works better when voters have an opportunity to judge liars and their programs.

In other cases, campaign promises have been closer to the actual programs of government. The victory of the Chilean center-left opposition parties in 1989 was based on government programs that were made public during the election campaign and eventually implemented; Chile's Concertación Democrática coalition was rewarded with reelection in 1993. The same transparency and consistency between campaign promise and government performance was evident in the case of the right-wing ARENA's victory in El Salvador in the 1989 election; ARENA was rewarded with another national election victory in 1994. Fernando Henrique Cardoso was elected president of Brazil in 1994 on the basis of his record as finance minister. And Ernesto Zedillo won the fairest-ever presidential election in Mexico in 1994 based on his record and his promises, which were eventually implemented while he was in office.[14]

Three trends were evident in elections in Latin America and the Caribbean in the late 1980s and early 1990s. First, in the midst of crisis, voters tended to vote against the incumbent party in virtually every country where fair, competitive elections were held (Colombia was the principal exception). Second, in a number of these elections, key politicians lied, but voters kept the opportunity to pass judgment on them or their parties at the next election. Third, by the mid-1990s "sincere" campaigning had become more common. Incumbents had little choice but to run on their record; more important, challengers in many countries, ranging from giant Brazil to tiny El Salvador, chose to contest power on the basis of a transparent program. This suggests that the behavior of voters helps to explain the course that history is actually taking in these countries and that democratic procedures, albeit on a lag, are working.

Experiences in former communist Europe bear some resemblance to Latin America's. Where free, fair, and competitive elections have been held repeatedly, voters troubled by economic or other distress have voted against the incumbents in Lithuania, Ukraine, Poland, Hungary, Bulgaria, and Rumania.[15] Where economic performance was better, as in the Czech Republic and Slovenia, voters retained the incumbent, center-hugging, coalitions while reshuffling the relative weights of parties. In former communist Europe, too, many supporters of Communist Parties discovered a gap between campaign promises and actual government performance—for example, in Poland and Hungary but most clearly in Bulgaria, where, in 1996–97, electoral defeat and massive demonstrations were aimed at the Bulgarian Socialist Party government. Voters in these countries have kept and exercised their right to reward or punish parties in successive elections, thereby also helping to explain and shape the actual course of politics and policy in these countries.

Ordinary citizens, in short, played an important role in the process of democratization in some European countries and, to a lesser degree, in some Latin American countries, but they have played a decisive role in the processes of consolidation of democracy in both of these regions. The Anglophone Caribbean, long accustomed to punishing or rewarding parties and politicians in competitive elections, had led the way. And even Mexico, a laggard in the process of democratic transition, has experienced significant change in the values of citizens who are readier for democracy than those who rule in their name. The attitudes of citizens and their behavior as voters have come to matter at long last.

"Democratic politics is a system of interactions and accountability between rulers and ruled," as Scott Mainwaring has aptly reminded those scholars who underestimate the significance of citizens for democratic politics.[16] First in the Anglophone Caribbean, and now more generally in Latin America and Central and Eastern Europe, scholars and politicians err if they ignore the protagonism of citizens in explaining key aspects about the practice of democratic politics and policies.[17]

Soldiers, Democratization, and Democracy

"If there is one characteristic common to all our cases it is the omnipresent fear, during the transition, and often long after political democracy has been installed, that a coup will be attempted and succeed," wrote Guillermo O'Donnell and Philippe Schmitter in the mid-1980s.[18] They also noted that such coups virtually never happened. A dozen years later, their findings stand. The fear of the coup haunts new democracies almost everywhere. As noted in chapter 3, there have been various coup attempts in Iberoamerica, but nowhere since 1976 (in Argentina) has the military overthrown a civilian president elected in free and fair elections held according to constitutional procedures.[19] In former communist Europe, as well, democratic transitions have not been interrupted by military coups. Worrying about such coups, O'Donnell and Schmitter also noted accurately, may make them less likely because civilians undertake policies to avoid the conditions that might lead to coups.

Nevertheless, although the military has rarely acted alone to overthrow constitutional governments in recent years, it has in certain cases supported a freely elected civilian president who has undermined or scuttled constitutional government. In Latin America, the principal example was President Alberto Fujimori's *auto-golpe* in Peru in 1992. In Eastern Europe, the clearest case is that of President Alyaksandr Lukashenka in Belarus in 1996. Whereas in Peru the unconstitutional government was short-lived, the prospects for a return to democratic practices seem more dire in Belarus.

In times past, soldiers played a more complex role with regard to democratization. When the armed forces of Rumania joined civilians to overthrow the dictatorship of President Nicolae Ceauşescu, they were acting as militaries had in Latin America earlier in the twentieth century. In Chile in the late 1920s and early 1930s, in Argentina, Guatemala, and Venezuela in the mid-1940s, in Venezuela and Colombia in the late 1950s, for example, military coups (often with ample civilian participation) opened up the political system and led to free, fair, and competitive elections in due course. Samuel Huntington has called these (and other similar instances in countries elsewhere in the world) "breakthrough coups."[20] This democratizing role of the armed forces has faded in recent times.

The role of force in bringing about democratization, however, has not disappeared altogether. As noted in chapter 2, force—drawn out in prolonged civil war—was a necessary component for the eventual political openings in Nicaragua, El Salvador, and Guatemala. And, as noted earlier, U.S. military interventions in the Dominican Republic, Grenada, Panama, and Haiti were decisive contributors to their democratization.

The novelty in the 1980s and 1990s has been the role of the military high command in defending constitutional government against military coups. General officers repeatedly played a key role in putting down coup attempts in Argentina in the 1980s through 1990 and in Venezuela in the early 1990s; the same occurred in Guatemala during the presidency of Marco Vinicio Cerezo in the late 1980s (as in the Philippines to defeat a 1989 coup attempt). In Ecuador in the 1980s and in Panama and Paraguay in the 1990s (as in Spain in 1981), some senior officers supported coup attempts, but constitutionalist senior officers prevailed in the end. Force was used in Trinidad and Tobago to defeat uprisings in 1970 and 1990 and to put down repeated coup attempts in Dominica in 1979–81.

In the past, the armed forces overthrew governments for a wide array of reasons. Most often, they sought to impose their will on the society;[21] less often, but in key cases, they overthrew an oligarchical or dictatorial government in order to open up politics. In recent years, the military appears to have taken more seriously their oath to uphold and defend the constitution.[22] Professionalism, at long last, seems to be explaining the greater likelihood that the military high command will support democratic institutions.[23] That augurs well for the prospects for democracy and helps to explain its endurance.

Valuing Politicians

Few characters may be more disreputable than politicians in the eyes of the public. In the parlance of scholarship about Latin American politics, *populism* is a label often indiscriminately attached to a wide array of politicians, when in fact scholars often mean "irresponsible demagogues."

This book celebrates the skills of many politicians. They are architects of the functioning democracies of the Anglophone Caribbean, ready to make deals to govern, capable of gathering public support, but also honorably ready to acknowledge defeat at the polls, when that is the case. They are the statesmen who at last ended Central America's wars, opened politics and markets, labored long against rigidities in the U.S. government and in their own countries, and at times overrode the preferences of their own support-ers. They are the technopols, lords of the craft of enacting economic reforms, often (though not always) through the procedures of democracy and for the sake of advancing and consolidating democratic objectives.[24] They are the street-level politicians and the national leaders who construct, adapt, and reshape political parties, which are the essential instruments of democratic politics.[25]

Many politicians have fostered and sustained democratic politics against seemingly impossible odds. "We begin with the assumption that economic instability and recession pose serious threats to democratic consolidation," wrote Stephan Haggard and Robert Kaufman about an underlying premise in their path-breaking study of the political economy of democratic transi-tions.[26] Adam Przeworski turns this proposition around to add his conclu-sion that "democracy in the political realm works against economic re-forms."[27] And yet, they exaggerate.

Latin American democracies survived the great economic depression of the 1980s; democracy in East Central Europe is holding up, too, despite very severe economic downturns in the early 1990s. In both Latin America and East Central Europe, democratic governments have enacted economic re-forms with appreciable success.[28] They have changed substantially the eco-nomic framework that prevailed at the moment of democratic transition in their countries, and in some countries they have done so dramatically. Latin American economies grew in the first half of the 1990s. In December 1994, a major financial panic hit Mexico, with immediate adverse repercussions throughout the region. And yet, by the end of 1995, all Latin American econ-omies but Argentina, Mexico, and Uruguay had positive rates of growth of gross domestic product; so did all the economies in the Anglophone Carib-bean but Dominica. From 1991 to 1995, despite the aftershocks of the Mex-ican financial debacle, the gross domestic product of South America grew by a cumulative 20 percent; Central America (Nicaragua excepted) and Pan-ama cumulatively grew closer to 25 percent in those years.[29]

In Europe, Poland, the Czech Republic, Slovakia, and Slovenia were growing well by the mid-1990s; Hungary also had positive growth rates despite its economic difficulties.[30] All of these governments continued to enact economic reforms. On balance, in Central and Eastern Europe, the more democratic the former communist country had become, the more substantial the economic reforms it adopted and the better its economic performance had become.[31] Moreover, politicians were not fools. The evidence from public opinion surveys shows that voters rewarded politicians who carried out rapid economic reforms, and that is one reason they were adopted.[32]

Democracy was making several contributions to economic reform in this small but important set of East Central European countries. Democratic politicians understood that the enemies of market reforms were often also the enemies of democracy; their democratic survival was advanced by the turn away from bureaucratic control over economy and society. Democratic politics required argument and explanation, helping to build tolerance, at a minimum, and support over time for the changing economic strategies. Elections brought into power new leaders with new ideas, making it possible to begin reforms. Many early reformers were defeated in subsequent elections in Poland, Hungary, and Lithuania, and parties of former communists came into office; these former communists, however, continued the economic reforms. As a result of elections, therefore, most parties across the ideological spectrum in this set of countries came to endorse and promote market reforms, making them more likely to endure and succeed. As in Latin America so too in East Central Europe: the opposition is the most effective long-term guarantee that market reforms will hold. The double transition may, in fact, have made it easier to consolidate democracy and markets; the lack of a fuller democratic transition, in turn, may also retard a market transition, as is evident (except in the Baltics) in most of the new states heir to the old Soviet Union.[33]

Politicians have also worked within suboptimal political institutions. That is the message of a part of chapter 3 in this book, and the stronger view of scholars who entitle their book *The Failure of Presidential Democracy: The Case of Latin America*.[34] And yet, politicians have sustained constitutional government, expanded the suffrage, advanced economic reform, and in some countries, begun to address the enormous social problems evident in Latin America and the Caribbean and, to a different extent, also in former communist Europe.

Politicians work most effectively through political parties.[35] Throughout this book, arguments and evidence have been presented about the impressive capacity of politicians in Latin America and the Caribbean to invent and reinvent parties to meet new challenges. The experience of former Communist Parties in Europe bears a strong resemblance to the political creativity of these politicians in the Western Hemisphere. Politicians and parties work relentlessly to reduce the uncertainties inherent in democratic politics.[36]

The accomplishments of politicians and political parties to reduce uncertainty are detailed in various chapters in this book. In the Anglophone

Caribbean, politicians and parties have sought to protect these small island countries from the vagaries of international economic and political forces, and they have drawn benefits for their homelands thanks to their skill at navigating through the international system. In Central America, they worked hard and effectively to create political certainties to persuade the powerful to yield their power, an especially noteworthy achievement in countries wracked by civil and international war for many years. Technopols, in turn, have sought to fashion long-term economic policies and market rules to provide effective certainties to rational investors.

Above all, politicians talk, argue, and disagree, seemingly endlessly. That is what they should do. The alternative is abuse and imposition without consultation or participation. Talk and especially disagreement is at the heart of democratic politics. Deliberation is essential for democracy.[37] Deliberative democratic politics seeks to gather the informed consent of the governed and to harness it to advance public goals that are contested, disputed, and changed until a new basis for further progress is reached. Thus, democracy is an arduous, time-consuming, and difficult task; leadership in a democracy requires special talents.

No wonder Machiavelli wrote in *The Prince*: "There is nothing more difficult to carry out, nor more doubtful of success, nor more dangerous to handle, than to initiate a new order of things."[38] Democrats know this all too well, and politicians know it instinctively and keenly. And yet, the record of accomplishment in democratization and, despite many ongoing weaknesses, in constructing democratic politics in Latin America and the Caribbean is impressive and reassuring, albeit still surprising. The record is good enough to believe that Martín Fierro's legacy may have been overcome and that Rubén Darío may have turned out to be right, though a century late: Let Hope be the ever-lasting vision among us.

Notes

Introduction

1. José Hernández, *El gaucho Martín Fierro*, 8th. ed. (Buenos Aires: Editorial Sopena, 1961), verses 52–78; quotation from verse 72.

2. The intellectual guiding light for the Reagan administration's first-term policies that followed from this premise was Jeane Kirkpatrick's "Dictatorships and Double Standards," *Commentary* 68 (1979): 34–45.

3. For some of the gruesome evidence, see Jorge I. Domínguez, Nigel S. Rodley, Bryce Wood, and Richard Falk, *Enhancing Global Human Rights* (New York: McGraw-Hill, 1979), 93–102.

4. David Collier, ed., *The New Authoritarianism in Latin America* (Princeton: Princeton University Press, 1979).

5. Ecuador and the Dominican Republic do not appear in the index to this book. Peru's military government does receive extensive treatment.

6. This was exactly Douglas Chalmers' insight, which proved a much better guide to understanding Latin America's future than more determinist explanations. See his "The Politicized State in Latin America," in *Authoritarianism and Corporatism in Latin America*, ed. James M. Malloy (Pittsburgh: University of Pittsburgh Press, 1977).

7. Karen L. Remmer, "Redemocratization and the Impact of Authoritarian Rule in Latin America," *Comparative Politics* 17 (1985): 253. Six years later, however, Remmer called attention to, and rightly criticized, the continuing expectation of Latin Americanists that democratic regimes would fail. See her "New Wine or Old Bottlenecks? The Study of Latin American Democracy," *Comparative Politics* 23 (1991): 479–95. In this and other works, Remmer does much to shed light on the changes in political practices.

8. Mitchell A. Seligson, "Democratization in Latin America: The Current Cycle," in *Authoritarians and Democrats: Regime Transition in Latin America*, ed. James M. Malloy and Mitchell A. Seligson (Pittsburgh: University of Pittsburgh Press, 1987), 3–4.

9. Adam Przeworski, *Democracy and the Market: Political and Economic Reforms in Eastern Europe and Latin America* (Cambridge: Cambridge University Press, 1991), 161, 180.

10. Writing about the 1980s, Robert Kaufman and Barbara Stallings at first seem

to provide conclusive evidence that authoritarian regimes are much more likely to install "orthodox" economic policies. This finding occurs principally as a result of their case selection: they exclude the years under authoritarian rule in the 1980s in Argentina, Brazil, and Uruguay. Had they included those cases, the results would have been indeterminate. The nature of the political regime did not explain the likelihood of adopting orthodox economic policies. See their "Debt and Democracy in the 1980s: The Latin American Experience," in *Debt and Democracy in Latin America*, ed. Robert Kaufman and Barbara Stallings (Boulder: Westview, 1989), 211.

11. In an article published in 1987, I noted the marked decline in military coups. Despite a severe economic crisis and a Reagan administration policy tolerant of dictatorships, "no competitive civilian regime was overthrown in Latin America between 1980 and 1986," while various other countries "made transitions away from military rule." Nonetheless, I was unsure about the prospects for stable democracy, arguing that the political process then under way might be "not a transition 'to' democracy" but "a transition 'from' the past to an uncertain future for less governable societies." Democracy in Latin America has done much better. See Jorge I. Domínguez, "Political Change: Central America, South America, and the Caribbean," in *Understanding Political Development*, ed. Myron Weiner and Samuel P. Huntington (Boston: Little, Brown, 1987), 80.

12. See, for example, Russell J. Dalton, Scott C. Flanagan, and Paul Allen Beck, eds., *Electoral Change in Advanced Industrial Democracies* (Princeton: Princeton University Press, 1984).

13. Guillermo O'Donnell, *Modernization and Bureaucratic- Authoritarianism: Studies in South American Politics* (Berkeley: Institute of International Studies, University of California at Berkeley, 1973). See also Malloy, *Authoritarianism and Corporatism in Latin America*.

14. Michel Crozier, Samuel P. Huntington, and Joji Watanuki, *The Crisis of Democracy: Report on the Governability of Democracies to the Trilateral Commission* (New York: New York University Press, 1975).

15. For an eloquent argument along these lines, see Przeworski, *Democracy and the Market*.

16. See, for example, the discussion by one of Cardoso's premier critics, Robert Packenham, in his *The Dependency Movement: Scholarship and Politics in Development Studies* (Cambridge: Harvard University Press, 1992).

17. See, for example, Robert E. Scott, *Mexican Government in Transition* (Urbana: University of Illinois Press, 1959); and Susan Kaufman Purcell, ed., *Mexico in Transition: Implications for U.S. Policy* (New York: Council on Foreign Relations, 1988).

18. Beatriz Manz, *Refugees of a Hidden War: The Aftermath of Counterinsurgency in Guatemala* (Albany: State University of New York Press, 1988).

19. Jorge I. Domínguez, *Cuba: Order and Revolution* (Cambridge: Harvard University Press, 1978).

20. For an effective formulation and use of these arguments, see Theda Skocpol, *States and Social Revolutions: A Comparative Analysis of France, Russia, and China* (Cambridge: Cambridge University Press, 1979).

21. For a classic discussion of these issues, see Robert Packenham, *Liberal America and the Third World: Political Development Ideas in Foreign Aid and the Social Sciences* (Princeton: Princeton University Press, 1973).

22. The detailed history is rather more complex. In the mid-1940s, the United States attempted to foster Nicaragua's democratization despite Anastasio Somoza García's opposition. In 1958, the United States distanced itself from Fulgencio Batista's dictatorship in Cuba. And shortly thereafter, the U.S. Central Intelligence Agency supported plots that would in the end lead to the assassination of Rafael Trujillo in the Dominican Republic.

23. Cole Blasier, *The Giant's Rival: The USSR and Latin America*, rev. ed. (Pittsburgh: University of Pittsburgh Press, 1989).

24. See Kathryn Sikkink, *Ideas and Institutions: Developmentalism in Brazil and Argentina* (Ithaca: Cornell University Press, 1991).

25. Guillermo O'Donnell and Philippe C. Schmitter, *Transitions from Authoritarian Rule: Tentative Conclusions about Uncertain Democracies* (Baltimore: Johns Hopkins University Press, 1986), 5.

26. Ibid.

27. In this way, I differ to some extent from Przeworski's insightful analysis in *Democracy and the Market*.

Chapter 1: The Caribbean Question

This chapter originally appeared in *Democracy in the Caribbean: Political, Economic, and Social Perspectives*, ed. Jorge I. Domínguez, Robert A. Pastor, and R. DeLisle Worrell (Baltimore: Johns Hopkins University Press, 1993).

1. Ralf Dahrendorf, *Society and Democracy in Germany* (Munich, 1965; New York: Norton, 1979).

2. This chapter does not include Cuba, except for an occasional point. Obviously, Cuba's political regime is not liberal democratic.

3. For a historical perspective, see Anthony Payne, *The Politics of the Caribbean Community, 1961–79: Regional Integration amongst New States* (Manchester: Manchester University Press, 1980).

4. For a thoughtful discussion, see Anthony Maingot, *The United States and the Caribbean: Challenges of an Asymmetrical Relationship* (Boulder: Westview, 1994).

5. For excellent analyses of politics in two of the larger countries, see Anthony Payne, *Politics in Jamaica*, rev. ed. (New York: St. Martin's, 1995); Evelyne Huber Stephens and John D. Stephens, *Democratic Socialism in Jamaica: The Political Movement and Social Transformation in Dependent Capitalism* (Princeton: Princeton University Press, 1986); and Selwyn Ryan, *The Disillusioned Electorate: The Politics of Succession in Trinidad and Tobago* (Port of Spain: Inprint Caribbean, 1989). For wider coverage, see Anthony Payne and Paul Sutton, *Modern Caribbean Politics* (Baltimore: Johns Hopkins University Press, 1993).

6. See Myron Weiner and Samuel P. Huntington, eds., *Understanding Political Development* (Boston: Little, Brown, 1987), chap. 2.

7. World Bank, *World Development Report: 1990* (New York: Oxford University Press, 1990), tables 1 and A.1.

8. Data are from Inter-American Development Bank, *Economic and Social Progress in Latin America: 1989 Report* (Washington, D.C.: IDB, 1989), 463.

9. United Nations Economic Commission for Latin American and the Caribbean, *Preliminary Overview of the Economy of Latin America and the Caribbean: 1989*, LC/G. 1586 (New York: ECLAC, 1989), 18.

10. Samuel P. Huntington, "Will More Countries Become Democratic?" *Political Science Quarterly* 99 (1984): 201.

11. U.S. Arms Control and Disarmament Agency, *World Military Expenditures and Arms Transfers: 1987* (Washington, D.C.: Government Printing Office, 1988), table 1.

12. Dion E. Phillips, "Defense Policy in Barbados, 1966–88," *Journal of Interamerican Studies and World Affairs* 32 (1990): 69–102.

13. For a detailed reconstruction of these events, see Selwyn Ryan and Taimoon Stewart, *The Black Power Revolution 1970: A Retrospective* (St. Augustine: Institute for Social and Economic Research, University of the West Indies, 1995).

14. For an analysis, see Selwyn Ryan, *The Muslimeen Grab for Power: Race, Religion, and Revolution in Trinidad and Tobago* (Port of Spain: Inprint Caribbean, 1991).

15. See Anthony P. Maingot, "The Visions of Elites since Independence," paper prepared for the World Peace Foundation's Caribbean Project, October 1990; see also Maingot, "The Caribbean: The Structure of Modern-Conservative Societies," in *Latin America, Its Problems and Its Promise: A Multidisciplinary Introduction*, ed. Jan Knippers Black (Boulder: Westview, 1984).

16. For a fine discussion of the Caribbean in historical context, see Franklin Knight, *The Caribbean: Genesis of a Fragmented Nationalism*, 2d ed. (Oxford: Oxford University Press, 1990).

17. Robert A. Dahl, *Polyarchy: Participation and Opposition* (New Haven: Yale University Press, 1971), 110–11.

18. See also Selwyn Ryan, *Race and Nationalism in Trinidad and Tobago: A Study of Decolonization in a Multiracial Society* (Toronto: University of Toronto Press, 1972).

19. For a discussion of efforts to manage such cleavages in the Netherlands Antilles and Suriname by means of consociational pacts, see Arend Lijphart, *Democracy in Plural Societies* (New Haven: Yale University Press, 1977), chap. 6.

20. See Claus Offe, "Competitive Party Democracies and the Keynesian Welfare State," in his *Contradictions of the Welfare State* (Cambridge: MIT Press, 1984).

21. For a valuable assessment of Caribbean economic performance, see R. DeLisle Worrell, *Small Island Economies: Structure and Performance in the English-Speaking Caribbean since 1970* (New York: Praeger, 1987); and also his *Economic Policies in Small Open Economies: Prospects for the Caribbean*, Commonwealth Economic Papers 23 (London: Commonwealth Secretariat, 1992).

22. Data from World Bank, *World Development Report: 1990*, tables 1, 28, and A.1.

23. I am grateful to Javier Corrales for provoking this thought. See also Peter J. Katzenstein, *Small States in World Markets: Industrial Policy in Europe* (Ithaca: Cornell University Press, 1985).

24. See, e.g., Carl Stone, "Political Aspects of Postwar Agricultural Policies in Jamaica (1945–1970)," *Social and Economic Studies* 23 (1974): 145–76.

25. Charles Skeete, "Performance and Prospects of the Caribbean Group for Co-operation in Economic Development," paper prepared for the World Peace Foundation's Caribbean Project, October 1990.

26. Courtney Blackman, "CARICOM Private Sector Enterprise in the Global Marketplace," paper prepared for the World Peace Foundation's Caribbean Project, November 1990.

27. Maingot, "Vision of Elites since Independence."

28. Lijphart, *Democracy in Plural Societies*, chap. 6.

29. Maingot, "Vision of Elites since Independence."

30. Henry Wells, *The Modernization of Puerto Rico: A Political Study of Changing Values and Institutions* (Cambridge: Harvard University Press, 1969), 315.

31. Maingot, "The Caribbean," 365.

32. Skeete, "Performance and Prospects of the Caribbean Group."

33. For a discussion of the security aspects of the problem, see Ivelaw L. Griffith, *The Quest for Security in the Caribbean: Problems and Promises in Subordinate States* (Armonk, N.Y.: Sharpe, 1993).

34. Blackman, "CARICOM Private Sector Enterprise."

35. I am indebted to Frances Hagopian, Tufts University, for calling to my attention aspects of the complex relationship among patronage, parties, democratic regimes, and new economic strategies such as the one under consideration.

36. Carl Stone, *Politics versus Economics: The 1989 Elections in Jamaica* (Kingston: Heinemann, 1989).

37. Blackman, "CARICOM Private Sector Enterprise"; Swinburne Lestrade, "Considerations Relating to the Promotion of Foreign Investment in the Caribbean," paper prepared for the World Peace Foundation's Caribbean Project, August 1990.

38. The expression is C. E. Lindblom's, in *Politics and Markets* (New York: Basic Books, 1977), chap. 13.

Chapter 2: Democratic Transitions

This chapter originally appeared in *Democratic Transitions in Central America*, ed. Jorge I. Domínguez and Marc Lindenberg (Gainesville: University Press of Florida, 1997). A draft of that chapter benefited from comments by Patricia Coatsworth, Barbara Ellington, Jeffry Frieden, María Victoria Murillo, Ashutosh Varshney, Jennifer Widner, and Deborah Yashar. The views expressed here, however, are mine alone, as is responsibility for errors. Reprinted with permission from the University Press of Florida.

1. For a more general argument and evidence, see Marc Lindenberg, "World Economic Cycles and Central American Political Instability," *World Politics* 42 (1990): 397–421.

2. Honduras and Costa Rica are not analyzed here but are referred to whenever appropriate.

3. Guillermo O'Donnell and Philippe C. Schmitter, *Transitions from Authoritarian*

Rule: Tentative Conclusions about Uncertain Democracies (Baltimore: Johns Hopkins University Press, 1986), 7.

4. See the thoughtful discussion by Eduardo Vallarino, "La búsqueda por la democracia en Panamá," in *Transiciones Democráticas en Centro América*, ed. Jorge I. Domínguez and Marc Lindenberg (San José: Editorial Instituto Centroamericano de Administración de Empresas, 1994).

5. Robert A. Dahl, *Polyarchy: Participation and Opposition* (New Haven: Yale University Press, 1971), 15.

6. Samuel P. Huntington, *The Third Wave: Democratization in the Late Twentieth Century* (Norman: University of Oklahoma Press, 1991), 207.

7. For the general importance of such factors as contributors to democratization since the early 1970s, see ibid., 85–106.

8. Laurence Whitehead, "International Aspects of Democratization," in *Transitions from Authoritarian Rule: Comparative Perspectives*, ed. Guillermo O'Donnell, Philippe C. Schmitter, and Laurence Whitehead (Baltimore: Johns Hopkins University Press, 1986), 3.

9. Adam Przeworski, "Some Problems in the Study of the Transition to Democracy," in *Transitions from Authoritarian Rule: Comparative Perspectives*, ed. Guillermo O'Donnell, Philippe C. Schmitter, and Laurence Whitehead (Baltimore: Johns Hopkins University Press, 1986), 58–59.

10. O'Donnell and Schmitter, *Transitions from Authoritarian Rule: Tentative Conclusions*, chap. 3; Huntington, *Third Wave*, chap. 3.

11. See the excellent discussion in Vallarino, "La búsqueda por la democracia en Panamá."

12. For a general discussion of the importance of certain policy issues and military prerogatives, see Alfred Stepan, *Rethinking Military Politics: Brazil and the Southern Cone* (Princeton: Princeton University Press, 1988), chaps. 6 and 7.

13. For a discussion of elite settlements and elite accommodation, see Michael Burton, Richard Gunther, and John Higley, "Introduction: Elite Transformations and Democratic Regimes," in *Elites and Democratic Consolidation in Latin America and Southern Europe*, ed. John Higley and Richard Gunther (Cambridge: Cambridge University Press, 1992).

14. Vallarino, "La búsqueda por la democracia en Panamá."

15. O'Donnell and Schmitter, *Transitions from Authoritarian Rule: Tentative Conclusions*, 62–63.

16. See Daniel H. Wolf, "ARENA in the Arena: Factors in the Accommodation of the Salvadoran Right to Pluralism and the Broadening of the Political System," *LASA Forum* 23 (1992): 11.

17. See Vallarino, "La búsqueda por la democracia en Panamá."

18. Huntington, *Third Wave*, 190.

19. United Nations Economic Commission for Latin America and the Caribbean, *Preliminary Overview of the Economy of Latin America and the Caribbean: 1994*, LC/G. 1846 (New York: ECLAC, 1994), 39; Inter-American Development Bank, *Economic and Social Progress in Latin America: 1996 Report* (Washington, D.C.: IDB, 1996), 359.

Chapter 3: Parties, Institutions, Market Reforms

This chapter originally appeared in *Constructing Democratic Governance: Latin America and the Caribbean in the 1990s*, ed. Jorge I. Domínguez and Abraham F. Lowenthal (Baltimore: Johns Hopkins University Press, 1996). We are grateful for comments received on early draft versions from Alan Angell, Michael Coppedge, Rosario Espinal, Peter Hakim, Harvey Kline, Abraham Lowenthal, Marifeli Pérez-Stable, Rose Spalding, Michael Shifter, and Deborah Yashar. These versions were presented at meetings of the Harvard University comparative politics faculty group and of the Sawyer Seminar at the Harvard Center for International Affairs sponsored by the Mellon Foundation. We are also grateful for comments from meeting participants Eva Bellin, Daniel Goldhagen, Torben Iversen, Stanley Hoffmann, Stephen Krasner, Anthony Pereira, Theda Skocpol, and Deborah Yashar. We thank Linda Lowenthal for very fine editing. All mistakes are ours alone.

1. Jorge Amado, *Gabriela: Clove and Cinnamon*, trans. James L. Taylor and William L. Grossman (New York: Crest Books, 1964), 75, 80.

2. Reelections had occurred uninterruptedly only where there had been no competition (Cuba) or where doubts existed about the fairness of electoral procedures (Antigua, the Dominican Republic, Mexico, and Paraguay). Only in Colombia (except in 1982) and elsewhere in the Eastern Caribbean have fair elections resulting in repeated incumbent party victories been the norm.

3. United Nations Economic Commission for Latin America and the Caribbean, *Preliminary Overview of the Economy of Latin America and the Caribbean: 1994*, LC/G. 1846 (New York: ECLAC, 1994), 39.

4. On this linkage function of social movements, see Kay Lawson and Peter Merkl, eds., *When Parties Fail* (Princeton: Princeton University Press, 1988). For evidence from Latin America, see Arturo Escobar and Sonia E. Alvarez, eds., *The Making of Social Movements in Latin America: Identity, Strategy, and Democracy* (Boulder: Westview, 1992); Susan Eckstein, ed., *Power and Popular Protest: Latin American Social Movements* (Berkeley: University of California Press, 1989); and Jane Jaquette, ed., *The Women's Movement in Latin America: Participation and Democracy*, 2d. ed. (Boulder: Westview, 1994).

5. The Mexican case is complex for two other reasons. Civilians have ruled in Mexico, and despite important irregularities in Mexican elections, the evidence from public opinion polls shows that a plurality of voters preferred to vote for the Institutional Revolutionary Party (PRI) than for any of the opposition parties. See Jorge I. Domínguez and James A. McCann, "Shaping Mexico's Electoral Arena: The Construction of Partisan Cleavages in the 1988 and 1991 National Elections," *American Political Science Review* 89 (1995): 34–48.

6. See also Karen Remmer, "The Political Economy of Elections in Latin America, 1980–1991," *American Political Science Review* 87 (1993): 393–407.

7. For a discussion of bargains that may lead to democratic outcomes, see Adam Przeworski, *Democracy and the Market: Political and Economic Reforms in Eastern Europe and Latin America* (Cambridge: Cambridge University Press, 1991), chaps. 1 and 2.

8. Robert A. Dahl, *Polyarchy: Participation and Opposition* (New Haven: Yale Uni-

versity Press, 1971), 15. For a more elaborate discussion of the costs and benefits facing guerrillas and governments, see Matthew Soberg Shugart, "Guerrillas and Elections: An Institutionalist Perspective on the Costs of Conflict and Competition," *International Studies Quarterly* 36 (1992): 121–51.

9. For the general concepts, see Albert Hirschman, *Exit, Voice, and Loyalty* (New Haven: Yale University Press, 1970).

10. Michael Coppedge, *Strong Parties and Lame Ducks: Presidential Partyarchy and Factionalism in Venezuela* (Stanford: Stanford University Press, 1994).

11. Barriers to entry by new parties in the electoral law are, however, often low; in some cases, they have been lowered in recent years. This is why dissident politicians can form new parties instead of seeking to overthrow the government by force.

12. For a discussion of the historic role of Argentina's provincial parties, see Edward Gibson, *Conservative Parties and Democratic Politics: Argentina in Comparative Perspective* (Baltimore: Johns Hopkins University Press, 1996).

13. See Domínguez and McCann, "Shaping Mexico's Electoral Arena."

14. For a discussion of the utility of "reliability" and "responsibility" in parties, see Anthony Downs, *An Economic Theory of Democracy* (New York: Harper and Row, 1957), 96–113.

15. We recognize an anomaly. If this argument were correct in every instance, a major third party would have emerged in Jamaica in the early 1990s in response to the People's National party's turn from statism toward promarket policies and the continued resistance of the two dominant parties to changing the electoral law to lower the threshold for third-party membership in parliament. Our argument with regard to the Latin American cases requires, therefore, permissive electoral laws—proportional representation. This is exactly what the Anglophone Caribbean does not have.

16. See Margaret E. Keck, *The Workers' Party and Democratization in Brazil* (New Haven: Yale University Press, 1992).

17. For further discussion, see Jane S. Jaquette, "Rewriting the Scripts: Gender in the Comparative Study of Latin American Politics," in *Latin America in Comparative Perspective: New Approaches to Methods and Analysis*, ed. Peter H. Smith (Boulder: Westview, 1995).

18. See Juan J. Linz and Arturo Valenzuela, eds., *The Failure of Presidential Democracy: The Case of Latin America* (Baltimore: Johns Hopkins University Press, 1994); and Juan J. Linz, Arend Lijphart, and Arturo Valenzuela, eds., *Hacia una democracia moderna: la opción parlamentaria* (Santiago: Ediciones Universidad Católica de Chile, 1990). Further research suggests, however, that many other aspects of institutional design—not only parliamentarism—have a significant impact on the nature and quality of executive-legislative relations. See Arend Lijphart and Carlos H. Waisman, eds., *Institutional Design in New Democracies: Eastern Europe and Latin America* (Boulder: Westview, 1996). See also Adam Przeworski et al., *Sustainable Democracy* (Cambridge: Cambridge University Press, 1995), 43–46.

19. For a detailed analysis of the Brazilian case, see Frances Hagopian, *Traditional Politics and Regime Change in Brazil* (Cambridge: Cambridge University Press, 1996).

20. For an overview of supreme courts, see Joel G. Verner, "The Independence of Supreme Courts in Latin America: A Review of the Literature," *Journal of Latin American Studies* 16 (1984): 463–506.

21. For a general discussion of human rights issues during democratic transitions, see Manuel Antonio Garretón, "Human Rights in Processes of Democratization," *Journal of Latin American Studies* 26 (1994): 221–34.

22. For a general discussion, see R. Andrew Nickson, *Local Government in Latin America* (Boulder: Lynne Rienner, 1995); Jonathan Fox, "Latin America's Emerging Local Politics," *Journal of Democracy* 5 (1994): 105–16.

23. For a theoretical argument about the economic advantages of democracy over autocracy, see Mancur Olson, "Dictatorship, Democracy and Development," *American Political Science Review* 87 (1993): 567–76. See also special issues of two journals: *World Development* 21 (1993), on economic liberalization and democratization, and *Journal of Democracy* 5 (1994), on economic reform and democracy.

24. For a related argument, see Barbara Geddes and Artur Ribeiro, "Institutional Sources of Corruption in Brazil," *Third World Quarterly* 13 (1992): 641–61.

25. See, for example, Guillermo O'Donnell and Philippe C. Schmitter, *Transitions from Authoritarian Rule: Tentative Conclusions about Uncertain Democracies* (Baltimore: Johns Hopkins University Press, 1986), 62–63.

26. The greater allegiance of the right to democracy can be found to varying degrees (listing from south to north) in Argentina, Chile, Colombia, Panama, Costa Rica, Nicaragua, El Salvador, and Mexico. Opposition to some of the negative consequences of market reforms has strengthened the long-term prospects for parties of the left to varying degrees. Listing from south to north, this is evident in Argentina, Uruguay, Brazil, Panama, Nicaragua, El Salvador, and Mexico.

27. See the excellent discussion in Inter-American Development Bank, *Economic and Social Progress in Latin America: 1996 Report* (Washington, D.C.: IDB, 1996), pt. 3.

28. For a discussion of the earlier pattern, see Alfred Stepan, "The New Professionalism of Internal Warfare and Military Role Expansion," in *Armies and Politics in Latin America*, ed. Abraham F. Lowenthal and J. Samuel Fitch (New York: Holmes and Meier, 1986), 134–47.

29. This pattern has been common elsewhere as well. See Samuel P. Huntington, *The Third Wave: Democratization in the Late Twentieth Century* (Norman: University of Oklahoma Press, 1991), 234.

30. A number of scholars stress the prerogatives retained by the military after the transition to constitutional government and the threat that this poses to democracy. See Alfred Stepan, *Rethinking Military Politics* (Princeton: Princeton University Press, 1988), 68–127. See also Brian Loveman, "'Protected Democracies' and Military Guardianship: Political Transition in Latin America, 1978–1993," *Journal of Inter-American Studies and World Affairs* 36 (1994): 105–89; and Felipe Agüero, "The Military and the Limits to Democratization in South America," in *Issues in Democratic Consolidation: The New South American Democracies in Comparative Perspective*, ed. Scott Mainwaring, Guillermo O'Donnell, and J. Samuel Valenzuela (Notre Dame: University of Notre Dame Press, 1992). In contrast, Wendy Hunter shows how democracy has

helped to limit military prerogatives in Brazil. See her "Politicians against Soldiers: Contesting the Military in Postauthoritarian Brazil," *Comparative Politics* 27 (1995): 425–43.

31. To be sure, the main U.S. motivation for intervention has not always been the promotion of democracy. In Panama, the main motivation was to curtail drug trafficking and financial laundering, while in Haiti it was to make it easier to stop the flow of immigration and to return undocumented immigrants. Another important difference between the two interventions is that in Haiti the United States sought and obtained prior authorization from the United Nations Security Council and a commitment that other countries would eventually join a peacekeeping effort; in Panama, the United States acted unilaterally.

32. Jorge Luis Borges, "The Lottery in Babylon," in *Labyrinths: Selected Stories and Other Writings*, ed. Donald A. Yates and James E. Irby (New York: New Directions Books, 1964), 30.

Chapter 4: Ideas and Leaders

This chapter originally appeared in *Technopols: Freeing Politics and Markets in Latin America in the 1990s*, ed. Jorge I. Domínguez (University Park: Penn State University Press, 1997). I am grateful to Richard Feinberg, Javier Corrales, Stephanie Golob, João Resende-Santos, Jeanne Kinney Giraldo, Delia Boylan, Eva Bellin, Stanley Hoffmann, María Victoria Murillo, Theda Skocpol, Ashutosh Varshney, Jennifer Widner, Deborah Yashar, and the members of the Sawyer Seminar at the Harvard Center for International Affairs for their comments, criticisms, and suggestions on draft versions of this chapter; they are not responsible for my errors. Reprinted with permission from the Penn State University Press.

1. Karl Marx, *The Eighteenth Brumaire of Louis Bonaparte* (New York: International Publishers, 1963), 15.

2. I am grateful to Javier Corrales for this and many other insights.

3. For a powerful argument that Mexico's "technocratic revolution" has not been democratic, see Miguel Centeno, *Democracy within Reason: Technocratic Revolution in Mexico* (University Park: Pennsylvania State University Press, 1994), esp. chap. 8.

4. Robert Bates seems to hold this view. See his "Comment," in *The Political Economy of Policy Reform*, ed. John Williamson (Washington, D.C.: Institute for International Economics, 1994), 29–34.

5. This is why I part company with John Toye's "Comment," in Williamson, *The Political Economy of Policy Reform*, 35–38. I am grateful to Javier Corrales for calling this fine article to my attention.

6. Catherine M. Conaghan and James M. Malloy, *Unsettling Statecraft: Democracy and Neoliberalism in the Central Andes* (Pittsburgh: University of Pittsburgh Press, 1994), 174.

7. I am grateful to Jeanne Kinney Giraldo for this insight—and many others.

8. For examples dealing with an earlier era, see William Ascher, *Scheming for the Poor: The Politics of Redistribution in Latin America* (Cambridge: Harvard University Press, 1984). See also Eliza J. Willis, "Explaining Bureaucratic Independence in Brazil:

The Experience of the National Economic Development Bank," *Journal of Latin American Studies* 27 (1995): 625–61.

9. David Collier, ed., *The New Authoritarianism in Latin America* (Princeton: Princeton University Press, 1979), 403.

10. Guillermo O'Donnell, *Modernization and Bureaucratic-Authoritarianism: Studies in South American Politics* (Berkeley: Institute of International Studies, University of California at Berkeley, 1973), 79–89, quotations from 84, 87. For a more recent statement reiterating similar views, see Guillermo O'Donnell, "Democracy's Future: Do Economists Know Best?" *Journal of Democracy* 6 (1995): 23–28.

11. See, for example, Magali Sarfatti Larson, "Notes on Technocracy: Some Problems of Theory, Ideology, and Power," *Berkeley Journal of Sociology* 17 (1972/73): 29.

12. This definition benefits from Miguel Angel Centeno's thoughtful analysis in "The New Leviathan: The Dynamics and Limits of Technocracy," *Theory and Society* 22 (1993): 307–35. Centeno appears to be more skeptical, however, about the prospects for reconciling technocrats to democratic politics. For a persuasive argument that the distinction between "technician" and "politician" has been overdrawn in the scholarship on Mexico, see Juan D. Lindau, "Schisms in the Mexican Political Elite and the Technocrat/Politician Typology," *Mexican Studies* 8 (1992): 217–35; and Lindau, *Los tecnócratas y la élite gobernante mexicana* (Mexico: Mortiz, 1993).

13. For the relatively rare example of a book describing democratic technopols (though neither the word nor the concept as such is presented there), who are more effective at advancing the goals of democracy and efficiency than authoritarian technopols are, see Ascher, *Scheming for the Poor*.

14. I rely on three of Weber's essays: "Politics as a Vocation," "Science as a Vocation," and the sections on bureaucracy in *Wirtschaft und Gesellschaft* in *From Max Weber*, ed. H. H. Gerth and C. Wright Mills (London: Oxford University Press, 1958).

15. Weber, "Politics as a Vocation," 115.

16. Weber, "Science as a Vocation," 138, 147.

17. Weber, "Bureaucracy," in *From Max Weber*, ed. H. H. Gerth and C. Wright Mills (London: Oxford University Press, 1958), 198–99.

18. Some authoritarian technopols exhibit similar traits—a sense of proportion and action as teachers to the nation—as was the case in Chile in the second half of the 1980s and as has been the case more generally in Mexico.

19. Inter-American Development Bank, *Economic and Social Progress in Latin America: 1991 Report* (Washington, D.C.: IDB, 1991), 273.

20. I am grateful to Delia Boylan for this insight—and many others.

21. For qualifications on this point, and a fine synthesis of the evolution of economic thought in Latin America, see Albert Fishlow, "The State of Latin American Economics," in *Changing Perspectives in Latin American Studies*, ed. Christopher Mitchell (Stanford: Stanford University Press, 1988).

22. In the 1990s, this point has been made often by Harvard professor Jeffrey Sachs.

23. Aníbal Pinto and Oswaldo Sunkel, "Latin American Economists in the United

States," *Economic Development and Cultural Change* 15 (1966): 79–90; quotations on 80, 83.

24. For a detailed account of the circumstances and climate of ideas shaping IEERAL and Cavallo, see Enrique N'haux, *Menem-Cavallo: El poder mediterráneo* (Buenos Aires: Ediciones Corregidor, 1993). I am grateful to María Victoria Murillo for the reference.

25. Curiously, scholars often write as if the creation of teams were unique to the countries that they study. Mexicanists write about *equipos* and *camarillas*, for example, as if they were unique Mexican flowers. For a relatively rare comparative analysis that touches on some of these themes, see Catherine M. Conaghan, James M. Malloy, and Luis A. Abugattás, "Business and the 'Boys': The Politics of Neoliberalism in the Central Andes," *Latin American Research Review* 25 (1990): 3–30.

26. Cardoso has always been sharply criticized by many to his political left. See, for example, John Myer, "A Crown of Thorns: Cardoso and Counter-Revolution," *Latin American Perspectives* 2 (1975): 33–48.

27. Scott Mainwaring, "Brazilian Party Underdevelopment in Comparative Perspective," *Political Science Quarterly* 107 (1992/93): 677–707.

28. Alejandro Foxley, "Towards a Free Market Economy: Chile 1974–1979," *Journal of Development Economics* 10 (1982): 28–29.

29. For some comparative indicators of repression, see Jorge I. Domínguez, Nigel S. Rodley, Bryce Wood, and Richard Falk, *Enhancing Global Human Rights* (New York: McGraw-Hill, 1979), 93–102.

30. United Nations Economic Commission for Latin America and the Caribbean, *Preliminary Overview of the Economy of Latin America and the Caribbean: 1989*, LC/G. 1586 (New York: ECLAC, 1989), 19–20.

31. For an excellent summary of this ideological consensus, see John Williamson, "What Washington Means by Policy Reform," in *Latin American Adjustment: How Much Has Happened?* ed. John Williamson (Washington, D.C.: Institute for International Economics, 1990). By "Washington," Williamson means not only U.S. government agencies but also "the technocratic Washington of the international financial institutions . . . and the think-tanks" (7). See also his *The Progress of Policy Reform in Latin America*, (Washington, D.C.: Institute for International Economics, 1990). Forty years ago, another ideological consensus had developed in Latin America around the influence of the United Nations Economic Commission for Latin America— another international pool of ideas that was in part implemented into policy. See Christopher Mitchell, "The Role of Technocrats in Latin American Integration," *Inter-American Economic Affairs* 21 (1967): 3–29; David C. Bruce, "The Impact of the United Nations Economic Commission for Latin America: Technocrats as Channels of Influence," *Inter-American Economic Affairs* 33 (1980): 3–28; and esp. Kathryn Sikkink, *Ideas and Institutions: Developmentalism in Brazil and Argentina* (Ithaca: Cornell University Press, 1991).

32. For a compatible argument, see John Markoff and Verónica Montecinos, "The Ubiquitous Rise of Economists," *Journal of Public Policy* 13 (1993): 37–68. I am grateful to Jeanne Kinney Giraldo for the reference.

33. See Scott Mainwaring, "Transitions to Democracy and Democratic Consolidation: Theoretical and Comparative Issues," in *Issues in Democratic Consolidation: The New South American Democracies in Comparative Perspective,* ed. Scott Mainwaring, Guillermo O'Donnell, and J. S. Valenzuela (Notre Dame: University of Notre Dame Press, 1992), 294, 308–12.

34. For the notion of idea carrier and its relationship to leaders and institutions, I am indebted to Peter A. Hall, introduction to *The Political Power of Economic Ideas: Keynesianism across Nations,* ed. Peter A. Hall (Princeton: Princeton University Press, 1989). See also Emanuel Adler, *The Power of Ideology: The Quest for Technological Autonomy in Argentina and Brazil* (Berkeley: University of California Press, 1987); and Sikkink, *Ideas and Institutions.*

35. For examples—from quite different empirical realms—of the utility of focusing on ideas to understand political and economic changes, see Ashutosh Varshney, "Ideas, Interests, and Institutions in Policy Change: Transformation of India's Agricultural Strategy in the Mid-1960s," *Policy Sciences* 22 (1989): 289–323; and Kathryn Sikkink, "Human Rights, Principled Issue Networks, and Sovereignty in Latin America," *International Organization* 47 (1993): 411–41.

36. Thomas C. Schelling, *The Strategy of Influence* (London: Oxford University Press, 1960).

37. For recent thoughtful discussions of these issues, see Conaghan and Malloy, *Unsettling Statecraft,* 220–24; see also Conaghan, Malloy, and Abugattás, "Business and the 'Boys.'"

38. On economic factors underlying the crisis in Mexico, see Jeffrey Sachs, Aaron Tornell, and Andrés Velasco, *The Collapse of the Mexican Peso,* Working Paper 95-7 (Cambridge: Center for International Affairs, Harvard University, 1995). On the closed nature of the policy-making process, see David Wessel, Paul B. Carroll, and Thomas T. Vogel Jr., "Peso Surprise: How Mexico's Crisis Ambushed Top Minds in Officialdom, Finance," *Wall Street Journal,* July 6, 1995. For the most part, the crisis was limited to Mexico. Despite a brief initial negative fallout from the Mexican crisis, the economies of Brazil and Chile continued on their high-growth path during 1995. Argentina was hit more severely; the country slipped into recession, and in May 1995 open unemployment rose to 18.6 percent. By year's end, however, Argentina's economic crisis was abating. For statistics, see United Nations Economic Commission for Latin America and the Caribbean, *Economic Panorama of Latin America: 1995* (New York: ECLAC, 1995), 17–31, 41–45, 55–64.

39. See convergent analysis by Alejandra Cox Edwards and Sebastian Edwards, "Markets and Democracy: Lessons from Chile," *World Economy* 15 (1992): 203–19.

40. U.S. Department of the Treasury, *Treasury News,* March 30, 1993, 4–5.

41. Conaghan and Malloy, *Unsettling Statecraft,* 202 and, more generally, chap. 7.

42. Ibid., 217–18.

43. Alejandro Foxley interview by Richard Feinberg, in Washington Exchange, *State of Latin American Finance* (Washington, D.C.: Inter-American Dialogue, 1992), 21–22.

44. Ibid., 22.

45. Karl Marx, "Theses on Feuerbach," in *Marx and Engels: Basic Writings on Politics and Philosophy*, ed. Lewis S. Feuer (Garden City, N.Y.: Anchor Books, 1959), 245; italics in the original.

Chapter 5: Norms of Mexican Citizenship

This chapter originally appeared in Jorge I. Domínguez and James A. McCann, *Democratizing Mexico: Public Opinion and Electoral Choices* (Baltimore: Johns Hopkins University Press, 1996). Questionnaire items used to construct tables and figures can be found in that volume.

1. Samuel P. Huntington, *The Third Wave: Democratization in the Late Twentieth Century* (Norman: University of Oklahoma Press, 1991), chap. 2; Larry Diamond, Juan J. Linz, and Seymour Martin Lipset, eds., *Democracy in Developing Countries*, 4 vols. (Boulder: Lynne Rienner, 1989); and Claus Offe, *Contradictions of the Welfare State* (Cambridge: MIT Press, 1984).

2. This proposition is consistent with the arguments of Guillermo O'Donnell and Philippe C. Schmitter, *Transitions from Authoritarian Rule: Tentative Conclusions about Uncertain Democracies* (Baltimore: Johns Hopkins University Press, 1986), 4–5, 26, 48.

3. For two fine surveys of Mexican politics that shed light especially on the years from the 1960s to the 1990s, see Roderic Ai Camp, *Politics in Mexico* (Oxford: Oxford University Press, 1993); and Wayne A. Cornelius and Ann L. Craig, *The Mexican Political System in Transition*, Monograph 35 (La Jolla: Center for U.S.-Mexican Studies, University of California at San Diego, 1991).

4. Among others, see George Philip, *The Presidency in Mexican Politics* (New York: St. Martin's, 1992); Samuel Schmidt, *The Deterioration of the Mexican Presidency* (Tucson: University of Arizona Press, 1991); Rogelio Hernández Rodríguez, "Inestabilidad política y presidencialismo en México," *Mexican Studies* 10 (1994): 187–216; Alicia Hernández Chávez, "Mexican Presidentialism: A Historical and Institutional Overview," *Mexican Studies* 10 (1994): 217–25; Lorenzo Meyer, "Historical Roots of the Authoritarian State in Mexico," in *Authoritarianism in Mexico*, ed. José Luis Reyna and Richard S. Weinert (Philadelphia: Institute for the Study of Human Issues, 1977); and Ann Craig and Wayne Cornelius, "Houses Divided: Parties and Political Reform in Mexico," in *Building Democratic Institutions: Parties and Party Systems in Latin America*, ed. Scott Mainwaring and Timothy R. Scully (Stanford: Stanford University Press, 1994).

5. During President Carlos Salinas's presidential term, about half of the state governors were removed from office.

6. For a comparative argument based on a different presidential system, see Nelson W. Polsby, "The Institutionalization of the U.S. House of Representatives," *American Political Science Review* 62 (1968): 145–46.

7. From 1938 to 1946, the official party was called the Party of the Mexican Revolution.

8. The following provide a general overview of politics in Mexico, with special attention to the 1980s and early 1990s: Carlos Bazdresch, Nisso Bucay, Soledad Loaeza, and Nora Lustig, eds., *México: auge, crisis, y ajuste*, 3 vols. (Mexico: Fondo de

Cultura Económica, 1992); Miguel Basáñez, *La lucha por la hegemonía, 1968–1990*, rev. ed. (Mexico City: Siglo XXI, 1990); Soledad Loaeza and Rafael Segovia, *La vida política mexicana en la crisis* (Mexico City: El Colegio de México, 1987); Pablo González Casanova, ed., *Las elecciones en México: evolución y perspectivas* (Mexico City: Siglo XXI, 1985); Carlos Martínez Assad, ed., *La sucesión presidencial en México, 1928–1988*, rev. ed. (Mexico City: Nueva Imagen, 1992); Soledad Loaeza, *El llamado de las urnas* (Mexico City: Cal y Arena, 1989); Juan Molinar, *El tiempo de la legitimidad: elecciones, autoritarismo, y democracia en México* (Mexico City: Cal y Arena, 1991); John J. Bailey, *Governing Mexico* (New York: St. Martin's, 1988); George W. Grayson, ed., *Prospects for Democracy in Mexico*, rev. ed. (New Brunswick: Transaction, 1990); and Wayne A. Cornelius, Judith Gentleman, and Peter H. Smith, eds., *Mexico's Alternative Political Futures*, Monograph 30 (La Jolla: Center for U.S.-Mexican Studies, University of California at San Diego, 1989).

9. The Mexican Academy of Human Rights and Civic Alliance/Observation 94 published various reports, among them *The Media and the 1994 Federal Elections in Mexico: A Content Analysis of Television News Coverage of the Political Parties and Presidential Candidates* and *Las elecciones federales en México según los noticieros "24 Horas" de Televisa y "Hechos" de Televisión Azteca, 30 de Mayo a 30 de Junio de 1994* (Mexico City: Observation 94, 1994).

10. Craig and Cornelius, "Houses Divided."

11. Inter-American Development Bank, *Economic and Social Progress in Latin America: 1991 Report* (Washington: IDB, 1991), 273.

12. For magisterial accounts of the relationship between the state and labor unions, see Ilán Bizberg, *Estado y sindicalismo en México* (Mexico City: El Colegio de México, 1990); and Kevin J. Middlebrook, *The Paradox of Revolution: Labor, the State, and Authoritarianism in Mexico* (Baltimore: Johns Hopkins University Press, 1995).

13. See several editions of United Nations Economic Commission for Latin America and the Caribbean, *Preliminary Overview of the Economy of Latin America and the Caribbean* (New York: ECLAC): *1988*, LC/G. 1536 , 17–18; *1992*, LC/G. 1751, 43–45; *1994*, LC/G. 1846, 41–42.

14. United Nations Economic Commission for Latin America and the Caribbean, *Preliminary Overview: 1992*, 41, 43–45; *1994*, 41–42.

15. Larry Diamond and Juan J. Linz, "Introduction: Politics, Society, and Democracy in Latin America," in *Democracy in Developing Countries*, ed. Larry Diamond, Juan J. Linz, and Seymour Martin Lipset (Boulder: Lynne Rienner, 1989), 12–13.

16. Seymour Martin Lipset, "The Social Requisites of Democracy Revisited," *American Sociological Review* 59 (1994): 3.

17. Terry Lynn Karl, "Dilemmas of Democratization in Latin America," *Comparative Politics* 23 (1990): 19; see also Terry Lynn Karl and Philippe C. Schmitter, "Modes of Transition in Latin America, Southern and Eastern Europe," *International Social Science Journal* 43 (1991): 269–84.

18. Edward N. Muller and Mitchell A. Seligson, "Civic Culture and Democracy: The Question of Causal Relationships," *American Political Science Review* 88 (1994): 635–52.

19. Diamond and Linz, "Introduction," 10. Lipset, too, argues that the emergence and consolidation of democracy are "linked to probabilities associated with the presence or absence" of various requisites, including political culture. See his "Social Requisites of Democracy Revisited," 16.

20. Gabriel A. Almond, "The Intellectual History of the Civic Culture Concept," in *The Civic Culture Revisited*, ed. Gabriel A. Almond and Sidney Verba (Boston: Little, Brown, 1980), 29.

21. Daniel Cosío Villegas, "The Mexican Revolution Then and Now," in *Is the Mexican Revolution Dead?* ed. Stanley R. Ross (New York: Knopf, 1966), 123–24.

22. Gabriel Almond and Sidney Verba, *The Civic Culture: Political Attitudes and Democracy in Five Nations* (Princeton: Princeton University Press, 1963), 414.

23. For a technical description of the surveys and a discussion of the political contexts in which they were taken, see Jorge I. Domínguez and James A. McCann, *Democratizing Mexico: Public Opinion and Electoral Choices* (Baltimore: Johns Hopkins University Press, 1996), app. 2. For the specific questions, see ibid., app. 1.

24. Almond and Verba, *The Civic Culture*, chap. 13.

25. Alberto Hernández Medina and Luis Narro Rodríguez, eds., *Cómo somos los Mexicanos* (Mexico City: Centro de Estudios Educativos, 1987), 10–12, 96–97. Their national survey ($N = 1,837$) was conducted between August and November 1982. The representation of Mexico's northern region is twice as great in this survey as in the 1980 census, while the representation of central Mexico is half as great. The southern region and the Federal District's share of the survey match well their share of the census. The representation of towns with a population below fifteen thousand is two-fifths as great as that of the census.

26. See, for example, Enrique Alduncín Abitia, *Los valores de los mexicanos: México entre la tradición y la modernidad* (Mexico City: Fondo Cultural Banamex, 1986); and Hernández Medina and Narro Rodríguez, *Cómo somos los mexicanos*, chaps. 6 and 8.

27. Richard R. Fagen and William S. Tuohy, *Politics and Privilege in a Mexican City* (Stanford: Stanford University Press, 1972), 122–27.

28. Seymour Martin Lipset, *Political Man* (Garden City, N.Y.: Anchor Books, 1960), chap. 4.

29. Rafael Segovia, *La politización del niño mexicano* (Mexico City: El Colegio de México, 1975), 124–26, 130.

30. Wayne A. Cornelius, *Politics and the Migrant Poor in Mexico City* (Stanford: Stanford University Press, 1975), 96, 150.

31. Henry A. Landsberger and Bobby M. Gierisch, "Political and Economic Activism: Peasant Participation in the *Ejidos* of the Comarca Lagunera of Mexico," in *Political Participation in Latin America*, ed. Mitchell A. Seligson and John A. Booth (New York: Holmes and Meier, 1979), 2:96.

32. John A. Booth and Mitchell A. Seligson, "The Political Culture of Authoritarianism in Mexico: A Reexamination," *Latin American Research Review* 19 (1984): 106–24.

33. On the unimportance of social class and religiosity and the importance of instrumental motivations in the context of electoral behavior, see Kenneth M. Cole-

man, "The Capital City Electorate and Mexico's Acción Nacional: Some Survey Evidence on Conventional Hypotheses," *Social Science Quarterly* 56 (1975): 502–9.

34. Miguel Basáñez, *El pulso de los sexenios* (Mexico City: Siglo XXI, 1990), pt. 3.

35. The Euro-Barometer Study, Number 31, was conducted in March-April, 1989. The principal investigators were Karl Heinz Reif and Anna Melich. The data were made available through the Inter-University Consortium for Political and Social Research (ICPSR Study Number 9322). Information on political interest is found on page 191 of the study codebook. The United States General Social Survey Cumulative Codebook, 1972–91, was produced by the National Opinion Research Center of the University of Chicago. Its principal investigators are James A. Davis and Tom W. Smith. These data were also made available through ICPSR (Study Number 9710). Information on political interest in 1987 (the most comparable year when the question was asked in the GSS) appears on page 380 of the codebook.

36. In mid-1993 the Salinas government sold off two public television stations to a private consortium partly in the hopes of generating some competition for TELEVISA.

37. Euro-Barometer Study 31.

38. For a discussion of church-state relations in contemporary Mexico, see Loaeza, *El llamado de las urnas*, pt. 3.

39. Alain Rouquié, *The Military and the State in Latin America*, trans. Paul E. Sigmund (Berkeley: University of California Press), 201–7, quotation from 204; see also David Ronfeldt, "The Modern Mexican Military," in *Armies and Politics in Latin America*, ed. Abraham F. Lowenthal and J. Samuel Fitch (New York: Holmes and Meier, 1986).

40. Basáñez, *El pulso de los sexenios*, 236–42.

41. The best description of the PRI nomination process remains Robert E. Scott's, *Mexican Government in Transition*, rev. ed. (Urbana: University of Illinois Press, 1964), 197–223.

42. For a discussion of institutional obstacles to democratization at the local level, see Jonathan Fox, "The Difficult Transition from Clientelism to Citizenship: Lessons from Mexico," *World Politics* 46 (1994): 151–85; and Jonathan Fox and Luis Hernández, "Mexico's Difficult Democracy: Grassroots Movements, NGOs, and Local Government," *Alternatives* 17 (1992): 165–208.

43. BANAMEX, *México social: 1990–91* (Mexico City: BANAMEX, 1991), 240, 247.

44. Huntington, *Third Wave*, 72–85.

45. The economic crisis of the 1980s hurt the nation so much and so evenly that perceptions of Mexico's economic situation failed to distinguish well the attitudes of Mexicans on other issues. On the other hand, the severity of the economic crisis no doubt may have predisposed Mexicans to think more openly about their political alternatives. See Domínguez and McCann, *Democratizing Mexico*, chap. 4.

46. E. E. Schattschneider, *The Semisovereign People: A Realist's View of Democracy in America* (Hinsdale, Ill.: Dryden, 1975), 1–18. The book was first published in 1960.

47. See Domínguez and McCann, *Democratizing Mexico*, Epilogue.

48. See, for example, Huntington, *Third Wave*; and Adam Przeworski, "Some

Problems in the Study of the Transition to Democracy," in *Transitions from Authoritarian Rule: Comparative Perspectives*, ed. Guillermo O'Donnell, Philippe C. Schmitter, and Laurence Whitehead (Baltimore: Johns Hopkins University Press, 1986).

49. Scott Mainwaring, "Transitions to Democracy and Democratic Consolidation: Theoretical and Comparative Issues," in *Issues in Democratic Consolidation: The New South American Democracies in Comparative Perspective*, ed. Scott Mainwaring, Guillermo O'Donnell, and J. Samuel Valenzuela (Notre Dame: University of Notre Dame Press, 1992), 308–10.

50. See Vikram Chand, "Civil Society, Institutions, and Democratization in Mexico: The Politics of the State of Chihuahua in National Perspective," Ph.D. diss., Harvard University, 1991.

51. Loaeza, *El llamado de las urnas*.

52. Domínguez and McCann, *Democratizing Mexico*, chap. 4.

53. José Antonio Crespo, "PRI: de la hegemonía revolucionaria a la dominación democrática," *Política y gobierno* 1 (1994): 48. See also Domínguez and McCann, *Democratizing Mexico*, chap. 6.

54. See Domínguez and McCann, *Democratizing Mexico*, Epilogue.

55. On the ephemeral nature of mass mobilization in other cases, see Guillermo O'Donnell and Philippe C. Schmitter, *Transitions from Authoritarian Rule: Tentative Conclusions about Uncertain Democracies* (Baltimore: Johns Hopkins University Press, 1986), 26.

56. For comparative analyses, see Grzegorz Ekiert, *The State against Society: Political Crises and Their Aftermath in East Central Europe* (Princeton: Princeton University Press, 1996), esp. pt. 3; see also Anthony Oberschall, "Opportunities and Framing in the Eastern European Revolts of 1989," in *Comparative Perspectives on Social Movements: Political Opportunities, Mobilizing Structures, and Cultural Framings*, ed. Doug McAdam, John D. McCarthy, and Mayer N. Zald (Cambridge: Cambridge University Press, 1996).

57. Ronald Inglehart, "The Renaissance of Political Culture," *American Political Science Review* 82 (1988): 1219.

58. Robert Fishman, "Rethinking State and Regime: Southern Europe's Transition to Democracy," *World Politics* 42 (1990): 436–37; Huntington, *Third Wave*, 258–65.

Chapter 6: Cuba in the 1990s

This chapter originally appeared in "Transition in Cuba: New Challenges for U.S. Policy" (Miami: Cuban Research Institute, Latin American and Caribbean Center, Florida International University, 1993); the research was funded by the Office of Research, U.S. Department of State, and the Bureau for Latin America and the Caribbean, U.S. Agency for International Development. Reprinted with permission from the Cuban Research Institute.

1. Computed from Banco Nacional de Cuba, *Economic Report: 1994* (Havana: Banco Nacional de Cuba, 1995), 4; and *Cuba: Economic Report: 1996 Summary*, courtesy of the Cuban Interests Section to the United States (January 1997). There is reason to think, however, that the decline of the Cuban economy in 1991 might have been sharper

than the official statistics suggest; in that case, the cumulative decline for 1989–93 would approach 50 percent. See Julio Carranza, "Cuba: los retos de la economía," *Cuadernos de Nuestra América* 9 (1992): 142.

2. Computed from Comité Estatal de Estadísticas, *Anuario estadístico de Cuba: 1989* (Havana: Comité Estatal de Estadísticas, 1989), 82. Global social product was the widest measure of aggregate economic performance until the change in the national accounts system in the early 1990s.

3. Computed from Banco Nacional de Cuba, *Economic Report: 1994*, 11; *Cuba: Economic Report: 1996 Summary*. See also discussion by Manuel Pastor Jr., *External Shocks and Adjustment in Contemporary Cuba*, Working Paper (Los Angeles: International and Public Affairs Center, Occidental College, 1992).

4. Ministerio de Economía y Planificación, *Cuba: informe económico, 1er. semestre 1996* (Havana: Ministerio de Economía y Planificación, 1996), courtesy of the Cuban Interests Section to the United States (July 1996), and interviews with informed persons.

5. For other discussions of scenarios for Cuba's future, see Carmelo Mesa-Lago and Horst Fabian, "Analogies between East European Socialist Regimes and Cuba: Scenarios for the Future," in *Cuba: After the Cold War*, ed. Carmelo Mesa-Lago (Pittsburgh: University of Pittsburgh Press, 1993); Edward Gonzalez and David Ronfeldt, *Cuba Adrift in a Postcommunist World*, R-4231–USDP (Santa Monica: RAND, 1992); and Edward Gonzalez, *Cuba: Clearing Perilous Waters?* (Santa Monica: RAND, 1996).

6. The text of the new constitution was published in *Granma*, September 22, 1993, 4–10.

7. For an assessment of the Cuban government's economic reforms, see Carmelo Mesa-Lago, *Are Economic Reforms Propelling Cuba to the Market?* (Miami: North-South Center, University of Miami, 1994).

8. Haroldo Dilla Alfonso, "Cuba: la crisis y la rearticulación del consenso político (notas para un debate socialista)," *Cuadernos de Nuestra América* 10 (1993): 34–35. See also his "Socialismo, empresas y participación obrera: notas para un debate cubano" (Havana: Centro de Estudios sobre América, 1992).

9. For a general discussion, see Jorge Pérez-López, *Cuba's Second Economy: From behind the Scenes to Center Stage* (New Brunswick: Transaction, 1995).

10. This information is from discussions with informed Cubans, August 1993.

11. Dilla, "Cuba," 37.

12. Computed from Comité Estatal de Estadísticas, *Anuario estadístico de Cuba: 1989*, 184.

13. See Carmen Diana Deere, Ernel Gonzales, Niurka Pérez, and Gustavo Rodríguez, *Household Incomes in Cuban Agriculture: A Comparison of the State, Cooperative, and Peasant Sectors*, Working Paper Series 143 (The Hague: Institute of Social Studies, 1993).

14. Carranza, "Cuba," 154.

15. The best information comes through the Buró de Información de Derechos Humanos, led by Ariel Hidalgo and Teté Machado (Miami: Buró de Información de

Derechos Humanos). See, among others, the following press releases: "Concilio Cubano define objetivos comunes" (October 29, 1995); "Acuse de recibo del gobierno a Concilio Cubano" (February 1, 1996); "Elige Concilio Cubano secretariado y delegado nacional" (February 12, 1996); and "Redada policiaca contra dirigentes de Concilio Cubano" (February 15, 1996). See also Amnesty International, *Cuba: Government Crackdown on Dissent* (London: International Secretariat, 1996).

16. For the text of Aldana's speech, see *Granma*, January 1, 1992, 3–5.

17. Raúl Castro Ruz, "Informe del Buró Político," *Granma*, March 27, 1996.

18. For a discussion, see Jorge I. Domínguez, "Leadership Strategies and Mass Support: Cuban Politics before and after the 1991 Communist Party Congress," in *Cuba at a Crossroads: Politics and Economics after the Fourth Party Congress*, ed. Jorge F. Pérez-López (Gainesville: University Press of Florida, 1994).

19. The enactment of the U.S. Helms-Burton Act in March 1996 was, in part, a direct consequence of the Cuban Air Force's downing on February 24, 1995, of two small aircraft piloted by Cuban Americans over international waters; a surviving Cuban American pilot had, however, violated Cuban air space earlier that day as well as on various occasions in preceding months. Some Cuban Americans may wish to provoke a U.S.-Cuban military confrontation as a means to destroy Castro's government.

20. My personal preferences are not pertinent to this book. Some of my views are presented in "The Secrets of Castro's Staying Power," *Foreign Affairs* 72 (1993): 97–107. I have also served as coordinator for the Inter-American Dialogue's Task Force on Cuba, whose most recent report is *Cuba in the Americas: Breaking the Policy Deadlock* (Washington: Inter-American Dialogue, 1995).

21. Guillermo O'Donnell and Philippe C. Schmitter, *Transitions from Authoritarian Rule: Tentative Conclusions about Uncertain Democracies* (Baltimore: Johns Hopkins University Press, 1986), 7.

22. This definition differs from that in ibid., 7–8.

23. The best realistic (albeit fictional) account is Carlos Fuentes, *The Death of Artemio Cruz*, trans. Sam Hileman (New York: Farrar, Straus, Giroux, 1964).

24. The Sandinistas were defeated in the February 1990 elections. Between 1990 and 1994, Nicaragua's GDP per capita in constant prices fell every year; in 1994, it grew a meager 0.4 percent. The cumulative decline from 1991 through 1995 was 11.1 percent. Its consolidated public sector deficit exceeded 8 percent of GDP every year between 1991 and 1995. The value of Nicaragua's exports fell between 1990 and 1992, though it recovered thereafter; in 1995, the value of exports finally matched the current price level reached in 1980. The value of imports rose every year but one in the early 1990s. The deficit on its balance of trade doubled between 1990 and 1992, when it reached $0.5 billion; though it declined thereafter, it was still higher in 1995 than in 1990. The deficit on the current account of the balance of payments doubled between 1990 and 1992, when it passed $1 billion; though it declined thereafter, in 1995 it remained at $850 million, well above the 1990 level. See several editions of United Nations Economic Commission for Latin America and the Caribbean, *Preliminary Overview of the Economy of Latin America and the Caribbean* (New York:

ECLAC): *1992*, LC/G. 1751, 41, 46, 53, 54; *1993*, LC/G. 1794, 38, 39, 43, 44; *1995*, LC/G. 1892–P, 48, 52, 55, 56, 59–60.

25. María Margarita Castro Flores, "Religiones de origen africano en Cuba: un enfoque de género," *Temas* 5 (1996): 69–70.

26. For the complex relationship between Cubans and tourists before the revolution, see Guillermo Cabrera Infante's hilarious as well as penetrating "Story of the Stick," in his *Three Trapped Tigers* (New York: Harper and Row, 1971), 177–208.

27. For this and other texts of Cuban constitutions, see Leonel-Antonio de la Cuesta, *Constituciones cubanas: desde 1812 hasta nuestros días* (New York: Ediciones Exilio, 1974). This book does not include the 1976 and 1992 Constitutions.

28. For one version of this argument, see Aurelio Alonso Tejada, "La economía cubana: los desafíos de un ajuste sin desocialización," *Cuadernos de Nuestra América* 9 (1992): 159–74.

29. For a Communist-party-sponsored survey, see Darío L. Machado, "¿Cuál es nuestro clima socio-político?" *El militante comunista* (September 1990): 2–12. For corroborating evidence, see a survey administered by Gallup–Costa Rica and sponsored by the *Miami Herald*: Mimi Whitefield and Mary Beth Sheridan, "Cuba Poll: The Findings," *Miami Herald*, December 18, 1994.

30. For a related discussion, see Adam Przeworski, *Democracy and the Market: Political and Economic Reforms in Eastern Europe and Latin America* (Cambridge: Cambridge University Press, 1991).

31. Mexican Americans are critical of authoritarian practices in Mexico. The main difference is that Mexican Americans are less politically active and influential than Cuban Americans. See Rodolfo O. de la Garza, Louis DeSipio, F. Chris Garcia, John Garcia, and Angelo Falcon, *Latino Voices: Mexican, Puerto Rican, and Cuban Perspectives on American Politics* (Boulder: Westview, 1992).

32. For a comparative analysis of democratic transitions in former communist Europe, see Juan J. Linz and Alfred Stepan, *Problems of Democratic Transition and Consolidation: Southern Europe, South America, and Post-Communist Europe* (Baltimore: Johns Hopkins University Press, 1996), pt. 4.

33. Minxin Pei, *From Reform to Revolution: The Demise of Communism in China and the Soviet Union* (Cambridge: Harvard University Press, 1994).

34. For a broader analysis and comparison, see James C. Scott, *Weapons of the Weak: Everyday Forms of Peasant Resistance* (New Haven: Yale University Press, 1985).

35. For a related discussion, see Aníbal Argüelles Mederos and Ileana Hodge Limonta, *Los llamados cultos sincréticos y el espiritismo* (Havana: Editorial Academia, 1991). See also Jorge I. Domínguez, "International and National Aspects of the Catholic Church in Cuba," *Cuban Studies* 19 (1989): 43–60.

36. María Isabel Domínguez, "La mujer joven en los 90," *Temas* 5 (1996): 34–35.

37. This information came from well-informed election observers in Cuba.

38. The Cuban government waited two months to report the proportion of blank and null ballots cast in the December 1992 elections. The government claimed that the number of null ballots was artificially inflated because of inadvertent and unintentional errors caused by improper ballot design. See *Granma*, February 27, 1993.

39. I have taken this idea from entirely different contexts, inspired by Stephen D. Krasner, "Sovereignty: An Institutional Perspective," *Comparative Political Studies* 21 (1988): 77–80. See also S. J. Gould and N. Eldredge, "Punctuated Equilibria: The Tempo and Mode of Evolution Reconsidered," *Paleobiology* 3 (1977): 115–51; S. J. Gould, "Darwinism and the Expansion of Evolutionary Theory," *Science* 214 (1982): 380–87; and N. Eldredge, *Time Frames: The Rethinking of Darwinian Evolution and the Theory of Punctuated Equilibria* (New York: Simon and Schuster, 1985).

Conclusion

1. Rubén Darío, "Salutación del Optimista," in *Poesía española contemporánea*, ed. Gerardo Diego (Madrid: Taurus, 1962), 36–38.

2. For a thoughtful essay on these issues, see Laurence Whitehead, "International Aspects of Democratization," in *Transitions from Authoritarian Rule: Comparative Perspectives*, ed. Guillermo O'Donnell, Philippe C. Schmitter, and Laurence Whitehead (Baltimore: Johns Hopkins University Press, 1986). See also Abraham F. Lowenthal, ed., *Exporting Democracy: The United States and Latin America* (Baltimore: Johns Hopkins University Press, 1991).

3. Defeat in war also contributed to democratization at the end of World War II in Germany, Italy, and Japan and in Greece in 1974.

4. United Nations Economic Commission for Latin America and the Caribbean, *Preliminary Overview of the Economy of Latin America and the Caribbean: 1995*, LC/G. 1892-P (New York: ECLAC, 1995), 48; World Bank, *World Development Report: 1990* (New York: Oxford University Press, 1990), 178–81. Formally, Cuba was the best performer in Latin America, but the quality of its statistics is insufficiently reliable.

5. See the valuable studies in Robert Kaufman and Barbara Stallings, eds., *Debt and Democracy in Latin America* (Boulder: Westview, 1989); and see, especially, Stephan Haggard and Robert R. Kaufman, *The Political Economy of Democratic Transitions* (Princeton: Princeton University Press, 1995).

6. For a similar analysis, see Juan J. Linz and Alfred Stepan, *Problems of Democratic Transition and Consolidation: Southern Europe, South America, and Post-Communist Europe* (Baltimore: Johns Hopkins University Press, 1996), 72–76. Guillermo O'Donnell and Philippe Schmitter underestimated the evidence already available when they wrote about the influence of international factors in democratization and democracy. See their *Transitions from Authoritarian Rule: Tentative Conclusions about Uncertain Democracies* (Baltimore: Johns Hopkins University Press, 1986), 19.

7. For an assessment of strategies to face up to this double transition, see Miguel Angel Centeno, "Between Rocky Democracies and Hard Markets: Dilemmas of the Double Transition," *Annual Review of Sociology* 20 (1994): 125–47.

8. See also the fine analysis in Samuel P. Huntington, *The Third Wave: Democratization in the Late Twentieth Century* (Norman: University of Oklahoma Press, 1991), 85–100.

9. Henry Kissinger, *A World Restored: Metternich, Castlereagh, and the Problems of Peace, 1812–1822* (Boston: Houghton-Mifflin, 1973), 1, 172.

10. O'Donnell and Schmitter, *Transitions from Authoritarian Rule*, 48.

11. See Grzegorz Ekiert, "Democratization Processes in East Central Europe: A Theoretical Reconsideration," *British Journal of Political Science* 21 (1991): 285–313; Anthony Oberschall, "Opportunities and Framing in the Eastern European Revolts of 1989," in *Comparative Perspectives on Social Movements: Political Opportunities, Mobilizing Structures, and Cultural Framings*, ed. Doug McAdam, John D. McCarthy, and Mayer N. Zald (Cambridge: Cambridge University Press, 1996); Giuseppe Di Palma, "Legitimation from the Top to Civil Society: Politico-Cultural Change in Eastern Europe," *World Politics* 44 (1991): 49–80; Doh Shull Chin, "On the Third Wave of Democratization: A Synthesis and Evaluation of Recent Theory and Research," *World Politics* 47 (1994): 341; and Linz and Stepan, *Problems of Democratic Transition and Consolidation*, 295. For a wider discussion of these themes prior to and during the democratic transitions, see Grzegorz Ekiert, *The State against Society: Political Crises and Their Aftermath in East Central Europe* (Princeton: Princeton University Press, 1996).

12. See Ekiert, *The State against Society*, pt. 3.

13. Susan Stokes, "Democracy and the Limits of Popular Sovereignty in South America," in *The Consolidation of Democracy in Latin America*, ed. Joseph S. Tulchin with Bernice Romero (Boulder: Lynne Rienner, 1995), 70, 79.

14. For the complex relationship between the nature of political regimes and the likelihood of citizen participation, see John A. Booth and Patricia Bayer Richard, "Repression, Participation, and Democratic Norms in Urban Central America," *American Journal of Political Science* 40 (1996): 1205–32.

15. For a comparative analysis of public opinion in Bulgaria, Czechoslovakia, Hungary, Poland, and Rumania, see William Mishler and Richard Rose, "Trajectories of Fear and Hope: Support for Democracy in Post-Communist Europe," *Comparative Political Studies* 28 (1996): 553–81. For an analysis of Polish voting behavior in three elections, see Robert E. Smith, Nathalie Frensley, and Tse-min Lin, "The Polish Democratic Consolidation: A Behavioral Analysis of Renewed Constituent Support for the Polish Left," paper prepared for the annual meeting of the American Political Science Association, August 1996.

16. Scott Mainwaring, "Transitions to Democracy and Democratic Consolidation: Theoretical and Comparative Issues," in *Issues in Democratic Consolidation: The New South American Democracies in Comparative Perspective*, ed. Scott Mainwaring, Guillermo O'Donnell, and J. Samuel Valenzuela (Notre Dame: University of Notre Dame Press, 1992), 304.

17. For a discussion of the contribution of social movements to democracy, see Arturo Escobar and Sonia E. Alvarez, eds., *The Making of Social Movements in Latin America: Identity, Strategy, and Democracy* (Boulder: Westview, 1992).

18. O'Donnell and Schmitter, *Transitions from Authoritarian Rule*, 23.

19. As noted earlier in this book, since 1976 military coups have overthrown elected civilian presidents in Grenada, Haiti, and Suriname. In 1979 in Bolivia, under military pressure, congress set aside the results of a national presidential election and, instead, chose the president of the senate, a civilian, as the interim president of the republic; this president was overthrown by the military in 1980.

20. Samuel P. Huntington, *Political Order in Changing Societies* (New Haven: Yale University Press, 1968), chap. 4.

21. For an able study of military government, see Karen Remmer, *Military Rule in Latin America* (Boulder: Westview, 1991).

22. In some cases, the military retains excessive though constitutionally recognized prerogatives. See Alfred Stepan, *Rethinking Military Politics: Brazil and the Southern Cone* (Princeton: Princeton University Press, 1988), chap. 7.

23. See the effect of this empirical change in Huntington's analysis of the role of the military in politics. In *Political Order in Changing Societies*, he wrote that "the most important causes of military intervention in politics are not military but political and reflect not the social and organizational characteristics of the military but the political and institutional structure of society" (194). In *The Third Wave*, in contrast, he saw military professionalism as a principal means to prevent coups (243–53).

24. For a more skeptical view of technopols, see Guillermo O'Donnell, "Do Economists Know Best?" *Journal of Democracy* 6 (1995): 23–28.

25. Among the most problematic politicians to celebrate, admittedly, are Brazil's. They are impressively talented but not always helpful in consolidating democratic politics or in fashioning appropriate economic policies. See, among others, Barry Ames, "The Congressional Connection: The Structure of Politics and the Distribution of Public Expenditures in Brazil's Competitive Period," *Comparative Politics* 19 (1987): 147–68; Scott Mainwaring, "Political Parties and Democratization in Brazil," *Latin American Research Review* 30 (1995): 177–97; and Frances Hagopian, "Democracy by Undemocratic Means? Elites, Political Pacts, and Regime Transition in Brazil," *Comparative Political Studies* 23 (1990): 147–66.

26. Stephan Haggard and Robert R. Kaufman, "The Challenges of Consolidation," in *Economic Reform and Democracy*, ed. Larry Diamond and Marc F. Plattner (Baltimore: Johns Hopkins University Press, 1995), 2. See also Haggard and Kaufman, *The Political Economy of Democratic Transitions*.

27. Adam Przeworski, *Democracy and the Market: Political and Economic Reforms in Eastern Europe and Latin America* (Cambridge: Cambridge University Press, 1991), 161. Nonetheless, see Adam Przeworski and Fernando Limongi, "Political Regimes and Economic Growth," *Journal of Economic Perspectives* 7 (1993): 51–69; they conclude the article by noting that "we do not know whether democracy fosters or hinders economic growth" (64).

28. On the economic reforms, see Sebastian Edwards, *Crisis and Reform in Latin America: From Despair to Hope* (Oxford: Oxford University Press, 1995).

29. United Nations Economic Commission for Latin America and the Caribbean, *Preliminary Overview: 1995*, 47.

30. Jeffrey Sachs and Andrew Warner, *Achieving Rapid Growth in the Transition Economies of Central Europe*, HIID Development Discussion Paper 544 (Cambridge: Harvard Institute for International Development, 1996); János Kornai, *Adjustment without Recession: A Case Study of Hungarian Stabilization*, Discussion Paper Series 33 (Budapest: Collegium Budapest and Institute for Advanced Study, 1996); Linz and Stepan, *Problems of Democratic Transition and Consolidation*, 439–49.

31. The one exception to this generalization was Slovakia, which scored weakly on democratic criteria but whose economy was growing well.

32. Amanda Rose, "Sachs Was Right: Economic Assessments under Rapid and Gradual Reform in Central and Eastern Europe," paper prepared for the annual meeting of the American Political Science Association, August 1996.

33. I owe much of this insight to my colleague Joel Hellman. Mistakes are mine alone.

34. Juan J. Linz and Arturo Valenzuela, eds., *The Failure of Presidential Democracy: The Case of Latin America* (Baltimore: Johns Hopkins University Press, 1994). See also Arend Lijphart and Carlos H. Waisman, eds., *Institutional Design in New Democracies: Eastern Europe and Latin America* (Boulder: Westview, 1996).

35. See the excellent compendium, Scott Mainwaring and Timothy R. Scully, *Building Democratic Institutions: Parties and Party Systems in Latin America* (Stanford: Stanford University Press, 1994).

36. For this insight, see Adam Przeworski, "Some Problems in the Study of the Transition to Democracy," in *Transitions from Authoritarian Rule: Comparative Perspectives*, ed. Guillermo O'Donnell, Philippe C. Schmitter, and Laurence Whitehead (Baltimore: Johns Hopkins University Press, 1986).

37. See Amy Gutmann and Dennis Thompson, *Democracy and Disagreement* (Cambridge: Harvard University Press, 1996).

38. Niccolò Machiavelli, *The Prince and the Discourses* (New York: Modern Library, 1950), chap. 6, 21.

Index

Library of Congress Cataloging-in-Publication Data

Domínguez, Jorge I., 1945–
    Democratic politics in Latin America and the Caribbean / Jorge I.
Domínguez.
        p.   cm.
    Includes bibliographical references (p.   ) and index.
    ISBN 0-8018-5752-X (alk. paper). —ISBN 0-8018-5753-8 (pbk.: alk. paper)
    1. Democracy—Latin America.   2. Latin America—Politics and govern-
ment—1980–   3. Democracy—Caribbean Area.   4. Caribbean Area—Politics and government—1945–   I. Title.
JL966.D66   1998
320.98—dc21   97-28400 CIP